IMAGES
of America

GEORGETOWN

ON THE COVER: Built in 1794, this was the winter residence of Thomas Sim Lee when he was not in his home state of Maryland, where he twice served as governor. Today, 3001–3009 M Street NW is the site of ever-changing commercial ventures. (Courtesy of the Historic American Buildings Survey.)

IMAGES
of America

GEORGETOWN

Canden Schwantes

ARCADIA
PUBLISHING

ISBN 978-1-4671-2236-8

Published by Arcadia Publishing
Charleston, South Carolina

Printed in the United States of America

Library of Congress Control Number: 2014933314

For all general information, please contact Arcadia Publishing:
Telephone 843-853-2070
Fax 843-853-0044
E-mail sales@arcadiapublishing.com
For customer service and orders:
Toll-Free 1-888-313-2665

Visit us on the Internet at www.arcadiapublishing.com

For my husband, Manny, who actually read this one, and for my family, who always encouraged my love of history

Contents

Acknowledgments

The collection of these images would not have been possible without the assistance of fellow historians at many locations in the Georgetown and Washington, DC, area. I would especially like to thank the staff, Anne McDonough and Laura Barry at the Historical Society of Washington, DC; Scott Scholz at the Dumbarton House; James Carder at Dumbarton Oaks Archives; and the Prints and Photograph Division staff at the Library of Congress. Many photographs are courtesy of the Historic American Buildings Survey (HABS).

Introduction

Georgetown has a varied history of successful industries and wealthy residents, from its founding as a tobacco inspection port to its days in the mid-20th century filled with the downtrodden and slums.

Before the arrival of Europeans in the area, the Anacostian tribe lived here, along the Potomac River near Rock Creek in the town of Tohoga. One of the first persons to document these natives and the landscape was Capt. John Smith, of the incorrectly attributed Pocahontas fame, who sailed down the Potomac River. The fertile soil he noted was ideal for the settlement of the New World, and many Scottish and German immigrants claimed this as home.

There was already a tobacco trade and warehouses along the river in what became the town of George. Founded in 1751, the small port town's original boundaries only extended north from the river a few blocks to Gay Street, now N Street NW. In fact, one of the original boundary stones can still be found in the backyard of the Laird-Dunlop House, on N Street NW. The western and eastern boundaries have remained static. The heights, where the university stands, marks the western edge, and, in the east, Georgetown is bounded by Rock Creek.

These limited boundaries had little effect on the colloquial naming of neighborhoods. Historic records seem to vary on where Georgetown was exactly. Homes that are currently on Georgetown lots were labeled as Tennellytown on maps, even when they were not at all near what is now considered Tenleytown today. During the Civil War, even Meridian Hill Park, north of the White House, was considered part of Georgetown Heights. When the town was in its prime, the outskirts claimed the name.

There is not a historical consensus regarding for which George the town was named. It may have been to honor King George II of England, since Maryland was still a colony at the time. Alternatively, the two previous owners of the land were George Gordon and George Beall. Beall did not necessarily support the development of a government-sponsored tobacco inspection port or its community commandeering his property. Since he had little choice in the matter, perhaps the prospect of financial compensation, a plot of land in the new town, and the honor of naming the city were considered fair consolation. The properties of the two George's were originally deeded as Knave's Disappointment and the Rock of Dumbarton. Georgetown was a much better-suited name to coexist with all the Williamsburgs and Jamestowns along the East Coast.

When the government was looking for a new place to settle after the Revolutionary War, Georgetown was an ideal place to begin. It had an established community, complete with taverns and boardinghouses for the commissioners to stay in as the district plans were laid out. As an added benefit for George Washington, who was given no money by Congress to fund the development of DC, Georgetown had expendable income. Supported by deep pockets, Georgetown residents invested in this new symbol of American independence on the condition that their community be included. What is now the District of Columbia, along the Potomac River and the Eastern Branch (Anacostia River), was originally the shape of a diamond to include both port towns of

Georgetown and Alexandria. Each was able to keep its independence and operated autonomously apart from the newly built city of Washington.

As the tobacco industry continued to prosper, so did the residents, resulting in grander homes and an expanding town as the successful merchants carried Georgetown into its heyday. Like most of the cities at the time, Georgetown's grand mansions were often built on the backs, literally and figuratively, of slaves. It was not long after the charter was written that a slave trade was opened in the area. A century later, at the time of the abolishment of slavery in the District of Columbia, in 1862, Georgetown had a sizeable black American population of both slaves and freedmen. The northwest corner of Georgetown, known as Herring Hill, became an established community of freedmen with its own shops, lawyers, and schools.

The tobacco industry continued to grow until it was stunted by a continuously silted Potomac River. The trade relied on the river, and without the ability to navigate it, a creative solution was found in the Chesapeake & Ohio Canal. The canal connected Georgetown to Cumberland, Maryland, allowing coal, salt, and, of course, tobacco to be carted in and out of the city. The canal was a staple of the community, and it even formed its own when families began to move into houseboats on the water. The business venture of the C&O Canal was never prosperous as a whole. It did, however, have a sizeable effect on continuing Georgetown's trade, especially considering that the Potomac River was no longer a viable option. Though beneficial for the area, the advent of the railroad and the connection of Georgetown to DC via the Q Street Bridge led to the closure of the C&O Canal, which has been part of the National Park Service since the 1930s. Today, the C&O Canal is a historic park with jogging trails and is an iconic feature of the Georgetown waterfront landscape.

With the expansion of the federal government and its surrounding environs, the municipality of Georgetown and other cities within the federal district were integrated. The streets were renamed to follow the numerical and alphabetical theme found in Washington. A thorough study of the roads will note that they do not run continuously east to west, a sign that they were not laid out to be the same road.

Since 1871, the city of Georgetown has been, politically speaking, nothing more than a neighborhood. However, even today, with the absence of a Metro station, Georgetown remains seemingly a separate town from Washington. The historic district of Old Georgetown retains a distinct 19th-century character. Even though most writings inaccurately refer to "the cobblestone streets of Georgetown," in reality, only a few streets are not paved to modern standards, but the comprehensive layers of this town can be seen in its residential, commercial, and social buildings.

One

Town Divided

Georgetown in the Civil War

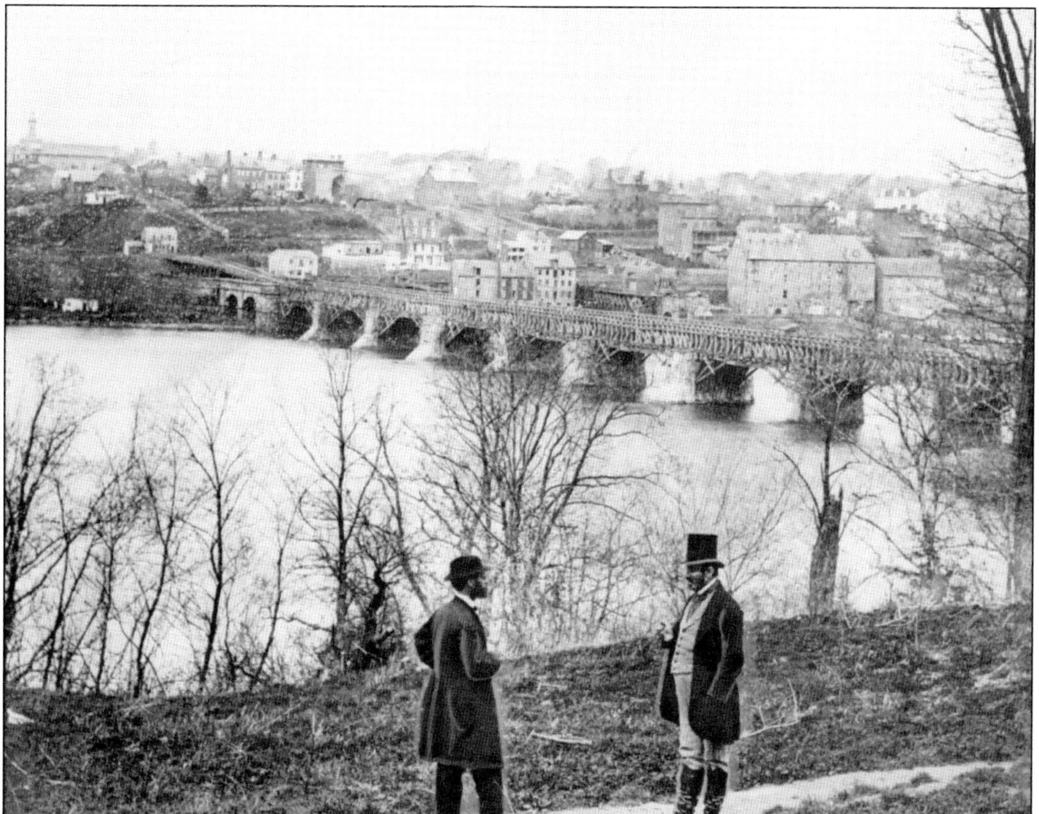

Two men stand in Virginia on the banks of the Potomac River with Georgetown in the background. This portion of Virginia was originally part of the District of Columbia but retroceded back in 1846. During the Civil War, Pres. Abraham Lincoln tried to have this former portion returned for security reasons, but he was rejected by the Senate. Despite the fact that it was technically part of a Confederate state, this portion of Virginia was always under Union control. (William Morris Smith, Library of Congress.)

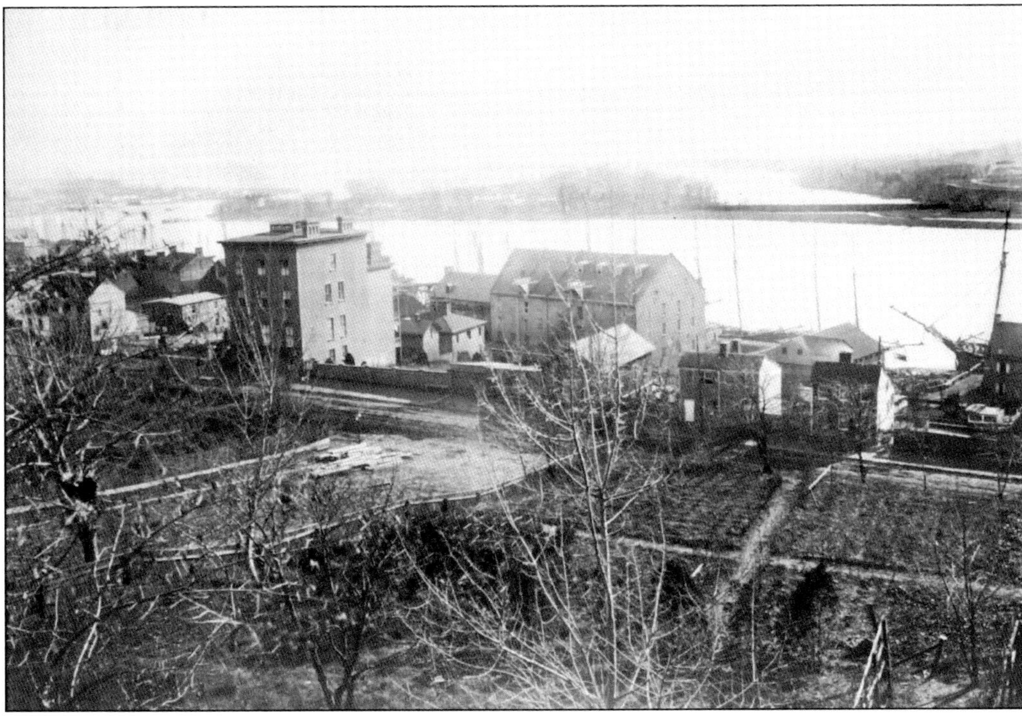

These two photographic prints show the view of Georgetown with the Potomac River, Mason's Island, and Washington, DC, in the background. These were taken during the Civil War, showing that the waterfront was very developed but that, only a few blocks north, the city continued to have more of a rural feel. At the beginning of 1861, most of the families in Georgetown were originally from the South. When the Southern states started to secede, it only took a few months for thousands of Union troops to set up camp in Georgetown. When these beaten soldiers returned from the first Battle of Manassas (Bull Run), the local "secesh" taunted them as they staggered down the main avenues. (Both, Andrew Russell, Library of Congress.)

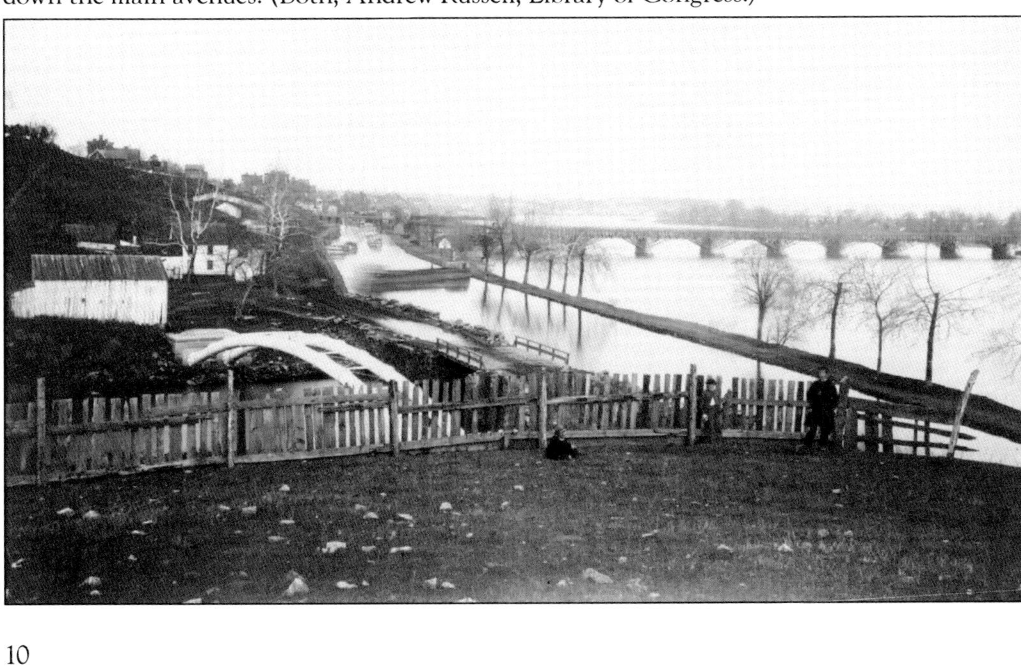

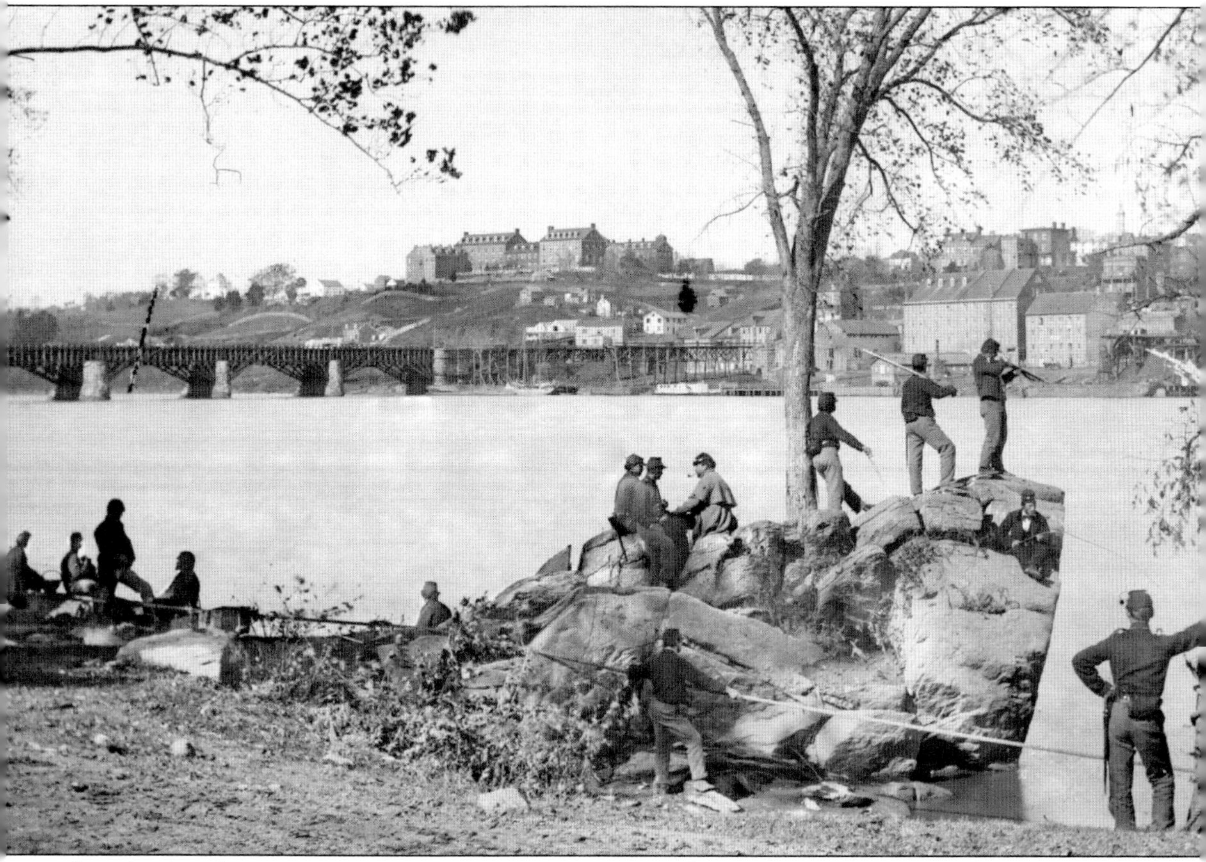

An island with many names—Anacostian, Mason's, and now Roosevelt Memorial Island—it was located between the Union troops in Georgetown and the seceded state of Virginia. Here, in 1861, Union soldiers rest on the rocks with a view of the recently completed Aqueduct Bridge and Georgetown in the background and the university upon the heights. (G.N. Barnard, Library of Congress.)

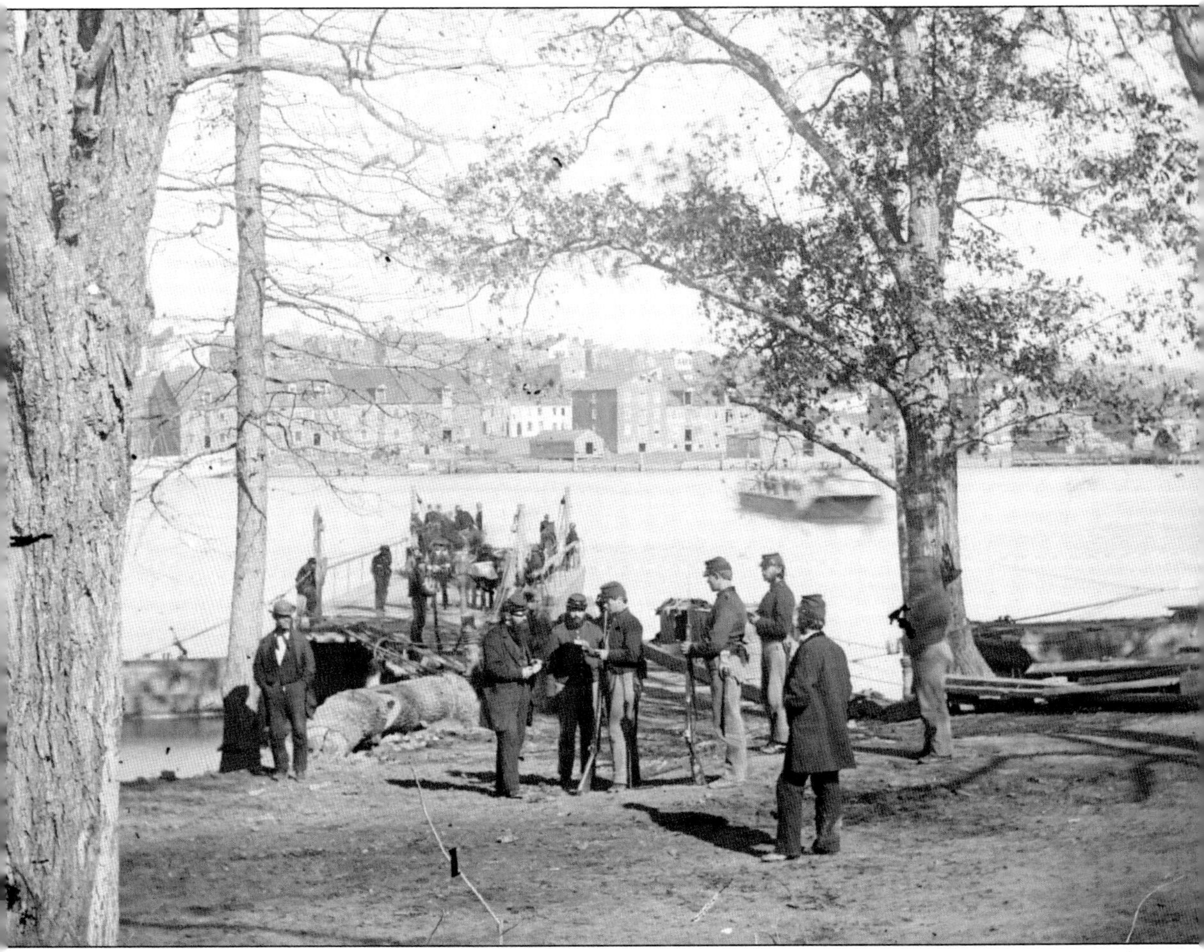

Mason's Island, as it was called in the 1860s, was only connected to Georgetown by ferry, though a pontoon bridge was eventually constructed. During the Civil War, only those with passes were allowed aboard the ferry *Georgetown*. Though it was technically part of the Union capital, most of its residents were Southern sympathizers. There are documented stories of Confederate soldiers sneaking into Georgetown to visit family. A cable connected Mason's Island to Georgetown for a small ferryboat. After heavy fighting upriver, bodies would be found caught on the cable. About once a week, these soldiers were buried in Georgetown in paupers' graves. (William Morris Smith, Library of Congress.)

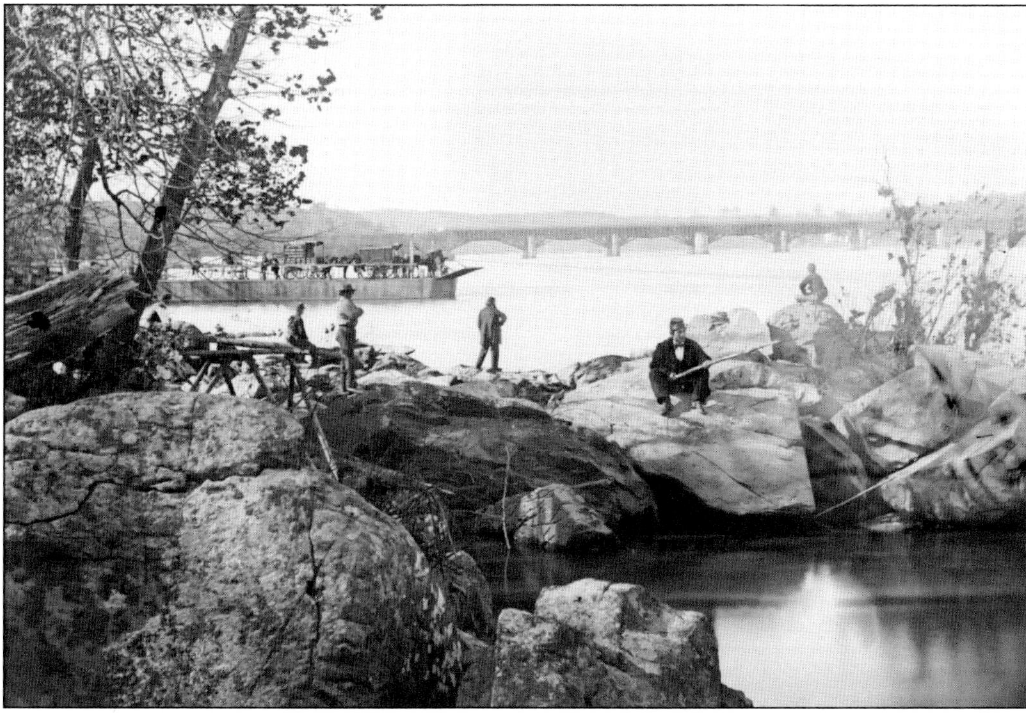

Soldiers are seen on the rocks of Mason's Island while, in the background, a Civil War traffic jam of horse-drawn carriages waits for the ferry. During the war, however, the Aqueduct Bridge, in the background, was converted into a wagon road, with just enough earthen forts on the Virginia side to allow for a retreat. (William Morris Smith, Library of Congress.)

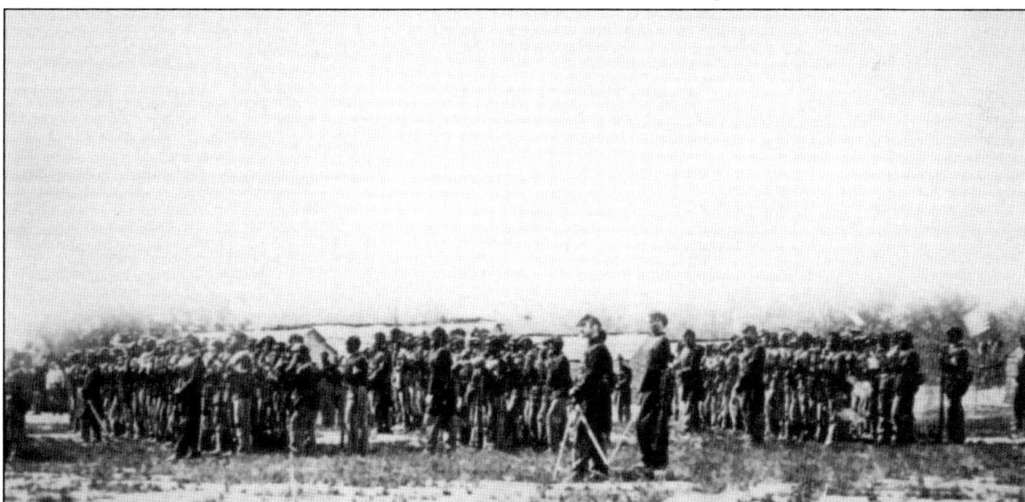

The strategic location of the island meant it was under Union control from the outset of the war. After the emancipation of the slaves in the district, the 1st US Colored Troops were stationed and trained here. Though the infantry regiment was comprised of freedmen and former slaves, the officers were all white. During the war, poet and nurse Walt Whitman visited the island and wrote about his observations. He visually measured the distance between the island and Georgetown as about 100 rods of muddy water. (Mathew Brady, Library of Congress.)

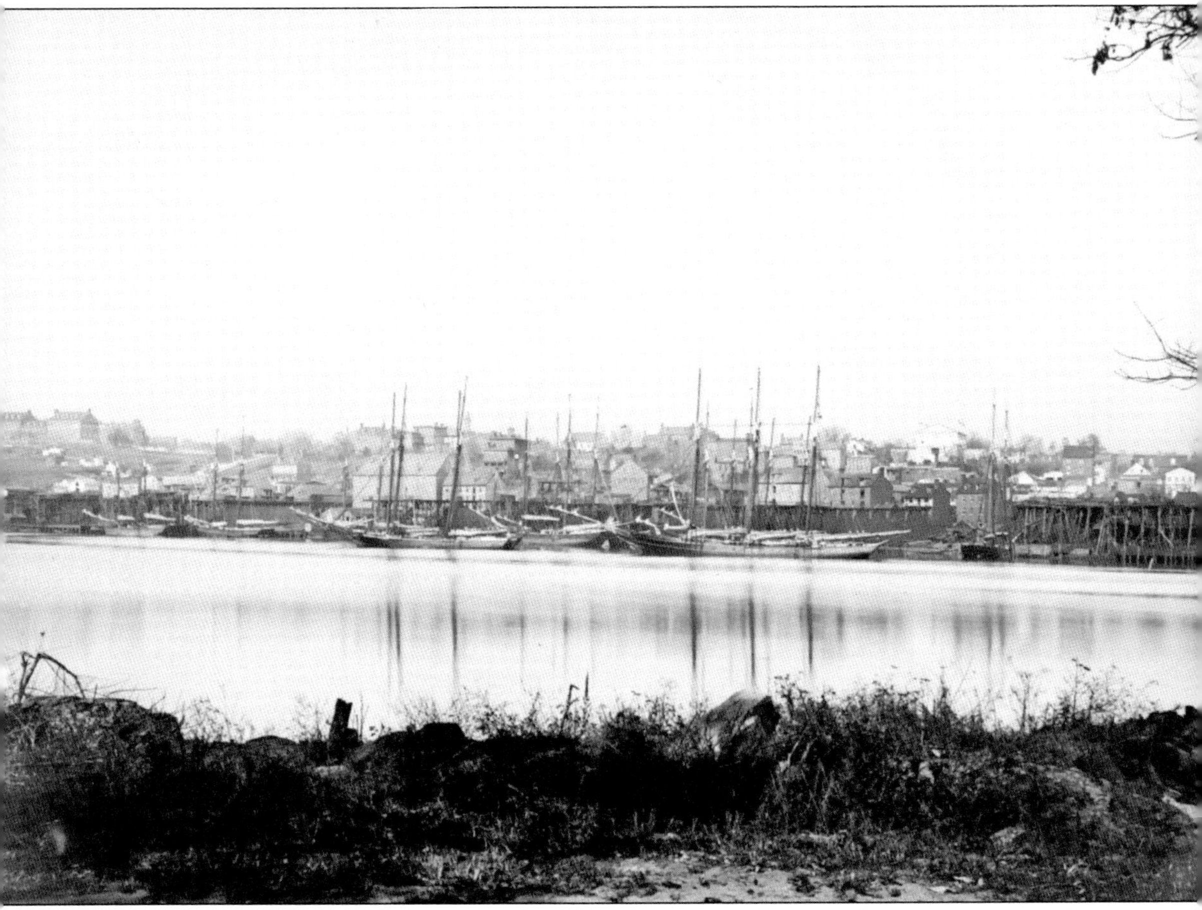

This image of Georgetown during the Civil War from across the river shows a panorama of many buildings still standing today. To the far left are Georgetown University's original buildings, moving to the right is Halcyon House, and at the far western edge of the developed part of the city is the chapel of the original Holy Trinity Church. Closer to the right, the large white building with three chimneys on each side is Tudor Place. (William Morris Smith, Library of Congress.)

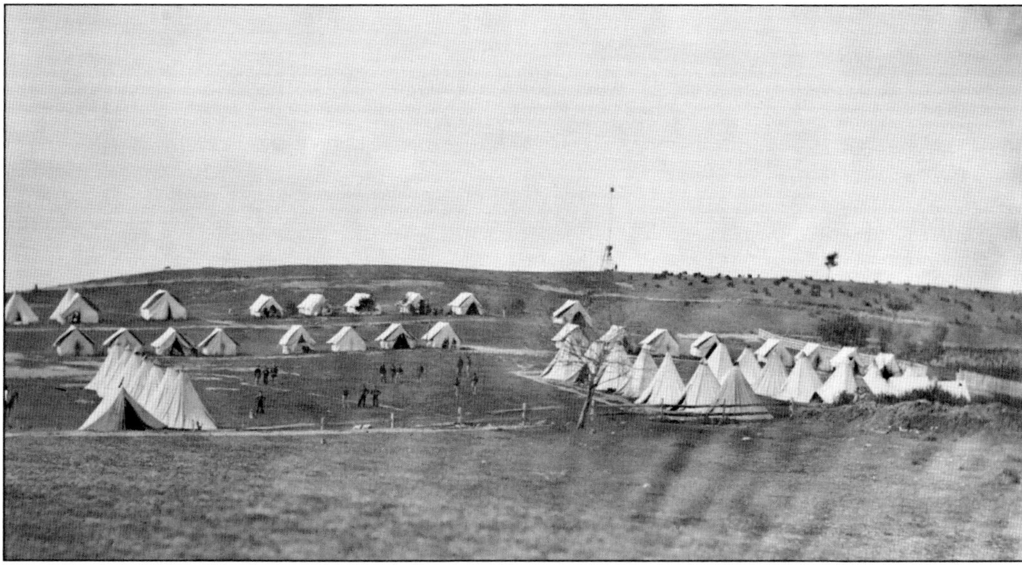

In the northern rural area above Georgetown, what is now the built-up neighborhood of Glover Park was just the "fields near Georgetown," which were used to establish the Signal Camp of Instruction. Union major Albert J. Myer discovered that the signals the Confederates were using were indeed his own, taught to them by his former assistant. After the first Battle at Manassas (Bull Run), Myer returned to set up a school to teach Union forces a new system he would develop. (William Redish, Library of Congress.)

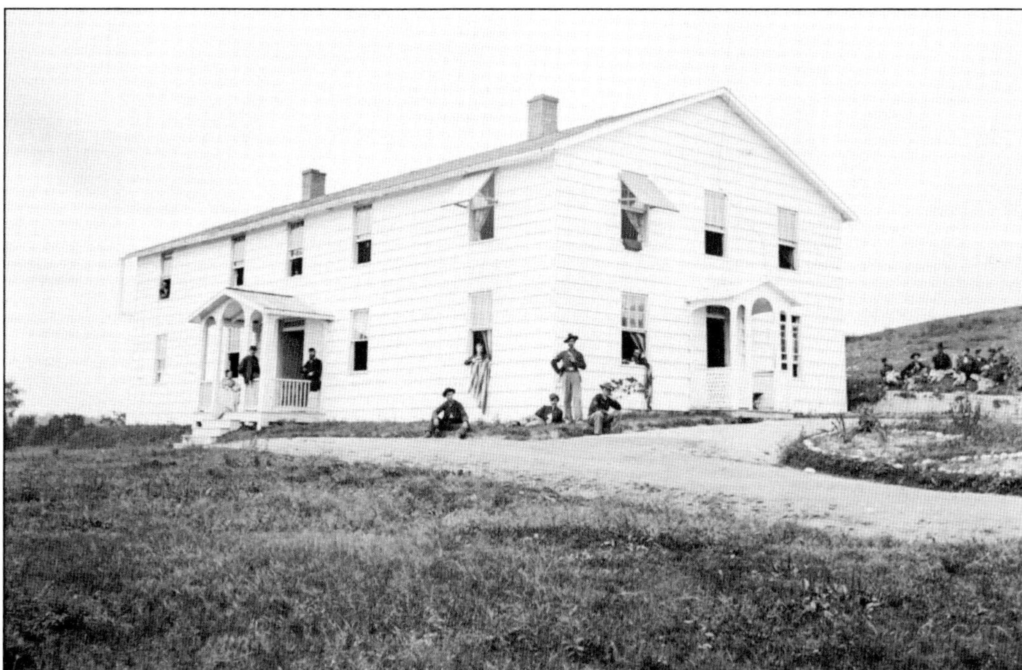

At Red Hill, Georgetown, where one could see miles into Virginia, the Signal Camp of Instruction had 100 two-man tents and a hospital. By later in the war, the soldiers had frame barracks—one for officers, seen here in August 1865, and one for enlisted men. (William Redish, Library of Congress.)

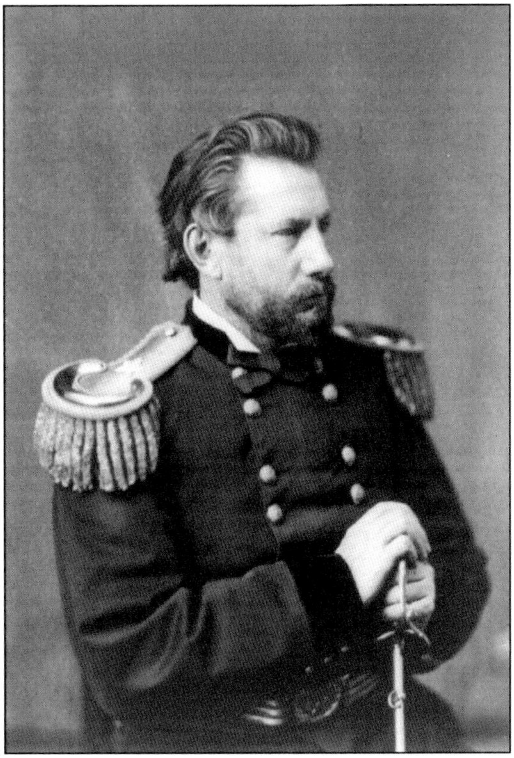

Albert Myer began to use the electric telegraph during the war, even though it was technically under the jurisdiction of the Military Telegraph Service and the secretary of war. Contention between Myer and Edwin Stanton, the secretary of war, over the telegraph led to Myer's dismissal from his duties as chief signal officer. (Mathew Brady, Library of Congress.)

When the Signal Corps camp was closed in 1865, the men posed here with the lowered flag and Albert Myer. As Myer had been relieved from duty, he appears here in civilian clothes. He would later be reinstated. (William Redish, Library of Congress.)

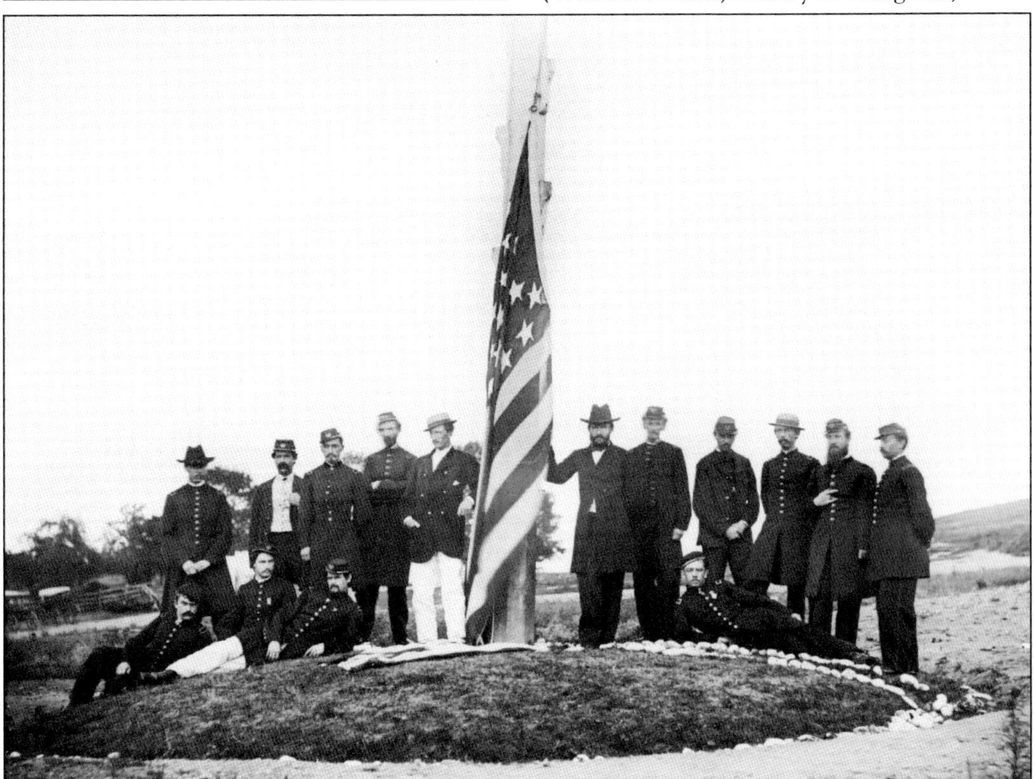

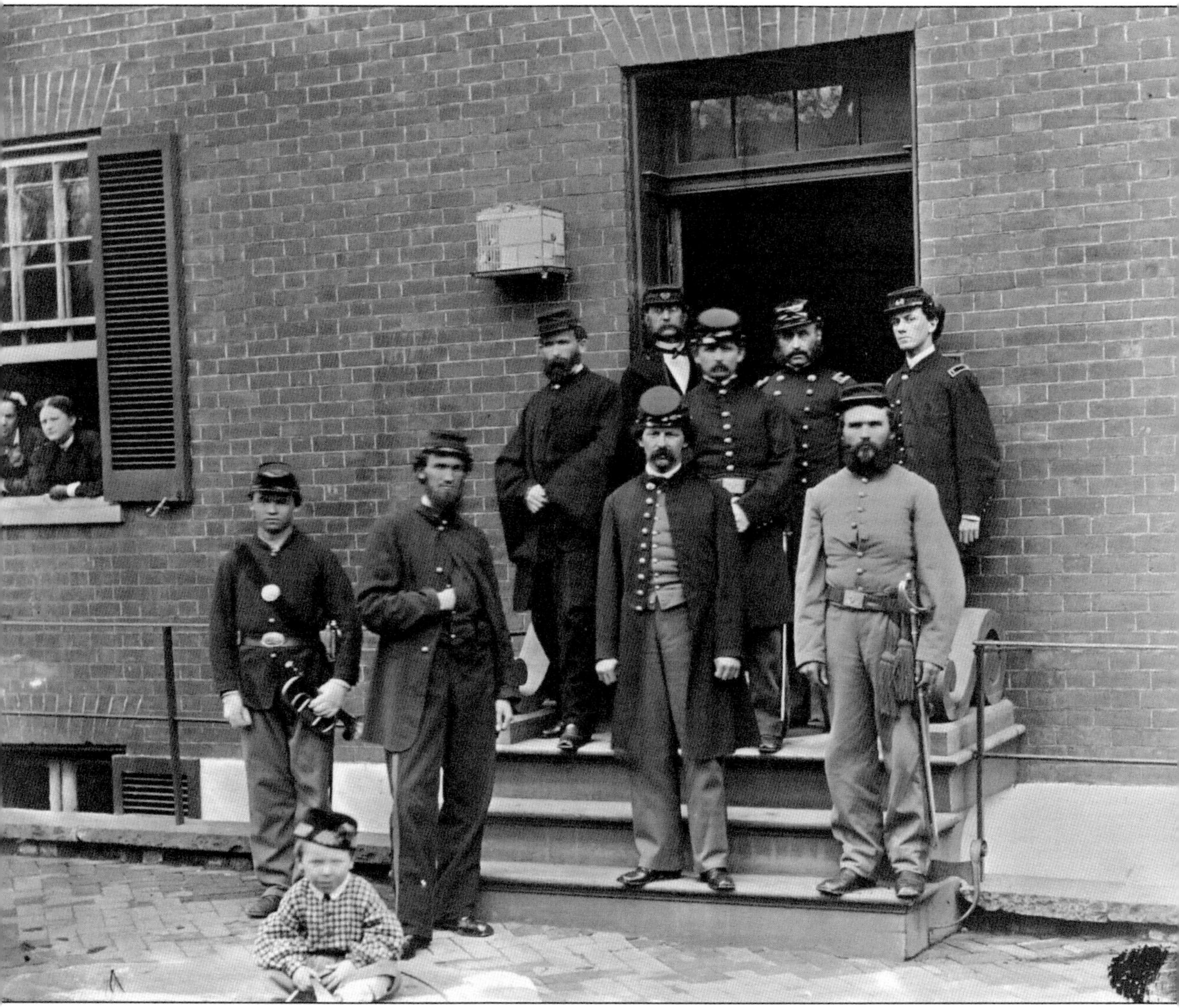

One Southern supporter was Lydia English, who ran the Seminary School for Girls in Georgetown. After the first Battle of Manassas (Bull Run), her school was taken over as a hospital for Union soldiers and renamed Seminary Hospital. In 1865, officers are seen here standing in front of the hospital. Since she could not stand to see the Union flag in front of her home, English moved around the corner and out of view. (Andrew Gardner, Library of Congress.)

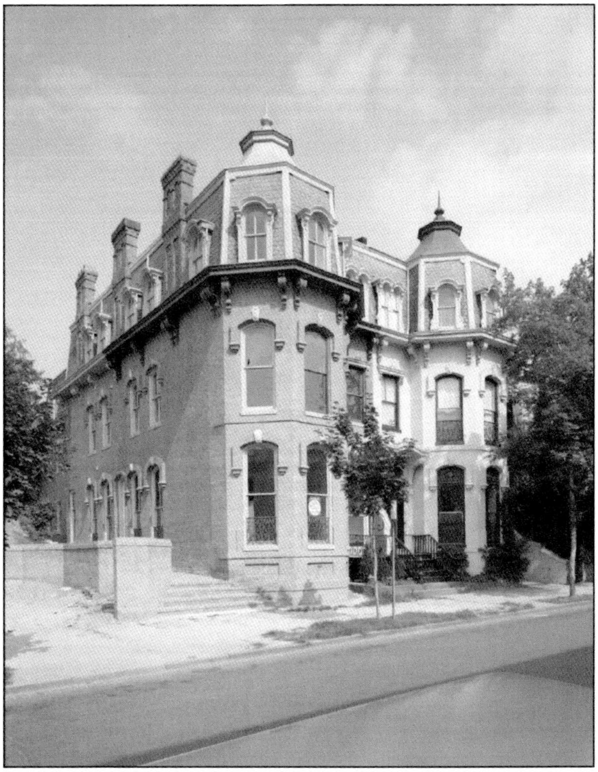

Dr. Grafton Tyler built this house in 1868, but, prior to its construction, he lived a few doors down in a much simpler home. Just like Lydia English, he did not want to see the Union flag hanging above Seminary Hospital, across the street, so he shuttered his windows for the entirety of the war. This house is a double mid-Victorian residence very ornately designed for the upper middle class, showing that, despite keeping his windows shut, Dr. Tyler did not suffer financially during the war, during which time he served as vice president of the American Medical Association. (HABS.)

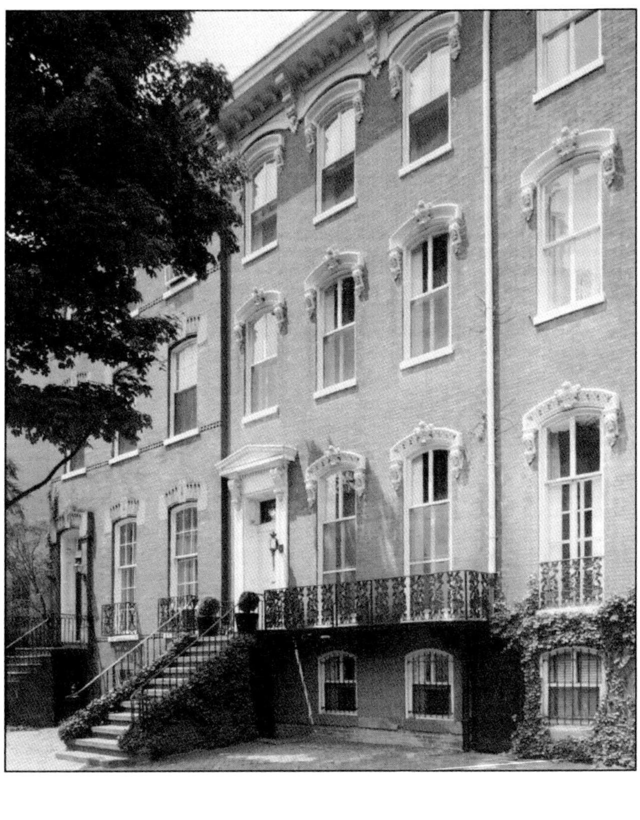

Many young boys from Georgetown families left to fight on the Confederate side. The Wheatley and Gordon families, who lived in these row houses, both had sons fighting for the South. Francis Wheatley was killed in action, and when his brother Walter snuck back into Georgetown to tell their mother in person, he was given away and arrested by Union troops. Though he could have been hung as a Confederate spy, he was kept in the Old Capitol Prison until the end of the war. (HABS.)

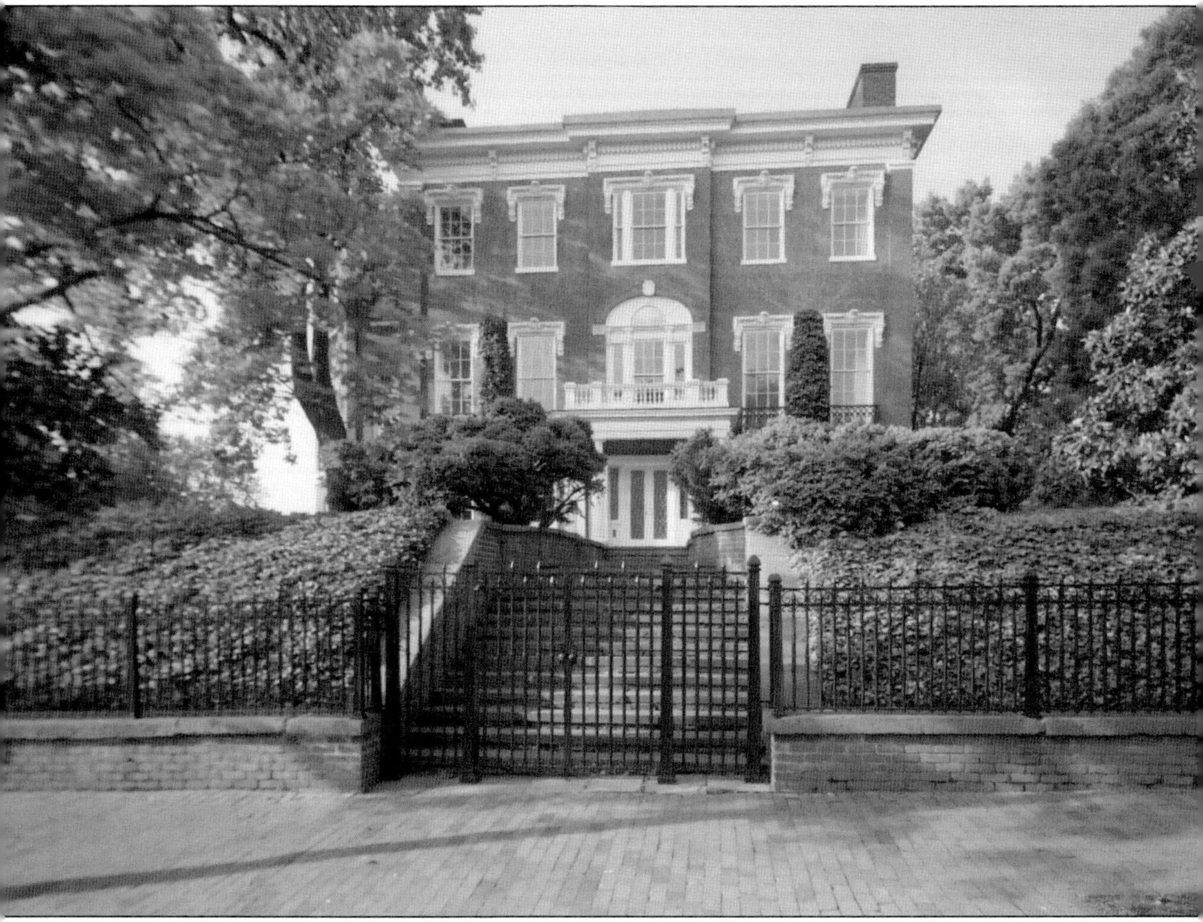

Gen. Henry W. Halleck, chief of staff to Gen. Ulysses S. Grant, owned this house during the Civil War. Legends say that Grant used the Scott-Grant house at the end of the war and as a summer home during his presidency. It is known that on May 18, 1865, Grant is documented as accepting Halleck's offer of use of the house, though Grant spent most of the summer traveling, so it was only for a few months that he resided here. It is unlikely that the house was used as a summer home given that it would not provide much more relief than the nearby White House. (HABS.)

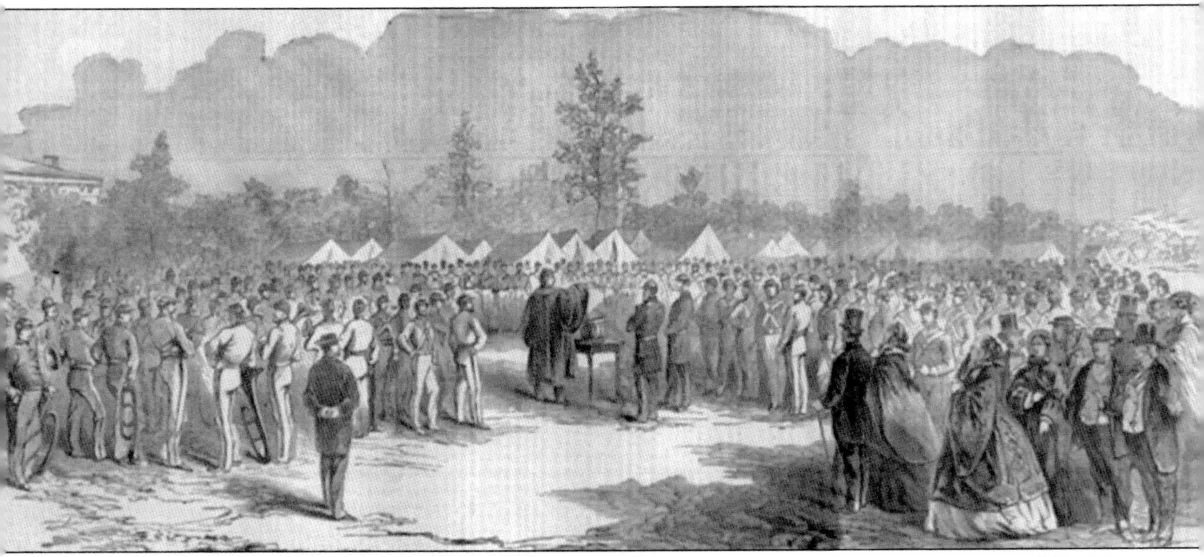

This sketch from 1861 shows Camp Cameron, the encampment of the 7th Regiment of the New York State Militia, and a service by the chaplain, Rev. Dr. Weston. The men were well cared for, with floored tents and so much food and so many care packages that the quartermaster had to order the post to forward no more to the troops. The area was known as Georgetown Heights at the time but is the current location of Meridian Hill Park, nearly a mile from Georgetown proper. (*Harper's Weekly*, May 25, 1861.)

During the Civil War, Forrest Hall was a military prison used as a detention center for deserters from Union forces, as well as spies. Called "the Last Ditch," the prison, in what used to be the ballroom, held more than 500 men and women. Famed Confederate spy Belle Boyd was kept here until moved to Old Capitol Prison. (HABS.)

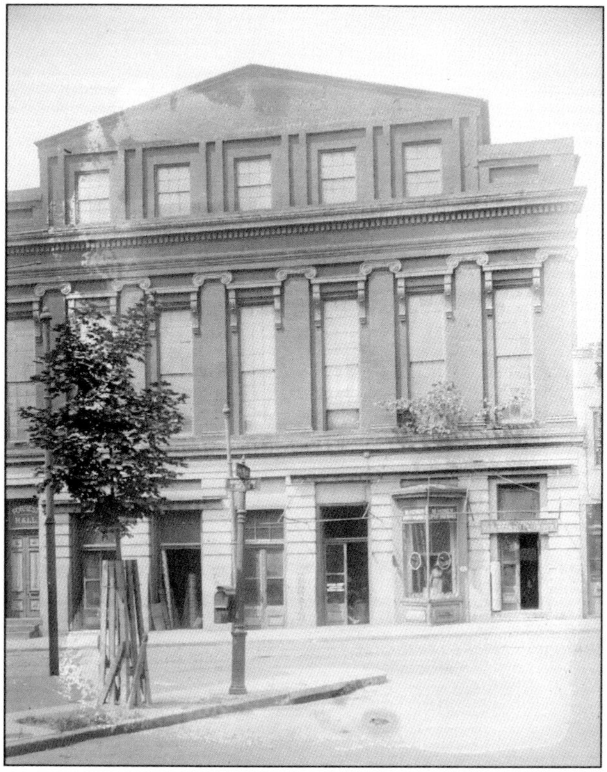

In June 1861, Georgetown College buildings became the quarters for the 69th Regiment of the New York State Militia. (*Harper's Weekly*, June 1, 1861.)

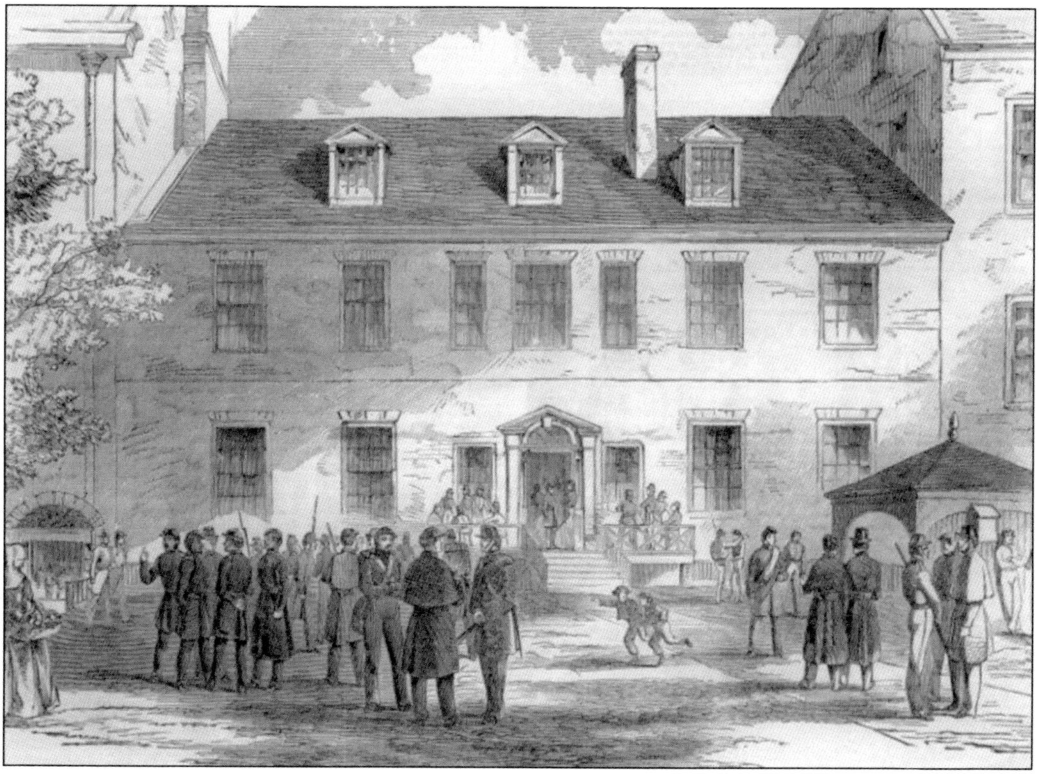

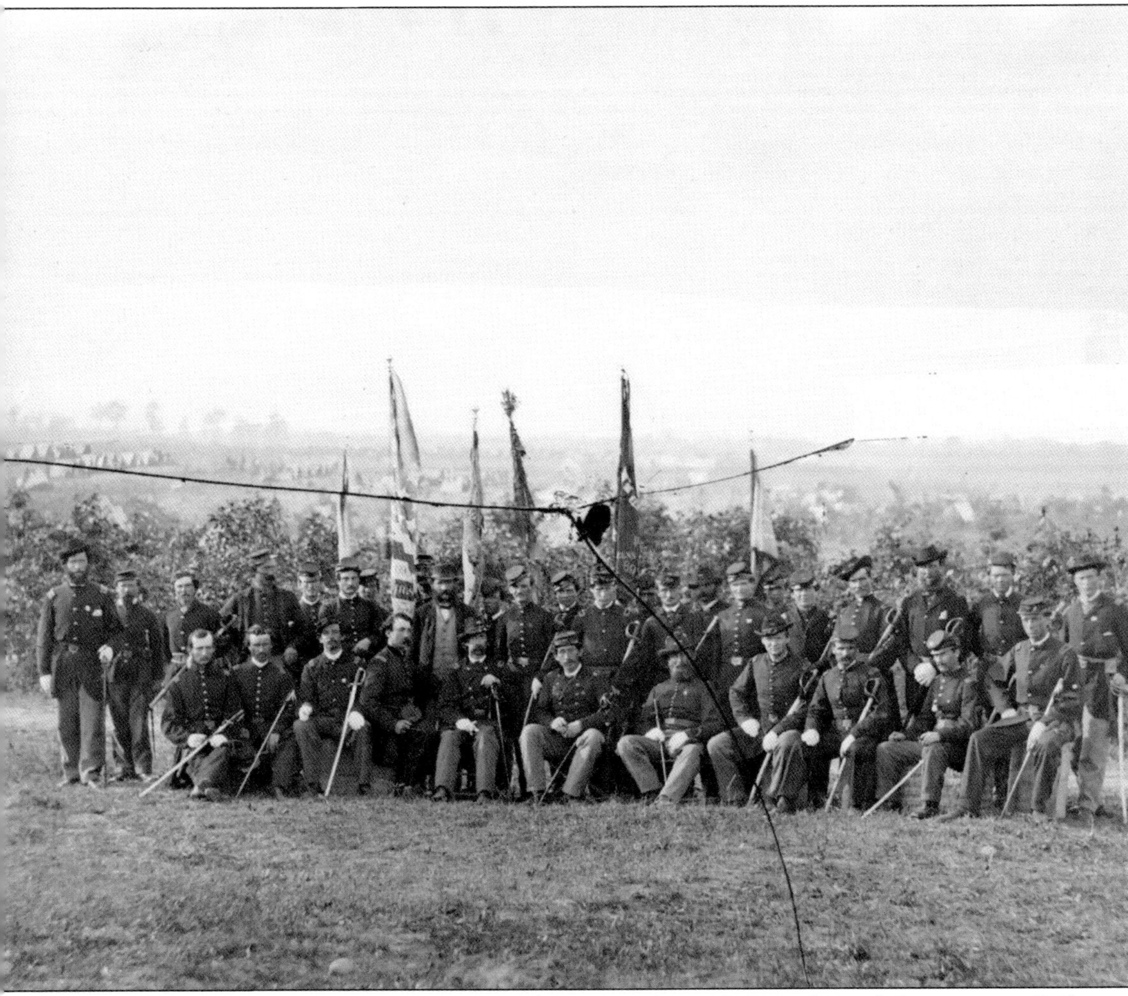

The 69th Regiment, pictured here, was known as the Irish Brigade, and Georgetown College, a Catholic university, was a fitting place for them. Of the 1,500 men, most were staunch Catholics. The grounds of the college were used for training, target practice, and living quarters. Georgetown residents and the Jesuit priests of the college commented with praise on the conduct of the Irish Brigade. Gen. Robert Nugent was the last commander of what was left of the brigade at the end of the war. He led the men in the Grand Review down Pennsylvania Avenue NW on May 23, 1865. (Library of Congress.)

Two

College Town
Georgetown University

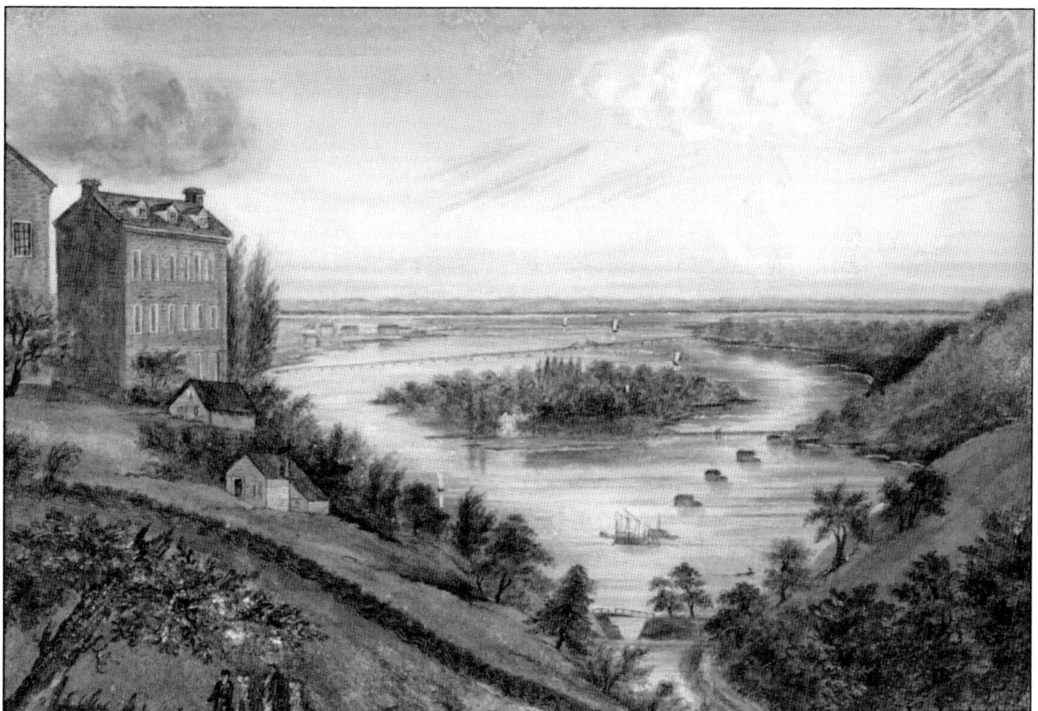

This painting shows Georgetown College's original buildings on the far left. The first building, Old South, has since been demolished. The Long Bridge and the beginnings of the Aqueduct Bridge can be seen on the river. This painting was done in 1838, only a few years after the bridge construction began. (Dumbarton House, the National Society of the Colonial Dames of America.)

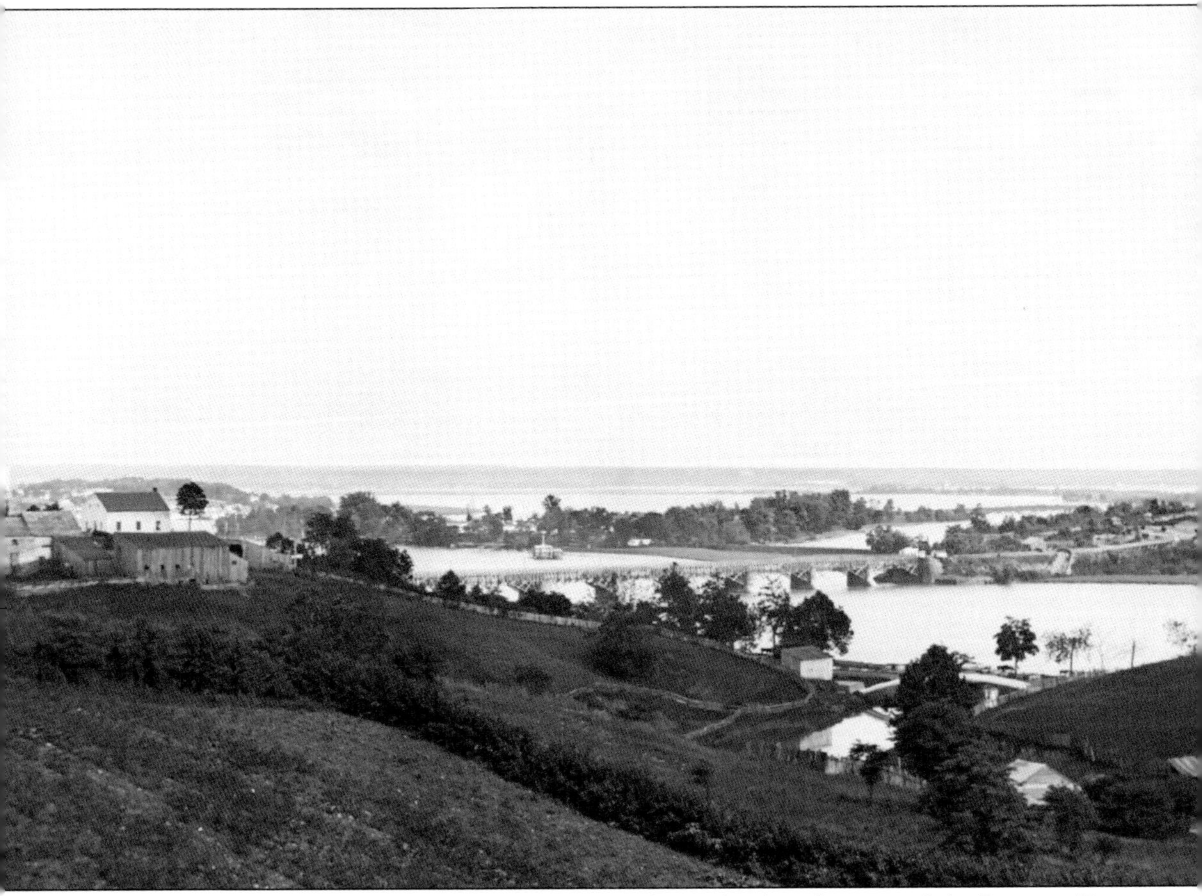

This view from Georgetown Heights looks across the undeveloped town and the Potomac River in 1865. At this point, Georgetown College was nearly a century old, with sizable buildings, but they must be behind the photographer. When Archbishop John Carroll was tasked with deciding the location of this new Jesuit school, he feared the alternative site of "Jenkins Hill" would be too rural. Ironically, Capitol Hill, as it is known today, is the exact center of town. (William Morris Smith, Library of Congress.)

John Carroll founded the first Catholic university in the United States in 1789 as Georgetown Academy, with college, preparatory, and elementary programs. In 1817, Georgetown awarded its first two bachelor's degrees. Carroll was the archbishop of Baltimore and the first Catholic bishop in the United States. This statue of him was unveiled in May 1912. (Harris Ewing Photography.)

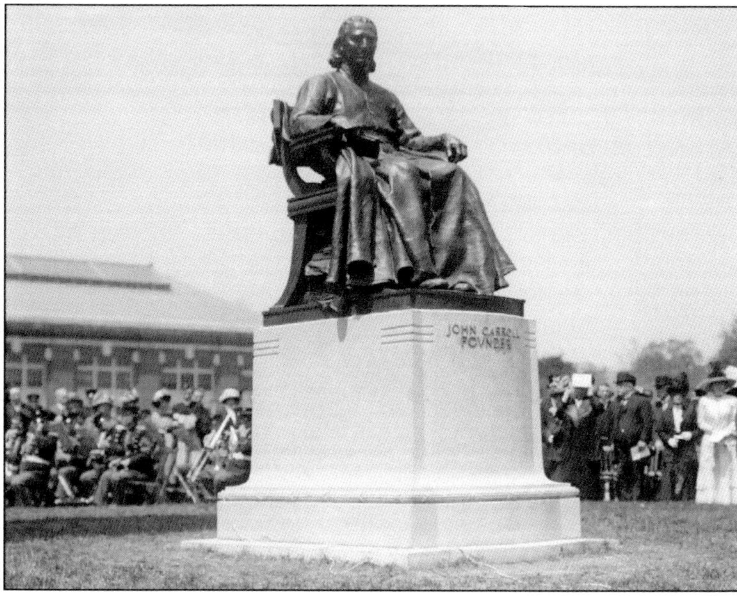

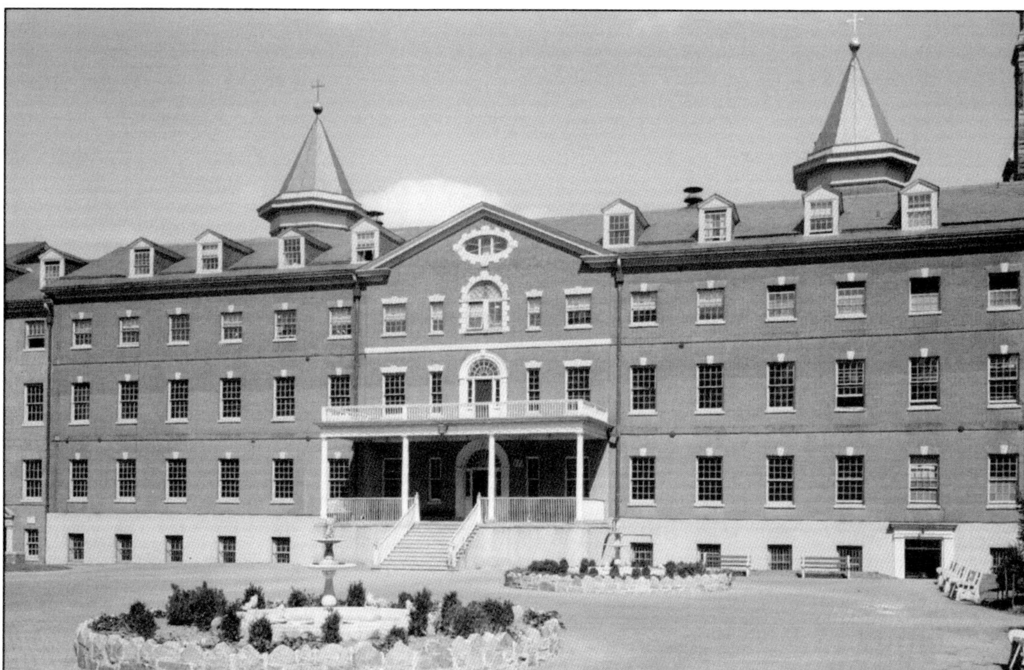

The oldest remaining building on Georgetown's campus, Old North, was constructed in 1794, after John Carroll purchased land to expand the campus. Three years after the completion of the building, George Washington visited his two nephews, students at the school, and spoke from the porch of Old North, a place now used for visiting presidents. (HABS.)

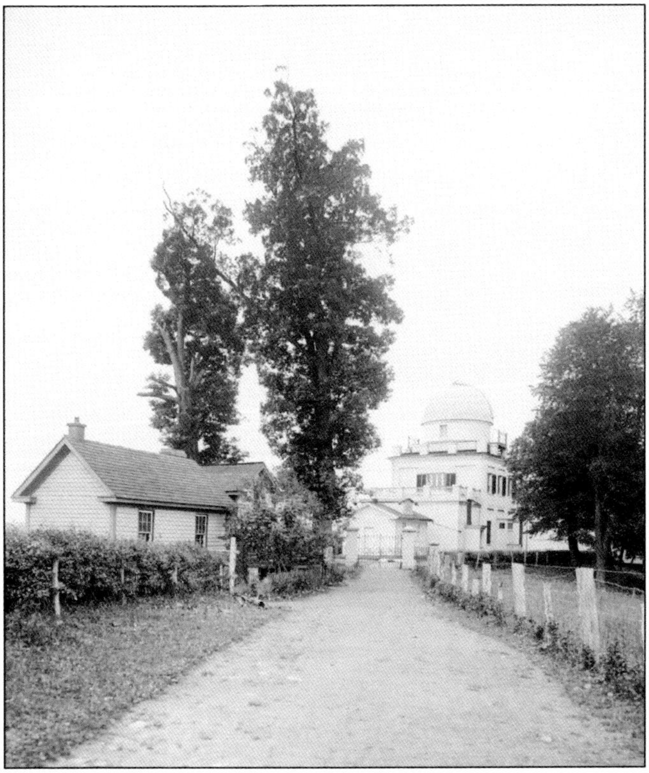

Built in 1844, the Georgetown University Observatory is one of the oldest college observatories in the United States. It was created under the supervision of its first director, Fr. James Curley. As the city of Washington continued to grow and electric power became ubiquitous, light pollution forced the observatory to close in 1972. It had been renamed the Heyden Observatory, after the last director, Francis Heyden, when this photograph was taken in the 1940s. (Detroit Publishing Company.)

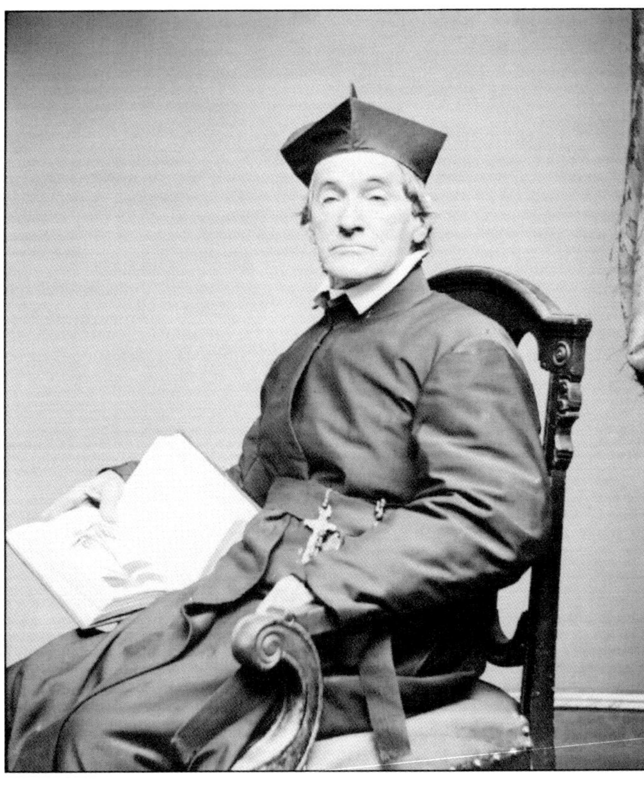

A professor in the physics department, Fr. James Curley used the observatory to determine the longitude and latitude of Washington, DC, as "38* 54' 26N" and "5h8m18.29s," respectively. His findings did not match up with those done by the Naval Observatory, but when the first transatlantic cable was laid in 1858, it proved him right. It was more of a coincidence in reality, as his methods were not entirely accurate. (Brady-Handy Photograph Collection, Library of Congress.)

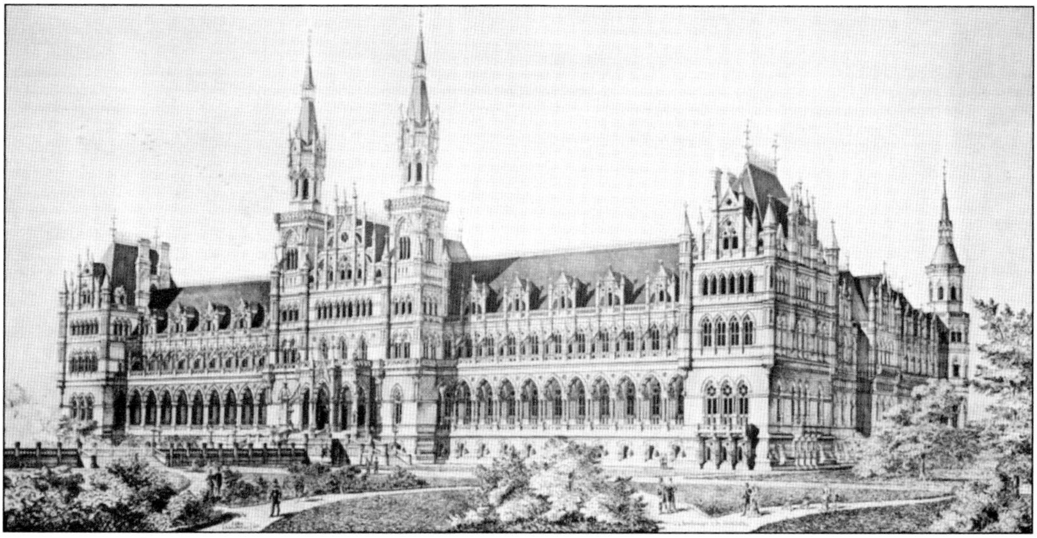

An 1876 preliminary drawing of Healy Hall shows that the final version was altered from the original plans. The most prominent difference is the single clock tower instead of two. While the general feel of the Gothic building is true to this design, many of the details changed. (HABS.)

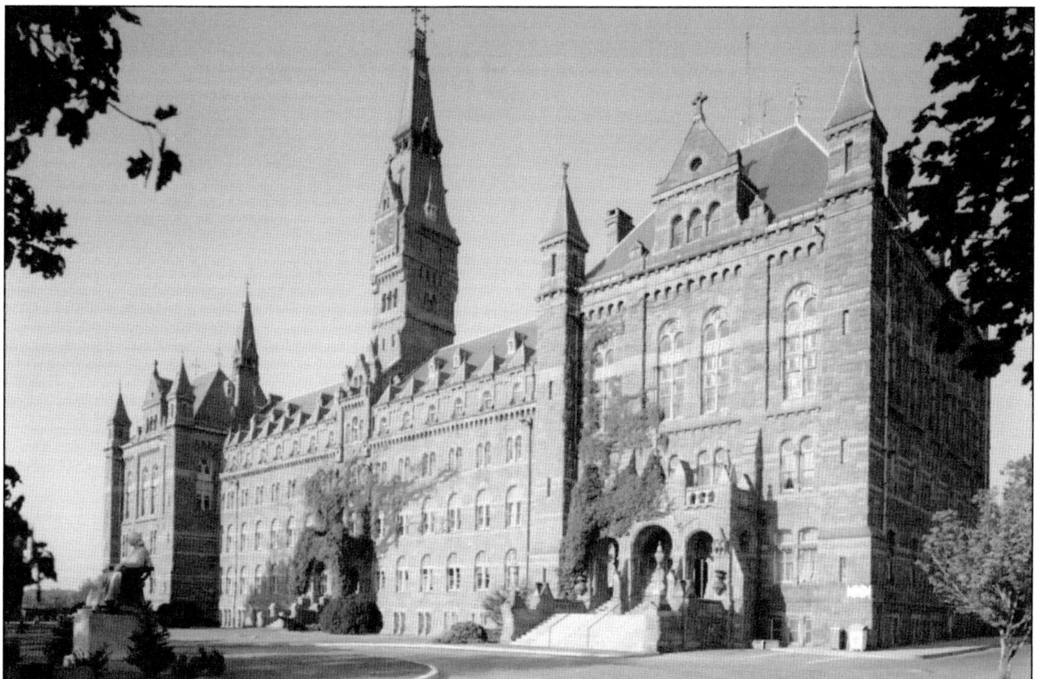

The most iconic image of Georgetown University, Healy Hall, was built from 1877 to 1879. The building was named for university president Patrick Healy, who is credited with reviving the struggling school after the Civil War. Healy was the son of a slave, though she was mixed-race and was in a common-law marriage with his father. Healy was able to earn his PhD in Europe and return to become the first American man of African heritage to head a predominately white university. (HABS.)

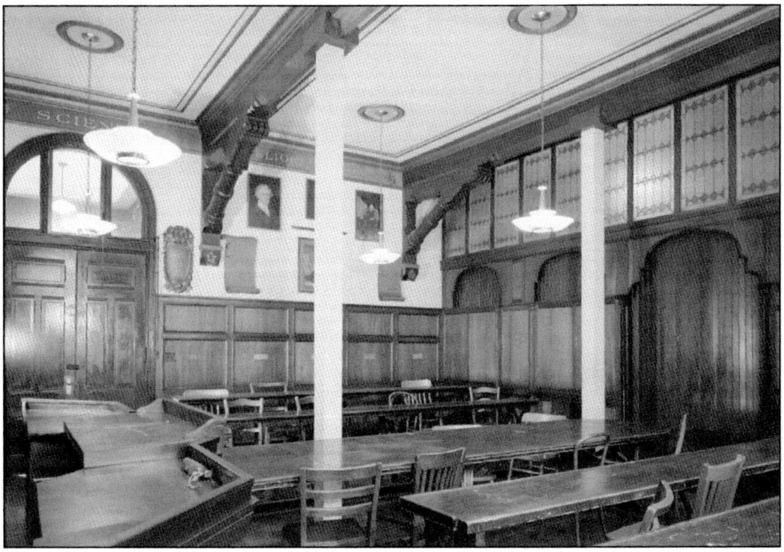

Healy Hall was built as both a dormitory and classrooms. The building also houses Riggs Library, Gaston Hall, Hall of Cardinals, and Carroll Parlor, which displays some of the university's art collection. This 1969 photograph shows a classroom on the first floor of Healy Hall. (HABS.)

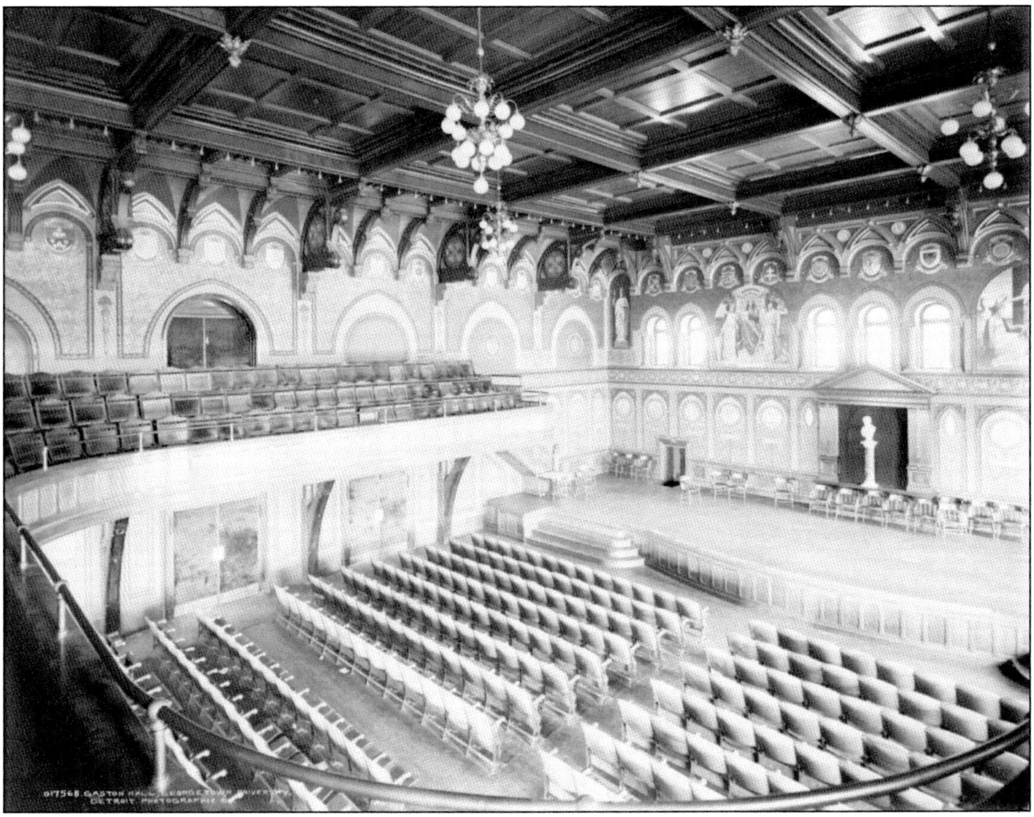

The 450-seat auditorium in Healy Hall is one of the iconic features of the university. It is named for William Gaston, Georgetown's first student, who became so at the age of 13. He was also the school's first dropout. Gaston Hall was not completed until 1909 due to the unexpected costs of building the rest of Healy Hall. (HABS.)

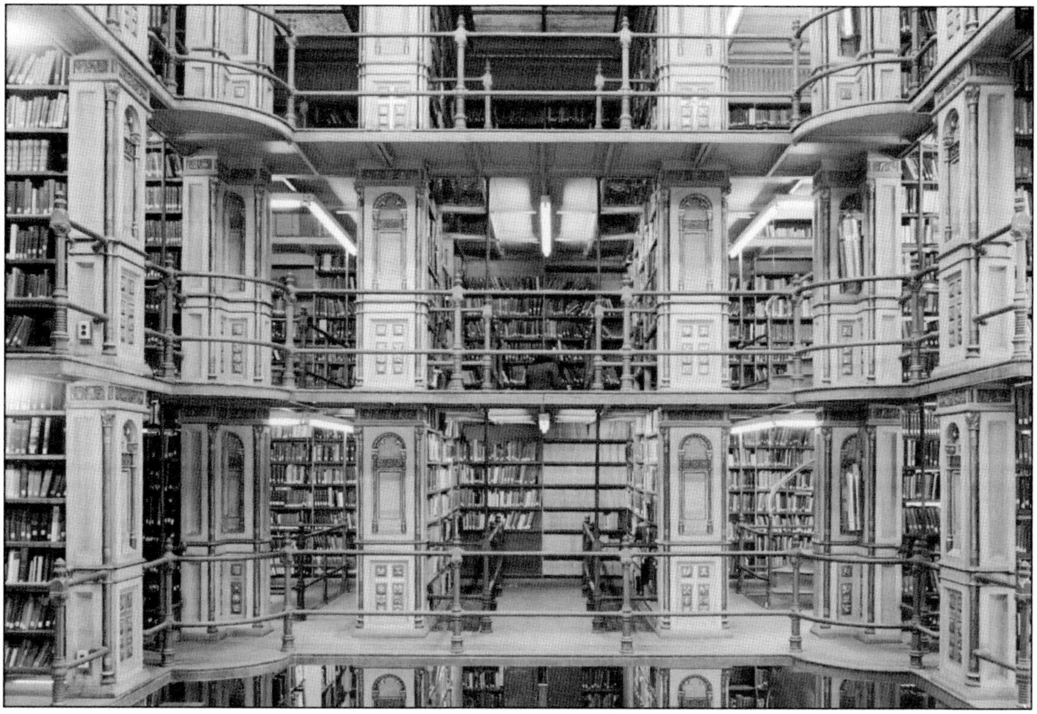

Riggs Library was funded by E. Francis Riggs of the Washington banking family in memory of his late father and in honor of his brother, an alumnus of the school. It was built in 1891 as part of Healy Hall and served as the main library on campus until 1970. Today, the stacks house over 35,000 volumes. (Detroit Publishing Company.)

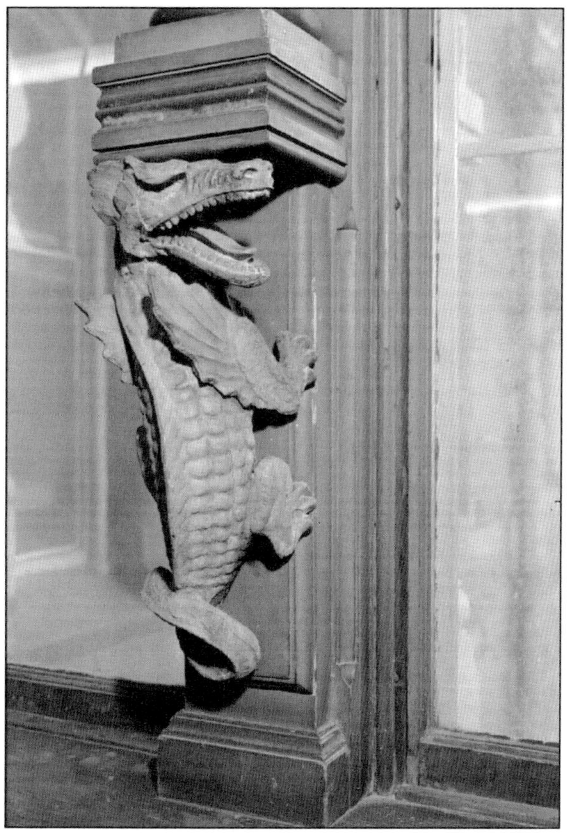

Riggs is one of the few remaining cast-iron libraries. Designed by Paul Pelz, who also worked on the Library of Congress, details include this cast-iron dragon. Cast-iron architecture was pervasive in the late 1800s and allowed for more slender columns. (HABS.)

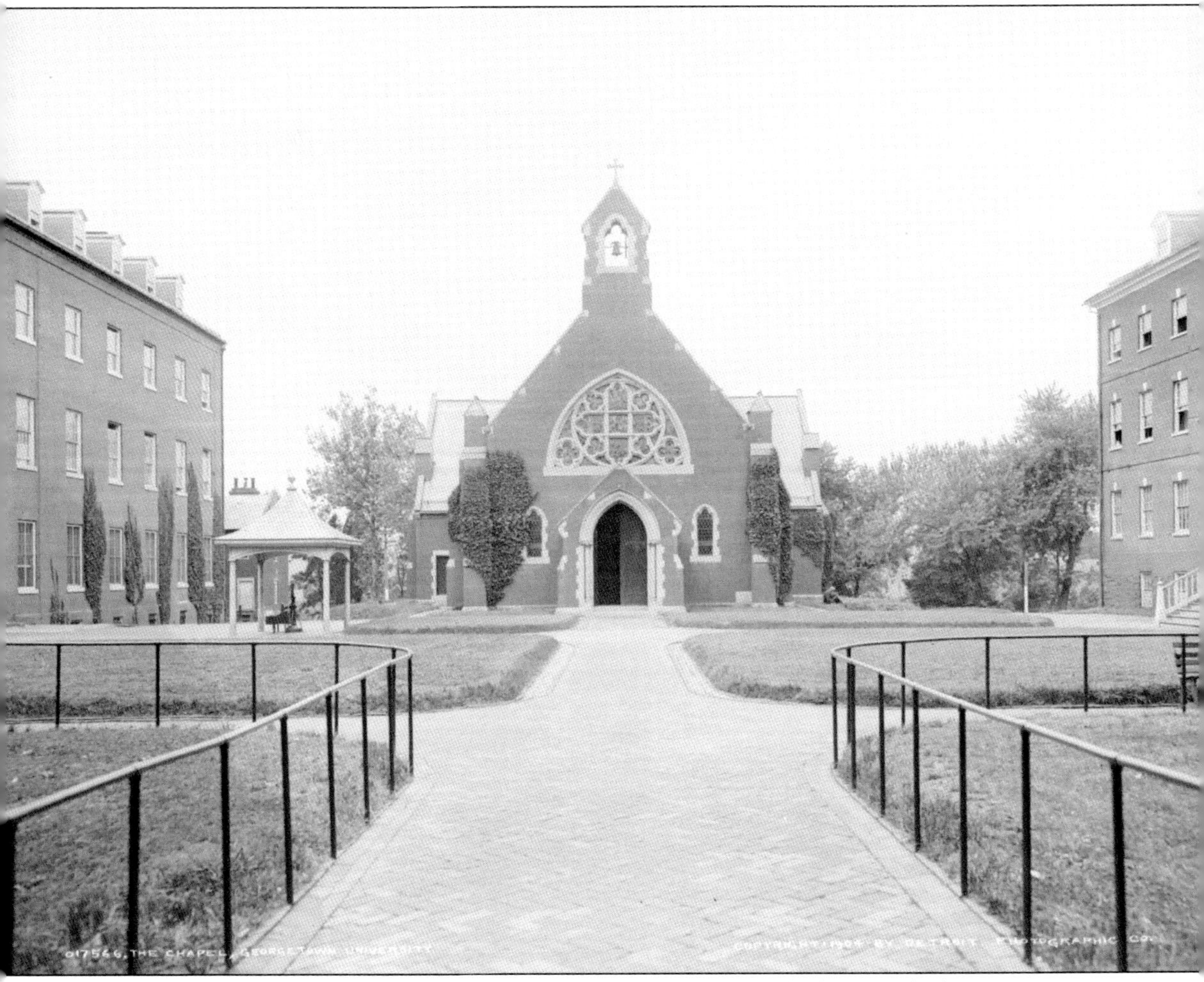

Dahlgren Chapel of the Sacred Heart has been the main chapel of the Catholic university since 1893. Its building was funded solely by donations from outside the university. It was a gift from John and Elizabeth Dahlgren in memory of their son. The iron cross hanging in the chapel is said to be made from parts of the *Ark* and the *Dove* sailing vessels, which brought the first Jesuit priests to Maryland. (Detroit Publishing Company.)

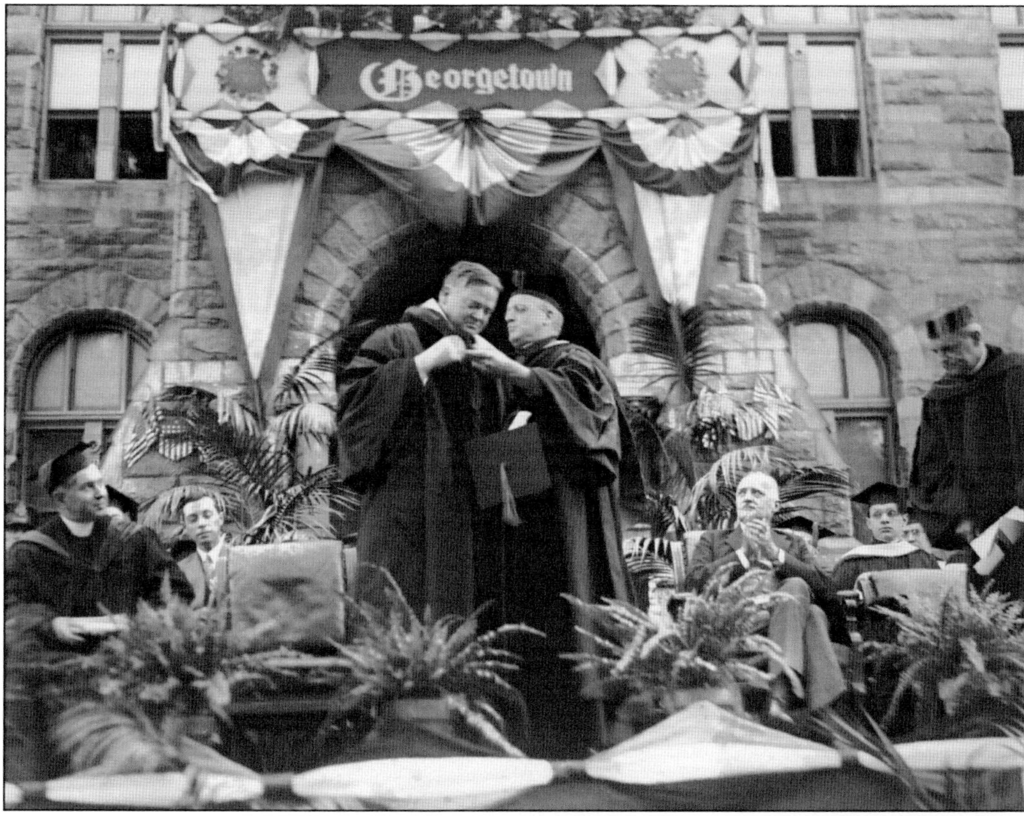

Herbert Hoover (center left), who was secretary of commerce at the time, receives an honorary degree from Georgetown University president Rev. Charles Lyons (center right) at the 1926 commencement. Two years later, Hoover would win the presidential election without any experience in elected office. (National Photo Company.)

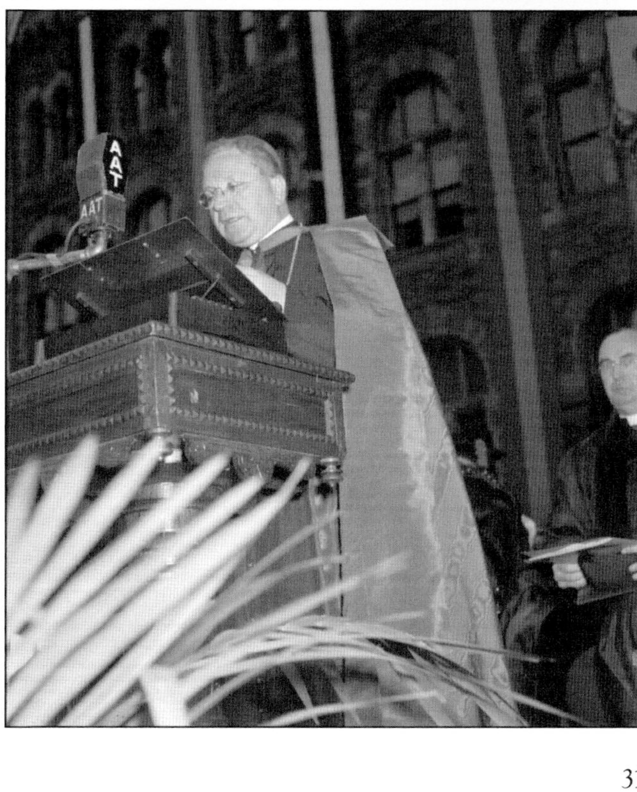

To celebrate the 150th anniversary of the founding of Georgetown, Rev. Amleto Giovanni Cicognani, apostolic delegate to the United States, reads a message from Pope Pius XI. It was Pope Pius VI who appointed John Carroll as the first Roman Catholic bishop in the United States 150 years earlier. (Harris Ewing Photography.)

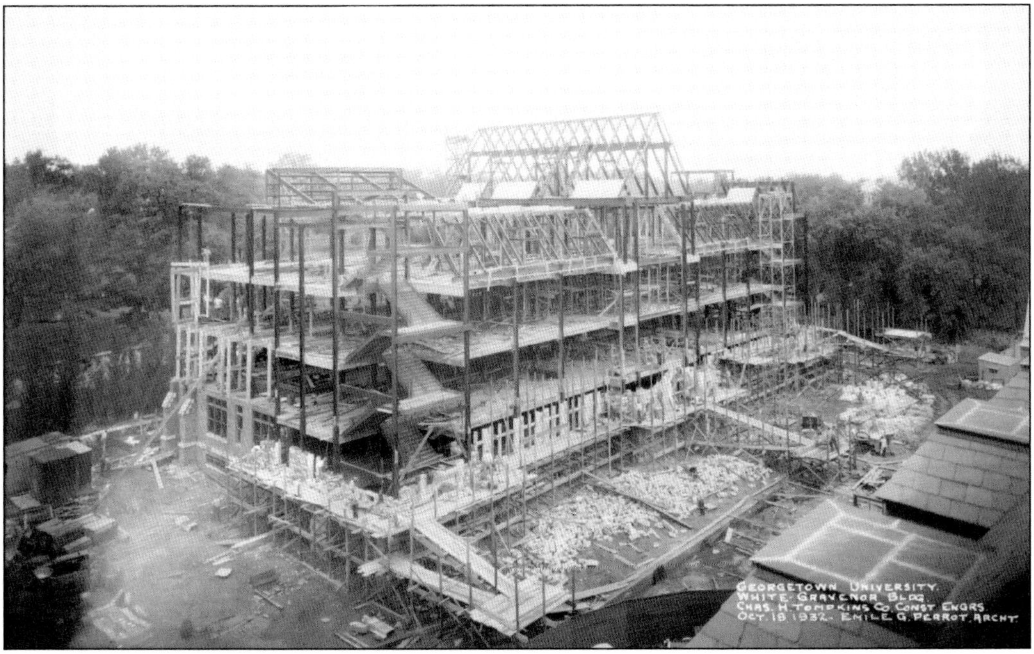

In 1634, two Jesuit priests, Andrew White and John Gravenor, landed in Maryland to establish a colony to educate the natives. The 1932 addition of this academic building to campus was named in honor of these two men. The 1634 date is carved above the door, alongside the founding date of 1789. (National Photo Company.)

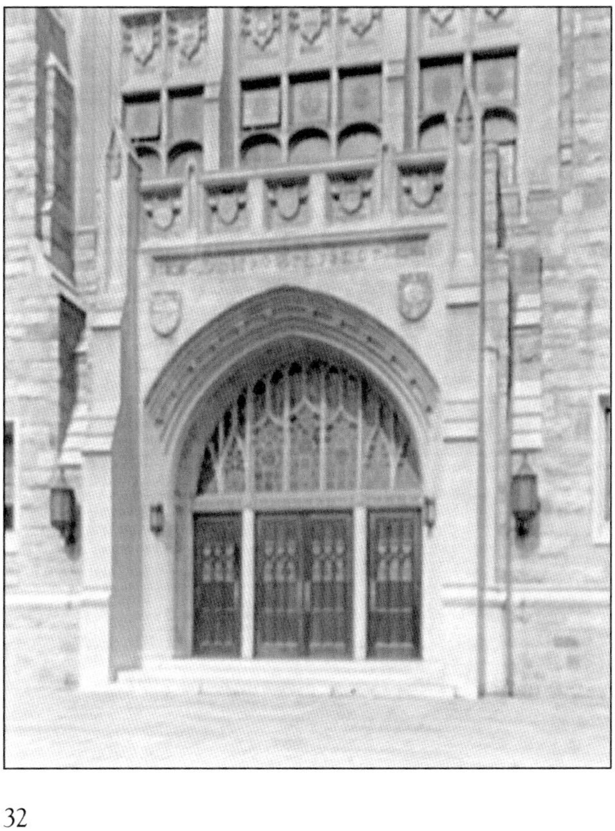

White-Gravenor is called a "sermon in stone" due the vast amount of religious symbolism on the building. Above the main entrance, there are 14 symbols of an academic field accompanied by the name of a Jesuit priest prominent in that study. Francisco Suarez and the lamp of learning represent philosophy, Athanasius Kircher represents science, and poet Robert Southwell represents the arts. There are five shields symbolizing academies founded by the Jesuits in Maryland: St. Mary's City (1634), Calverton Manor (1640), Newtown Manor (1677), Bohemia Manor (1745), and Georgetown Heights (1789). (Theodor Horydczak.)

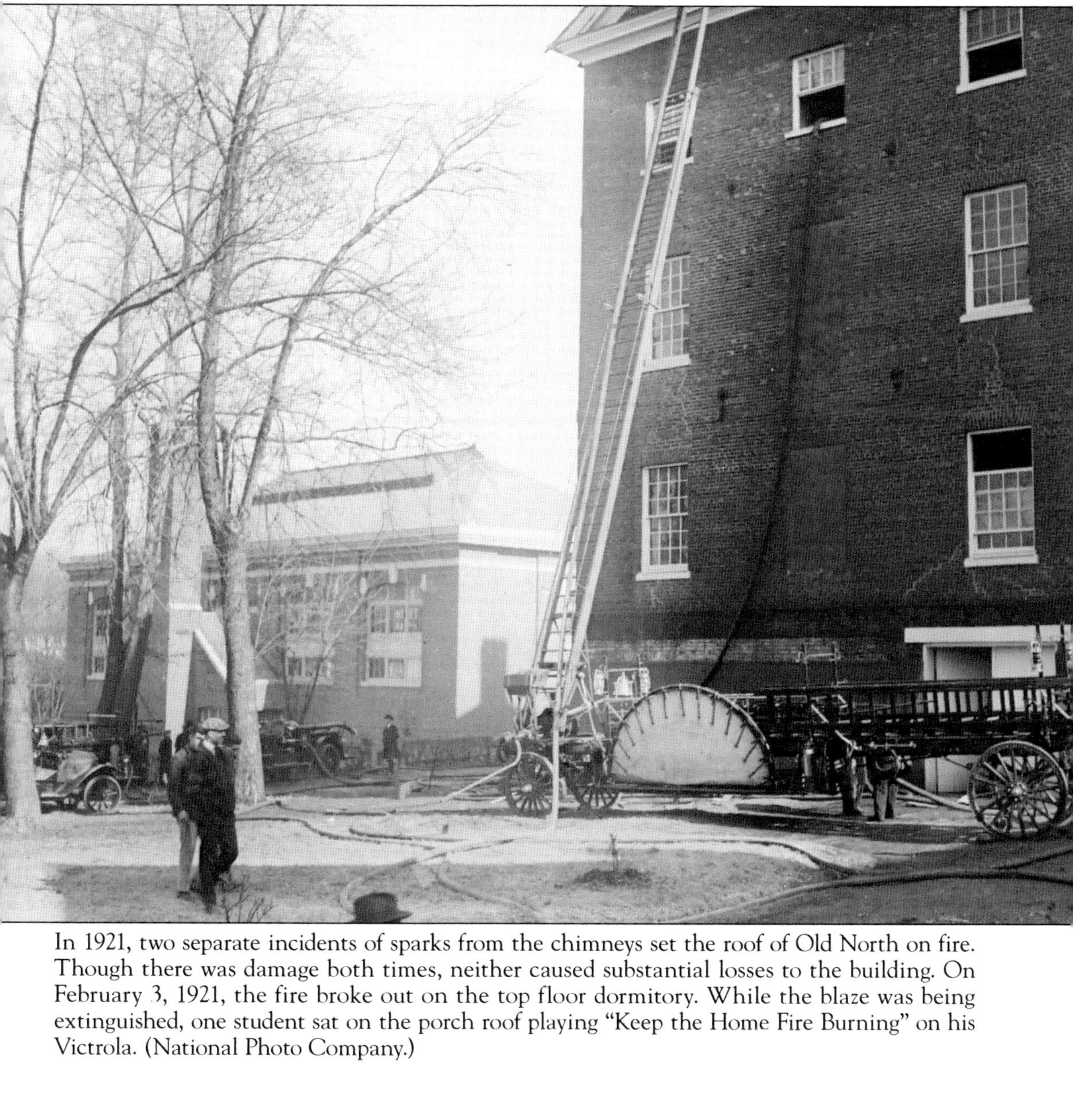

In 1921, two separate incidents of sparks from the chimneys set the roof of Old North on fire. Though there was damage both times, neither caused substantial losses to the building. On February 3, 1921, the fire broke out on the top floor dormitory. While the blaze was being extinguished, one student sat on the porch roof playing "Keep the Home Fire Burning" on his Victrola. (National Photo Company.)

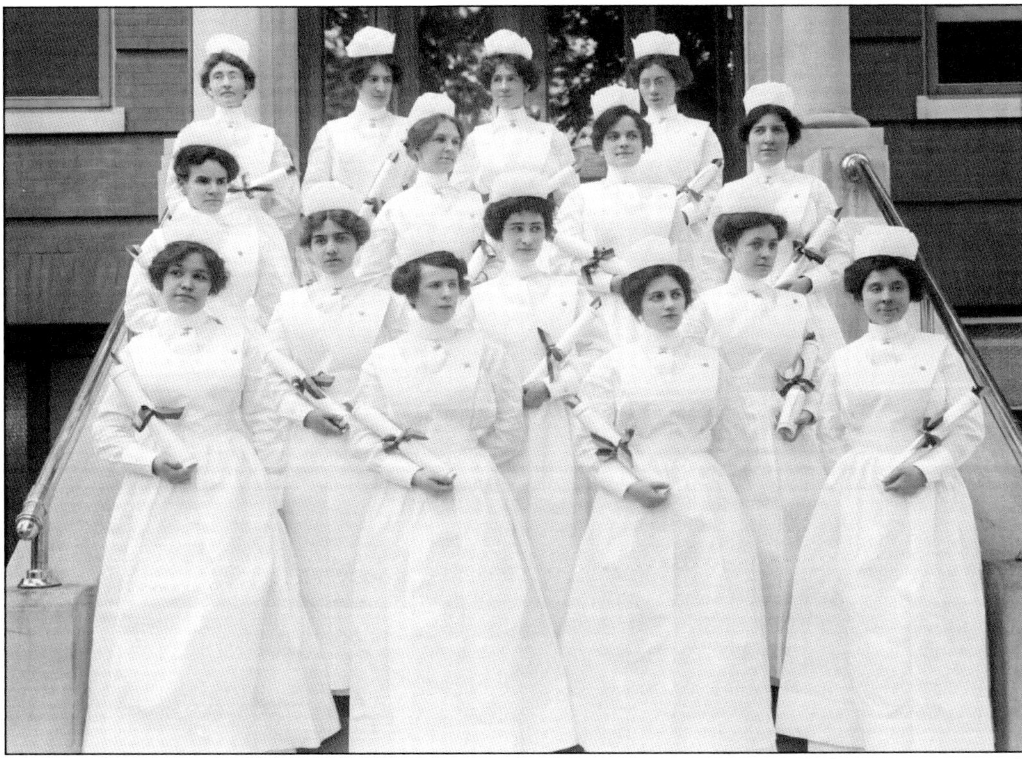

The Georgetown University Hospital Training School for Nurses was founded in 1903 to provide nursing staff for the recently established hospital at Georgetown. This 1914 graduating class of nurses included some of the first women to graduate from the university under any program. (National Photo Company.)

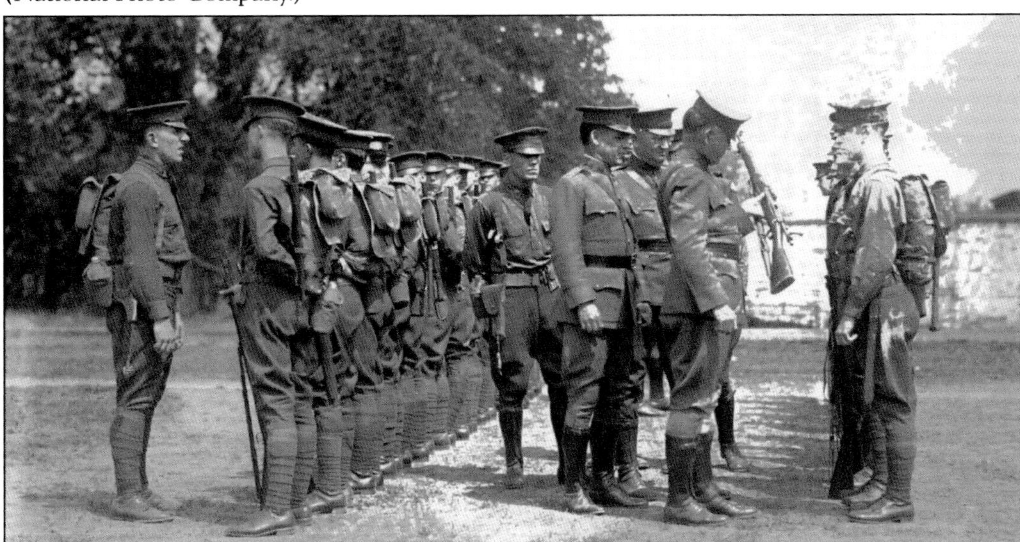

The Hoya Battalion was officially begun in the 1830s. The Georgetown Reserves are pictured here on May 5, 1923, a few days after the Military Day celebrations. A few years prior, during World War I, over 2,000 Georgetown men served. The first American to be killed in action, Denis R. Down, was a Georgetown University graduate. (National Photo Company.)

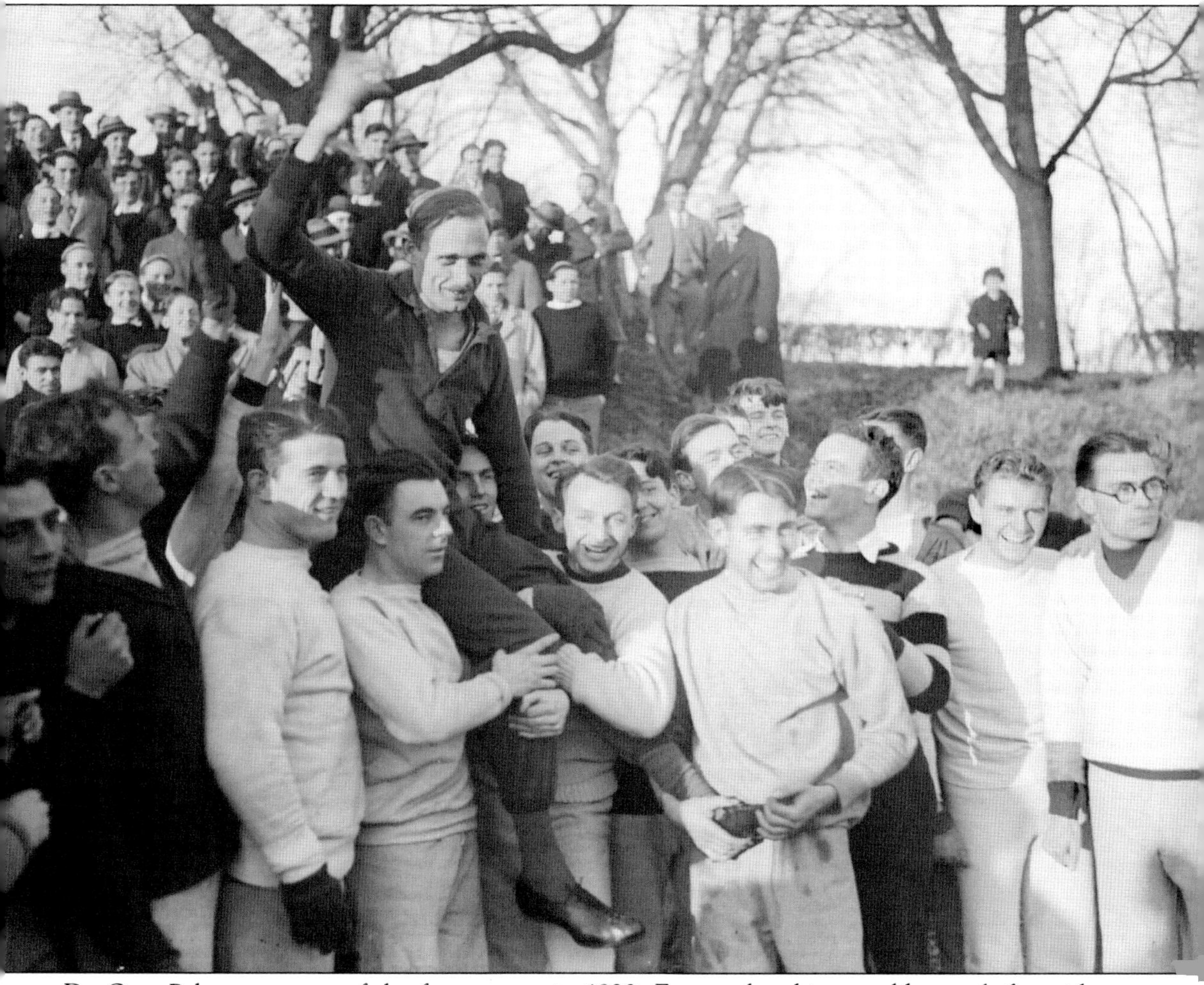

Dr. Otto Peltzer was one of the fastest men in 1920s Europe, breaking world records for mid-distance running. On his trip to America in December 1927, his first workout on American soil was taken over by eager Georgetown University students. The German athlete was touring American universities to study track conditions, but he was forbidden by the German Athletic Association to compete in races while in America so he could keep up his strength for the 1928 Olympics. Though he previously set world records for the 800-meter and 1,500-meter races, Peltzer never won an Olympic medal. (Harris Ewing Photography.)

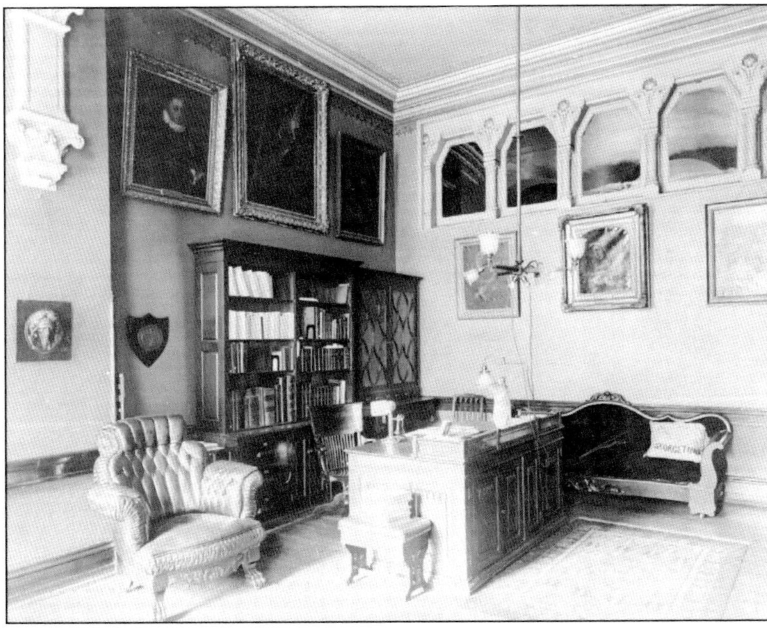

The 35th president of Georgetown College, Rev. Joseph Himmel, had his office here in 1910. Though founded two decades earlier as a Jesuit institution, it was only in 1805 that the Society of Jesuits became an active part of the administration and served in advisory roles. The university has always been separate from the Jesuits, though influenced by their teachings. (HABS.)

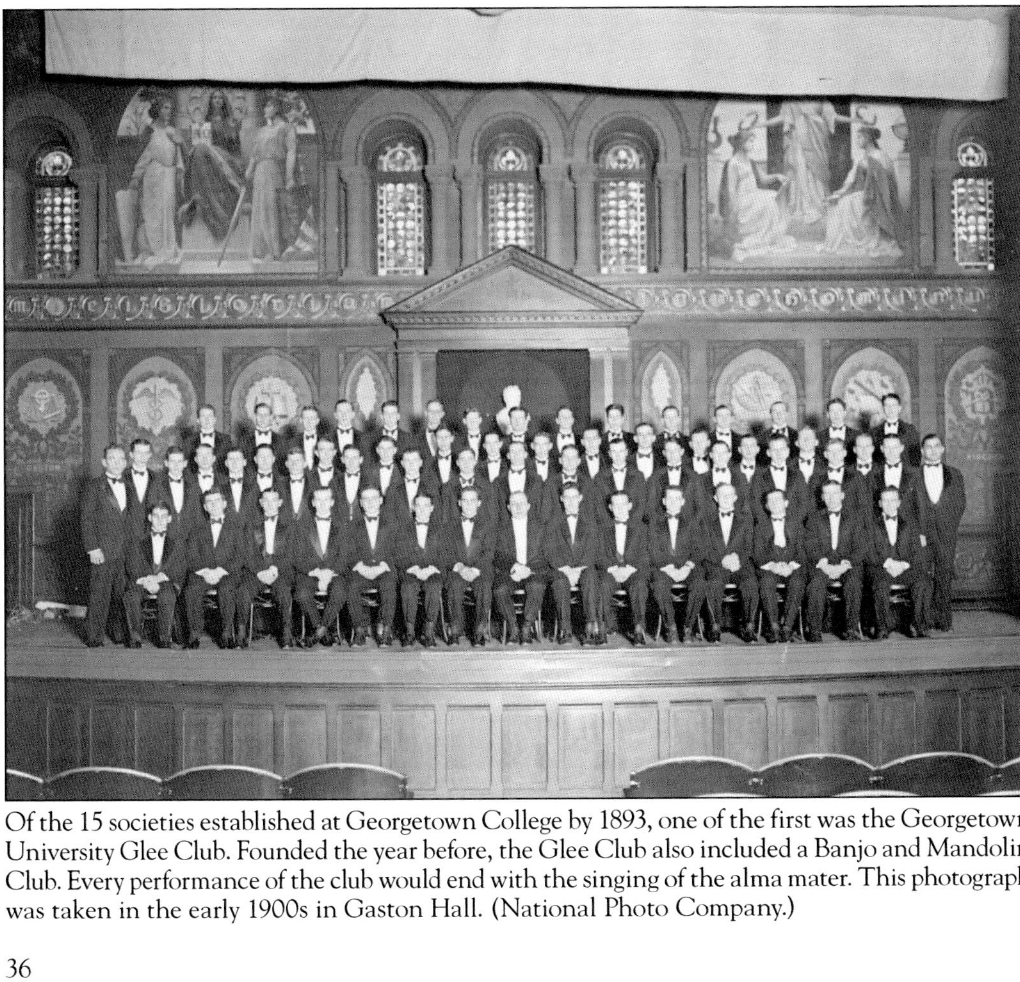

Of the 15 societies established at Georgetown College by 1893, one of the first was the Georgetown University Glee Club. Founded the year before, the Glee Club also included a Banjo and Mandolin Club. Every performance of the club would end with the singing of the alma mater. This photograph was taken in the early 1900s in Gaston Hall. (National Photo Company.)

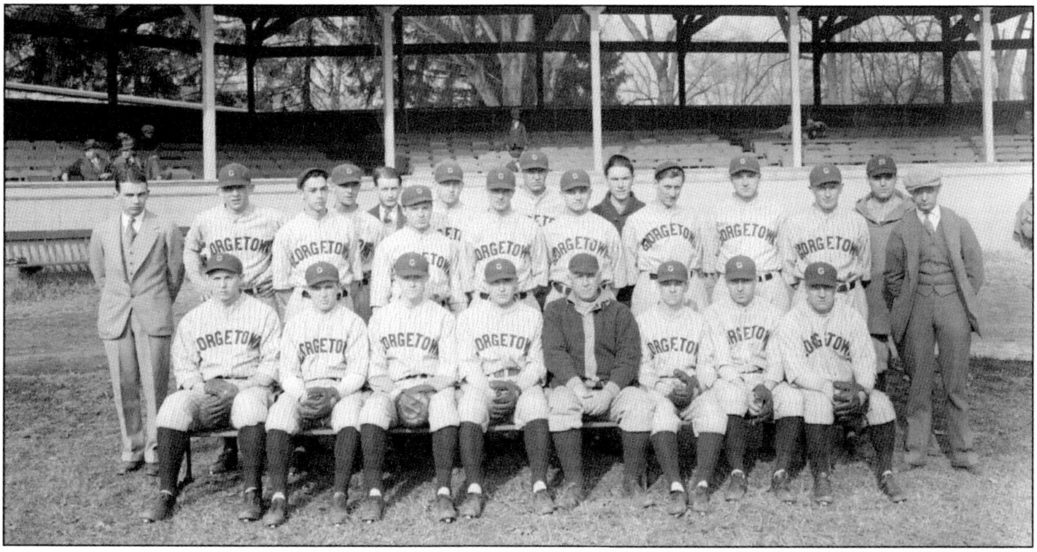

Georgetown's oldest sports team is the baseball team, which has played since 1866 and was formally organized in 1870. This photograph shows the team in 1926. All sporting teams at Georgetown are known as the Hoyas. This goes back to the classical education and the university chant, *Hoya Saxa*. A combination of Greek and Latin, it means "What Rocks!" and may refer to the defensive line of the football team. The Civil War took a toll on the size of the student body, dropping it to 17. After the war, the rowing team adopted the Prussian blue of the Union uniform and the cadet grey of the Confederate uniform. This has been the official color scheme of the Hoyas ever since. (National Photo Company.)

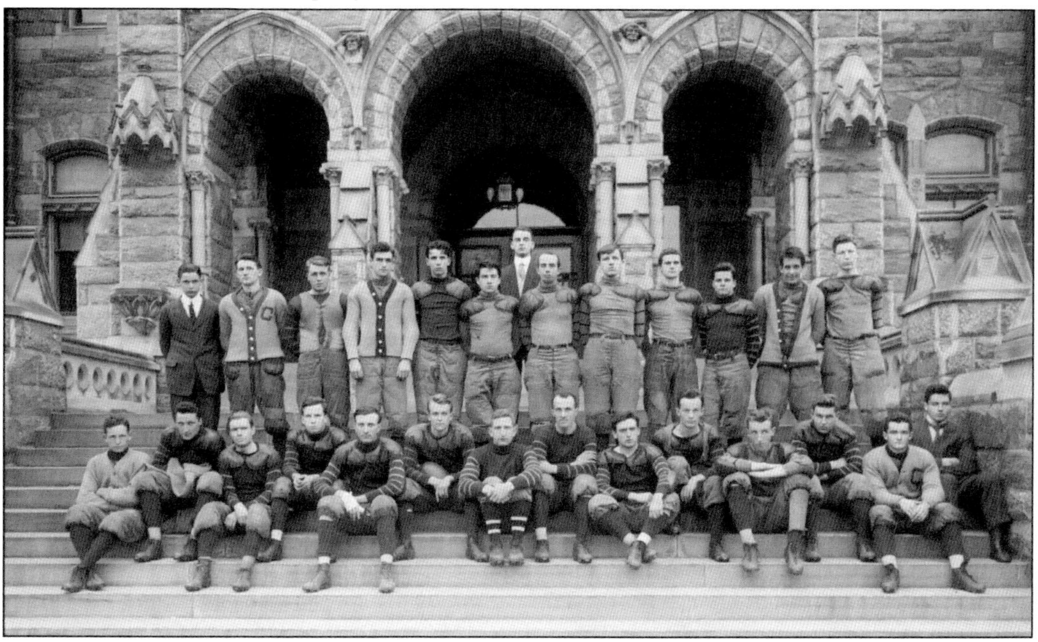

This photograph of the Georgetown University football team is from the 1910s. The football program was established in 1874, but, after the expensive nature of the game proved too much after World War II, the team was disbanded. Though an earlier, student-run, exhibition-only program was established, the university reintroduced an official team in 1970. (Harris Ewing Photography.)

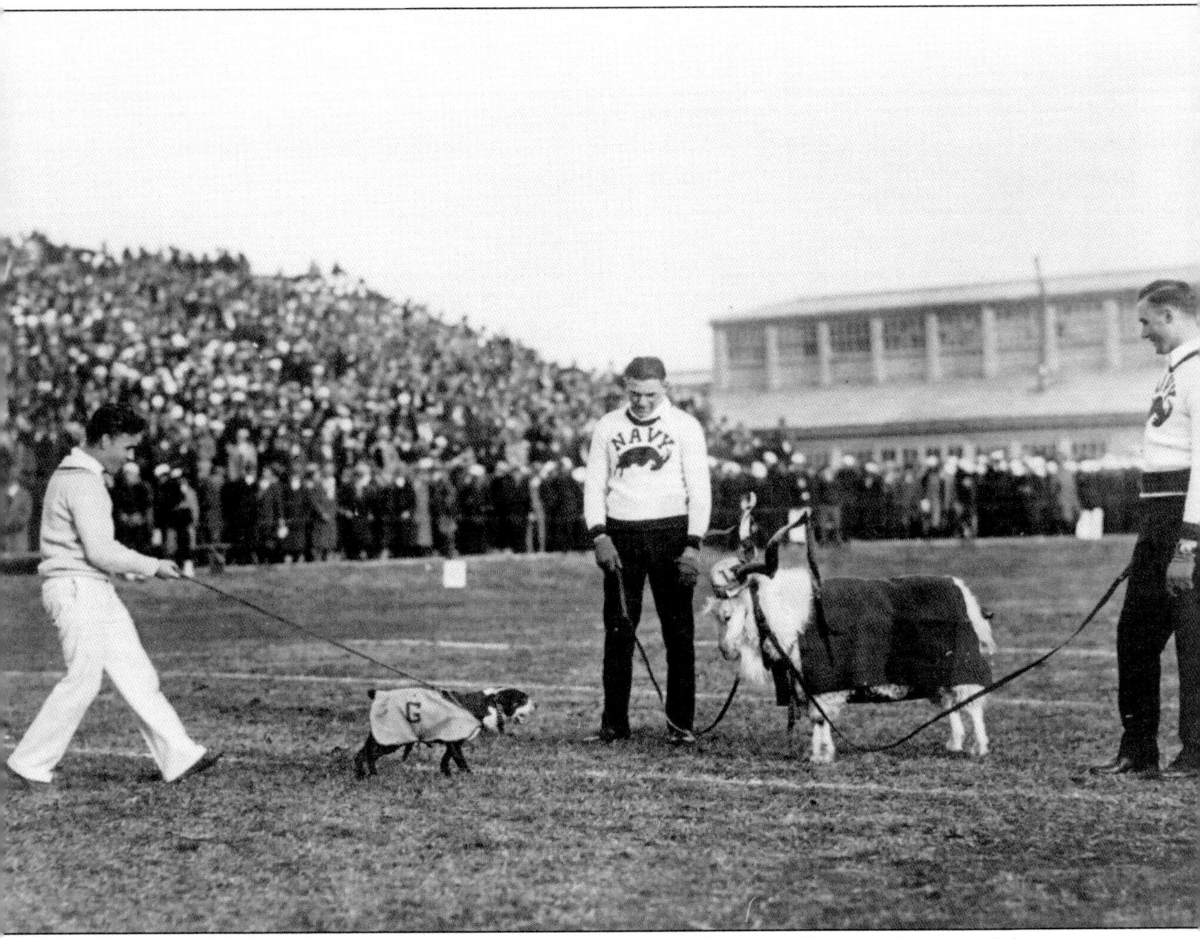

The 1920 Georgetown vs. Navy football game began with a friendly introduction of the mascots. A bulldog is the current mascot, but different breeds have been associated with the football team since the beginning of the 1900s, from bull terriers to Great Danes. These early dogs usually came with students and were cared for by individual students and the team rather than the school administration. Since 1962, English bulldogs named Jack have been the official mascots of Georgetown University. His care is entrusted to a group of students known as "Jack's Crew." The first bulldog was supposed to be named "Hoya," but he would only answer to Jack. (National Photo Company.)

Three

Home Town

Row Houses, Rentals, and Mansions

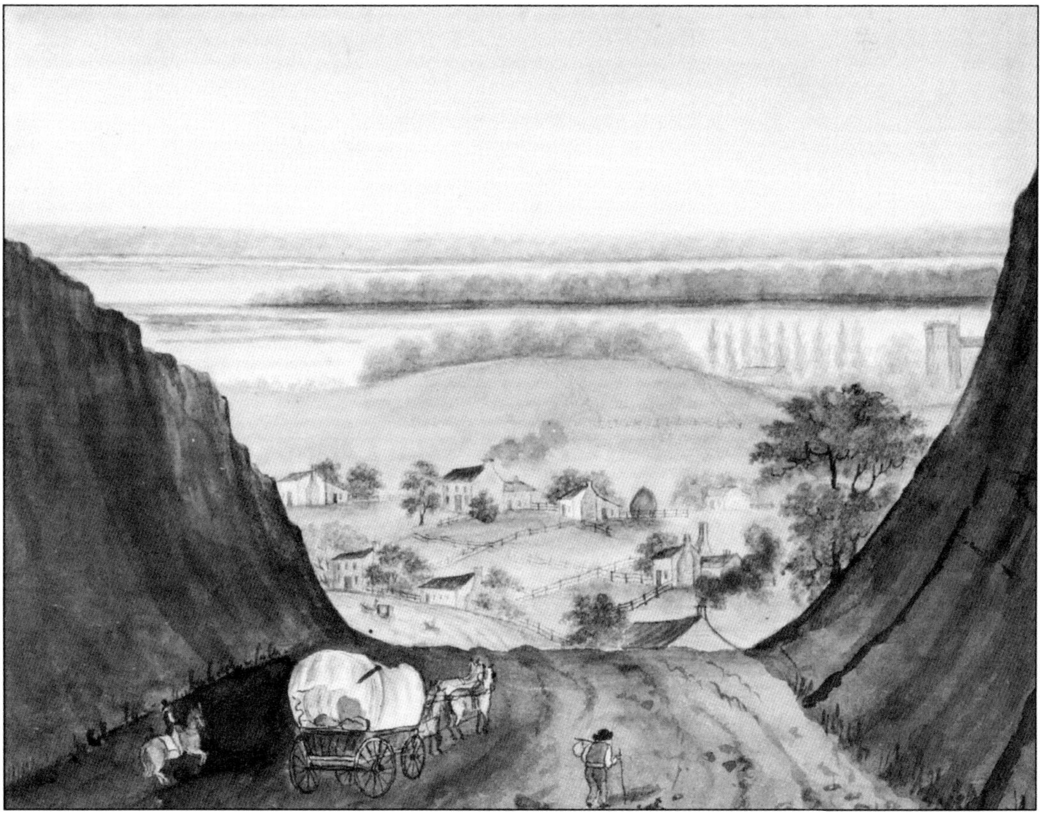

Looking down from Book Hill in the north of Georgetown to the Potomac River, this painting by resident Rebecca Nourse shows the time before the busy, commercial Wisconsin Avenue, now filled with residences and businesses, blocked the view to the Potomac. This was a time when Georgetown was but a few wooden buildings along the water. (Dumbarton House, National Society of the Colonial Dames of America.)

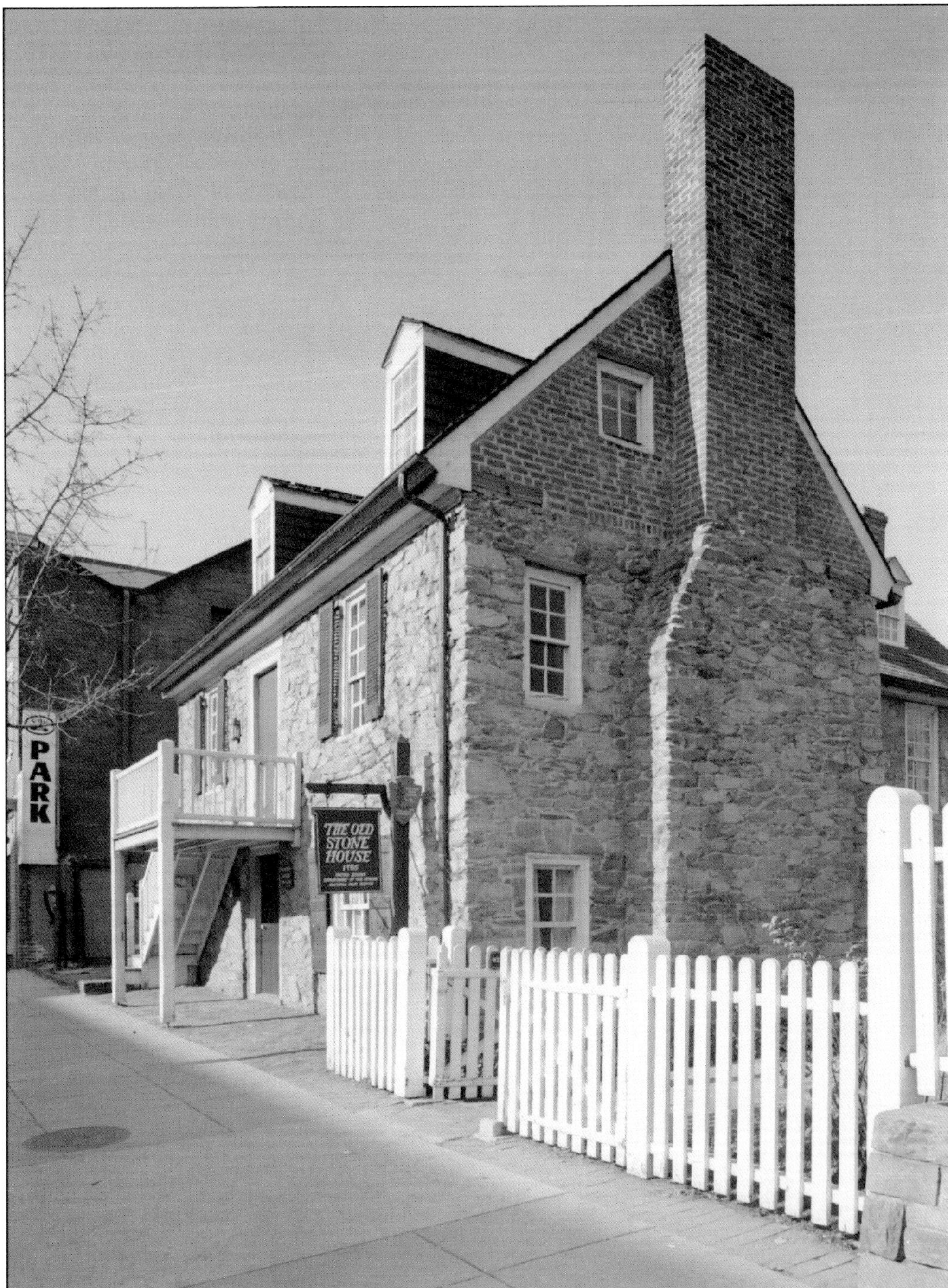

The oldest residence in the District of Columbia, the Old Stone House, at 3051 M Street NW, was built in 1765 by German immigrant Christopher Leyman. Built with stones quarried from the nearby Potomac River, this home remained intact due to the incorrect belief that it was the headquarters of the men who created the federal district. By the time the true history was discovered, it was a 200-year-old house and worth keeping on its own merits. (HABS.)

As Georgetown developed, homes were built, well before electric power. Dotting the sidewalks are old coal chutes. Coal was brought in on the C&O Canal and could be delivered directly to the house. Some homes would have coal chutes built directly into the side of the house, but this one is found on the sidewalk and likely connects to a nearby basement. (HABS.)

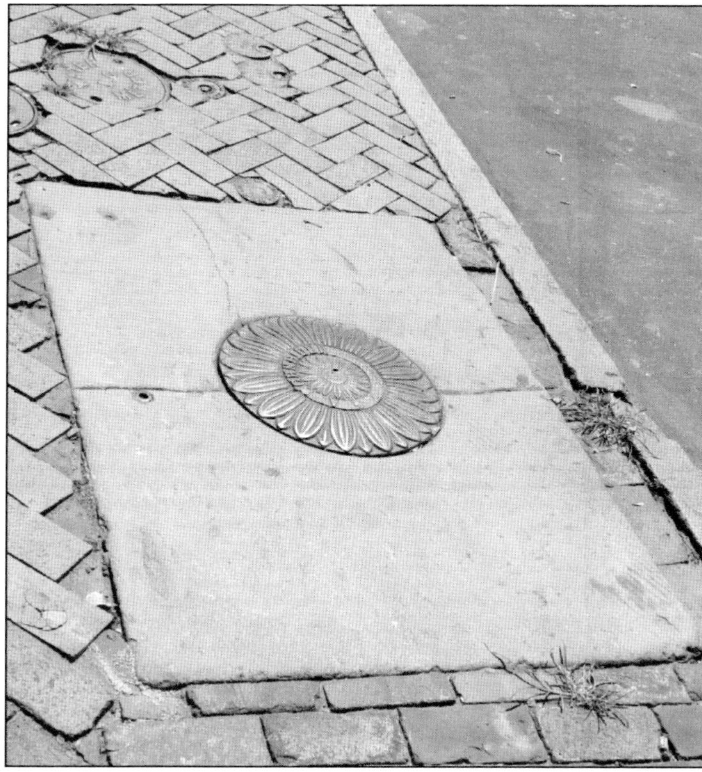

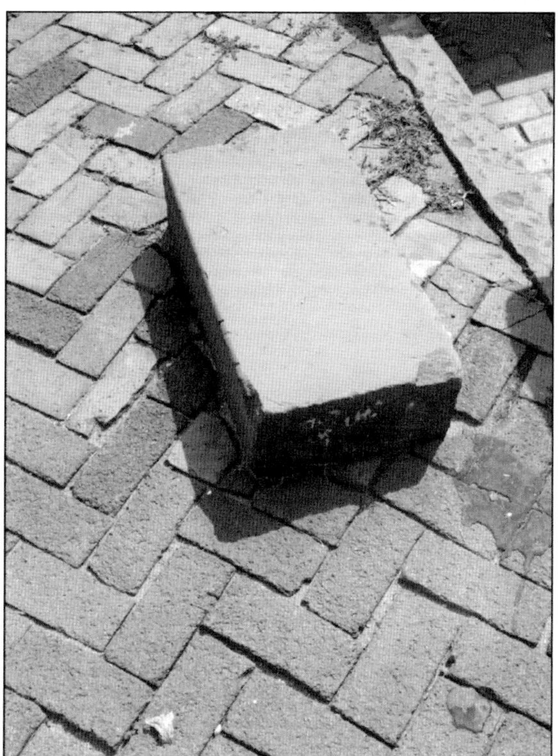

Before sidewalks and before roads were paved and when women often wore long dresses, these carriage stones would be placed in front of a house to assist a lady getting into and out of a carriage. (HABS.)

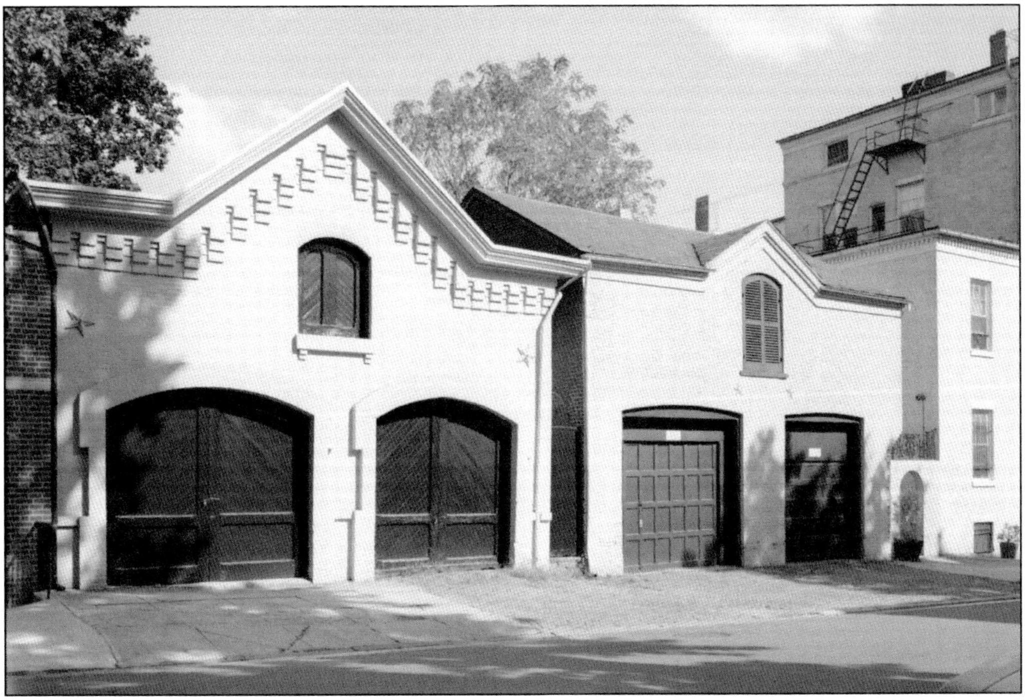

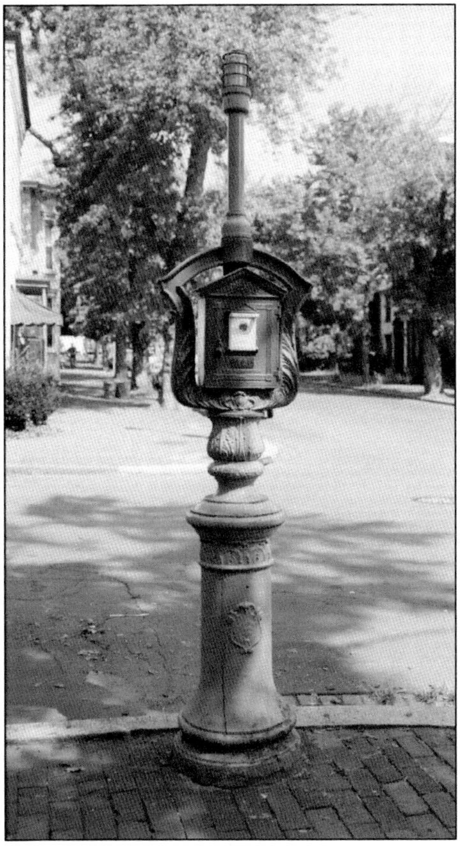

Thought to be from about 1857, these are a few of the last Victorian carriage houses remaining in Georgetown. Originally built to house horse-drawn carriages, many have been converted into modern garages or even small living quarters. (HABS.)

Before 911 operators, cell phones, and two-way radios, patrolmen and neighbors in need would use these call boxes, located on 30 street corners throughout Georgetown. A police officer could unlock the boxes to connect with his precinct to call for backup or to check in while on the beat. Installed in the mid-1800s, these could be used to call local police and fire authorities. By the 1960s, they were obsolete—but too large and heavy to move. They are now part of an art project throughout the District of Columbia that provides historical anecdotes or paintings relevant to the area. (HABS.)

Original firefighting companies were not a part of the local government. The Vigilant Fire Company was founded as the first in Georgetown in 1817. This building was constructed as their second firehouse in 1844 and remained in use until 1883, when the company, now District of Columbia Fire Company No. 5, moved around the corner. The lore of their jokes and tomfoolery was so strong that the Georgetown Fire Company fined 25¢ to any member who mentioned the name "Vigilant Fire." (HABS.)

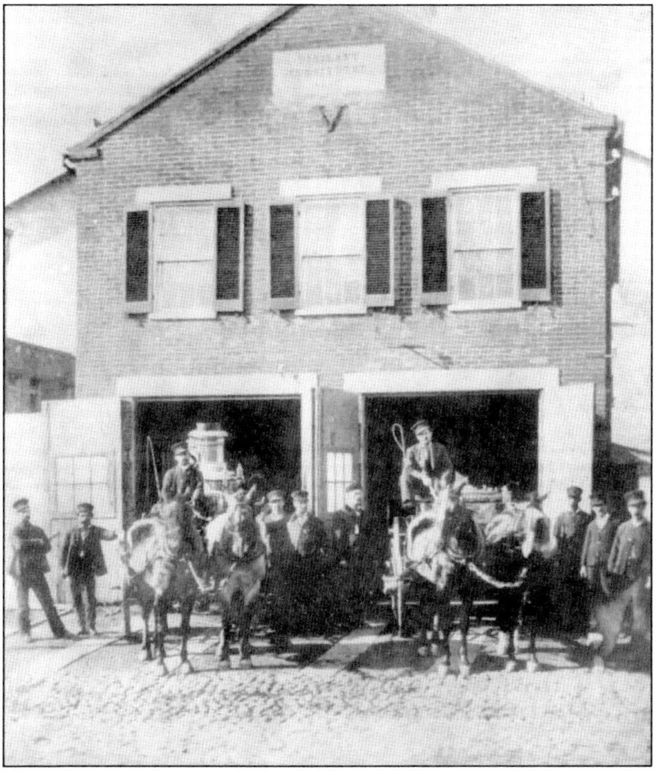

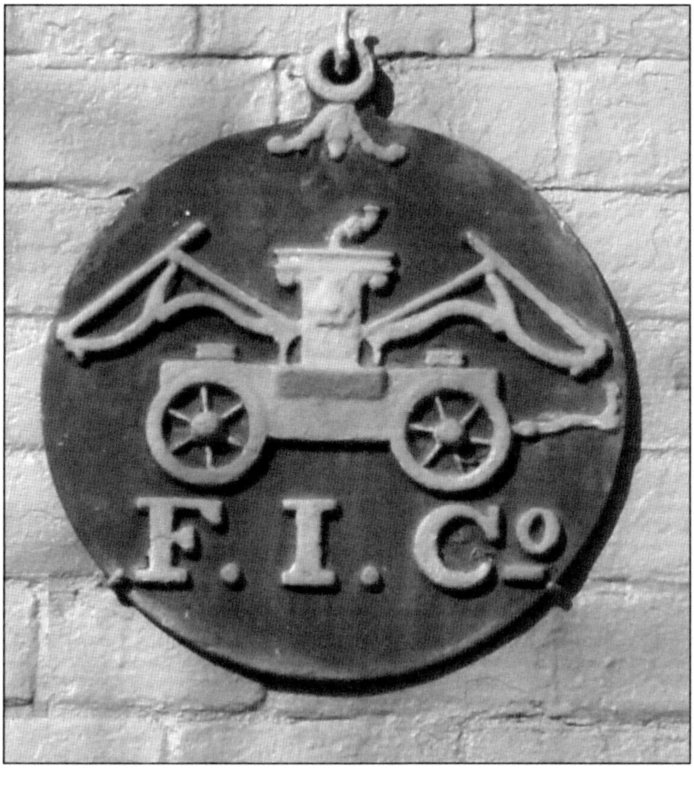

Fire marks were designated symbols to show that the owner of that house was a paying member to a fire insurance company. Before volunteer and city-funded firefighting companies, there were private companies who expected payment for their services—and often did not get it. A monthly subscription service assured that firefighters would get paid and supported both these private insurance companies and the volunteer brigades, who were sometimes given bonuses if they were the first to arrive. (Author's collection.)

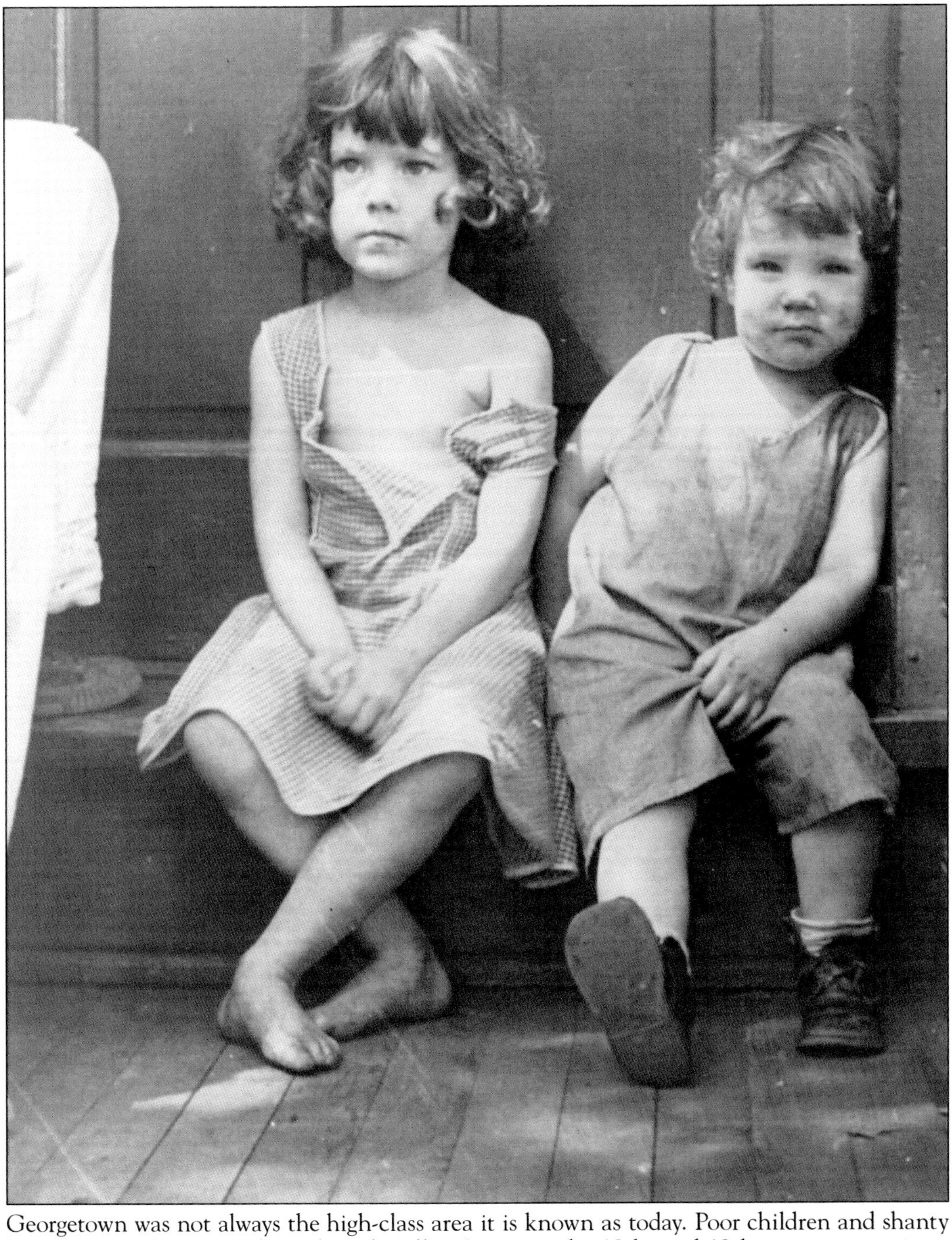

Georgetown was not always the high-class area it is known as today. Poor children and shanty houses were often seen along the sidewalks. Amongst the 18th- and 19th-century mansions, pockets of poverty could be found. The Gilded Age of the 1920s took hold more on Massachusetts Avenue in Washington, leaving Georgetown behind. However, not long after this photograph was taken in 1935, many moving to the area to work for the federal government under New Deal programs began to purchase homes in the more affordable Georgetown. (US Farm Security Administration, Office of War Information.)

The exact date the Medley-Sewell house was constructed is unknown, but it is known that there was a building here in 1798. The lot was purchased by Bernard Medley and then, shortly after, by Clement Sewell. Sewell was the first proprietor of the famed City Tavern, still standing on M Street NW. (HABS.)

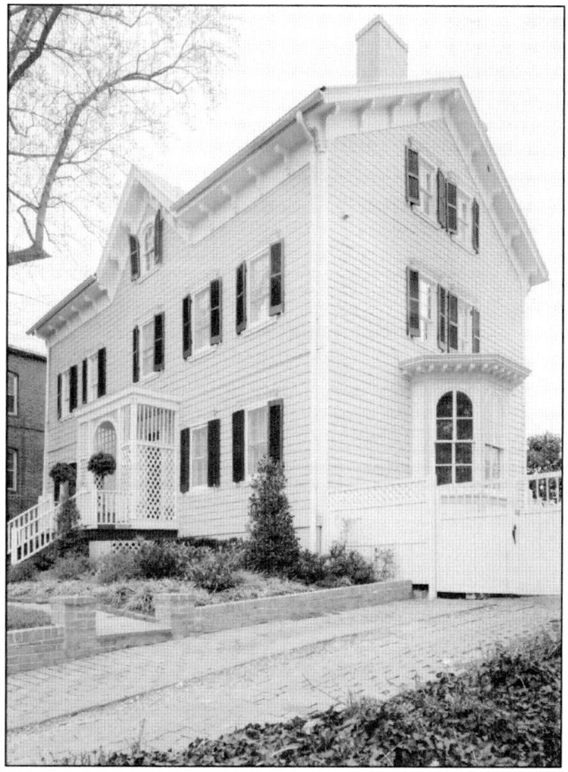

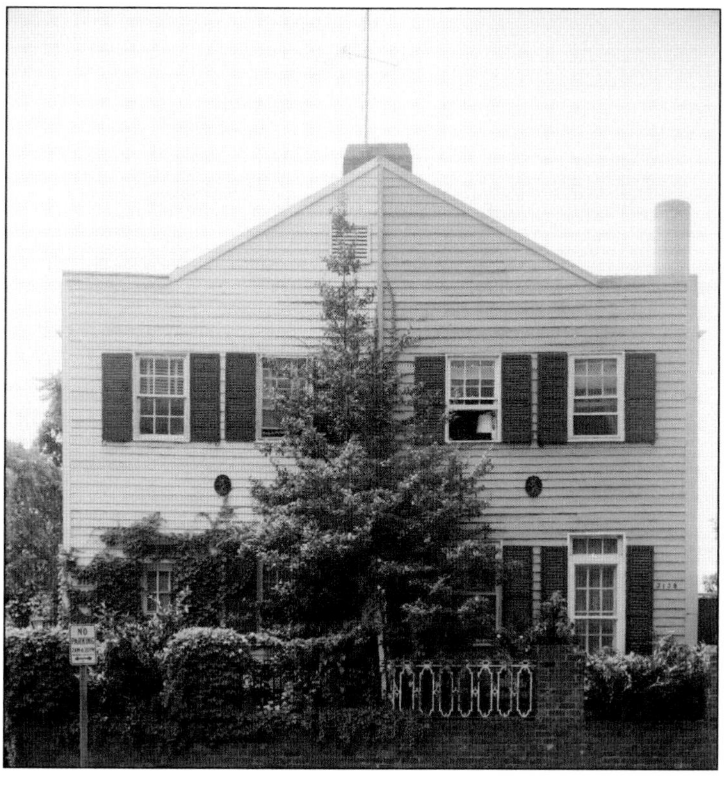

The Brickyard Hill House, built c. 1800, remains as a rare example of a stand-alone, wood-frame house in the Georgetown waterfront district, and it is one of the oldest in the area. It can be seen in the backyard of George Bernard's Civil War photograph from Mason's Island. It was owned by the Peters, one of the leading families of Georgetown, as one of their many property investments in Georgetown and DC. (HABS.)

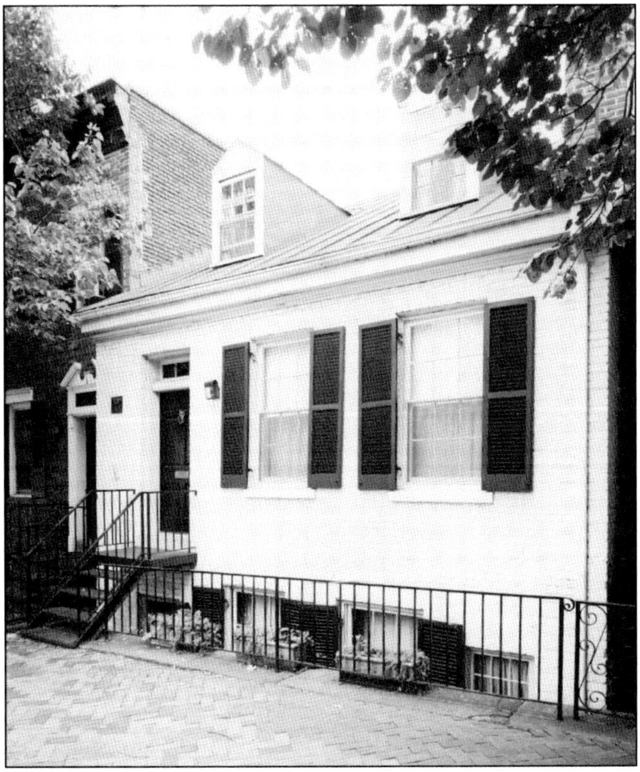

The McCleery House was built in 1800 as a modest-sized residence near the water. Built before the canal, the house seems to be only one level, but it was originally constructed as a two-story home. When the road was raised to accommodate the canal, the first floor was below street level. One can see that the sidewalk is about halfway up the first-floor windows. Oral histories of the house state that it was designed by James Hoban, the architect of the White House, but there is no written proof of this. (HABS.)

This cottage was likely built before the Civil War, but no exact date is known for the erection of this structure or when its namesake moved in. Emma Dorothy Eliza Nevitte Southworth, more commonly known as E.D.E.N. Southworth, was a well-known author, penning more than 60 novels. She lived here until her death in 1899. Before the house was demolished in the 1940s, it was a tourist trap with a café and postcards for sale. (Historical Society of Washington, DC.)

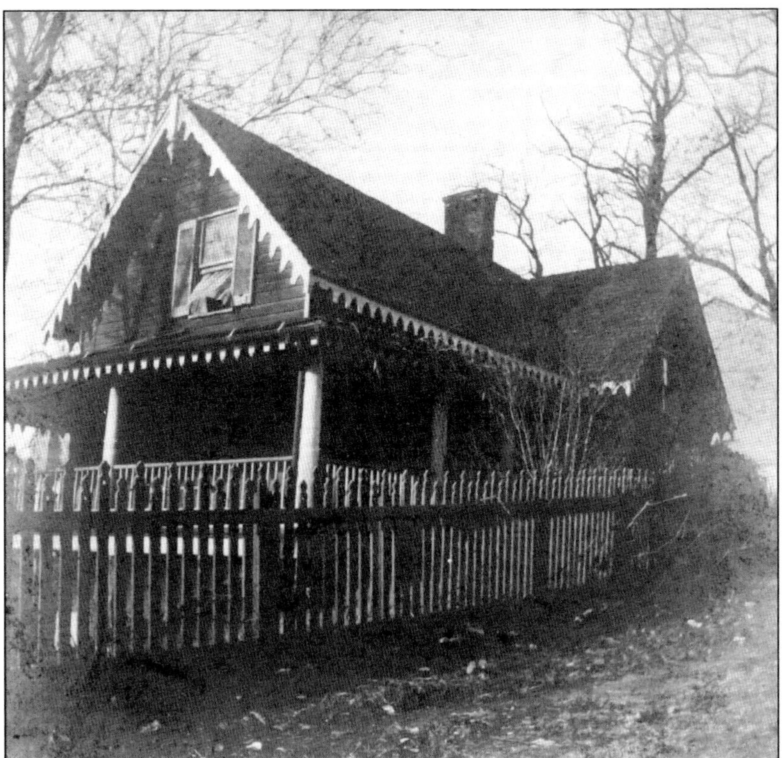

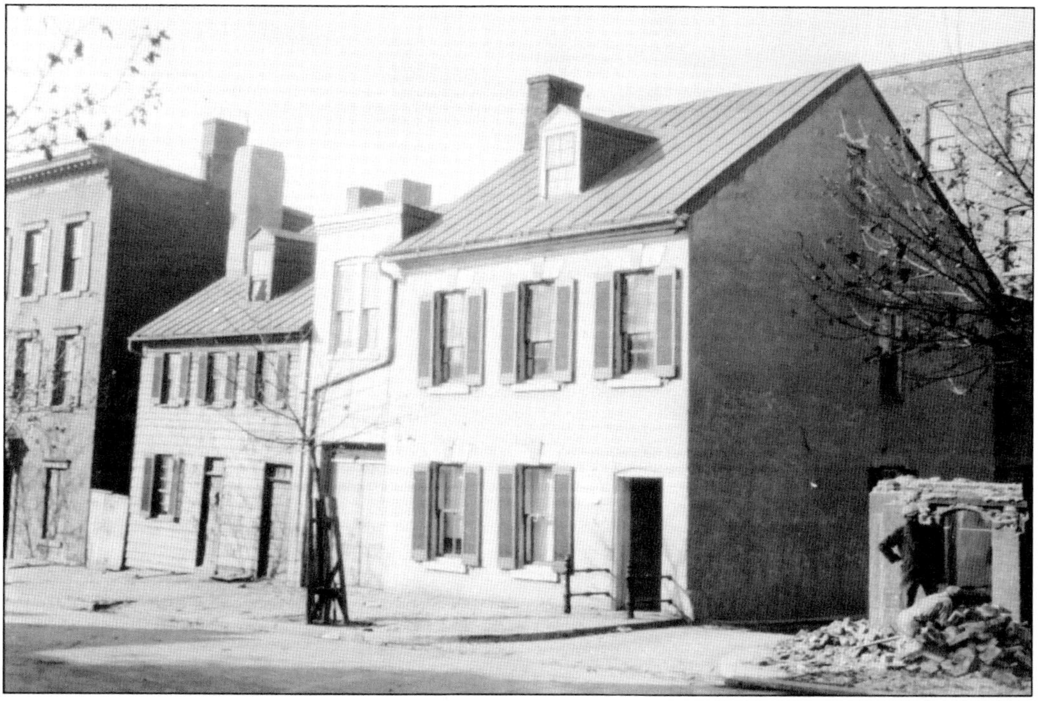

This small wooden home is largely unchanged from when it was built in 1810. The Adams-Mason House is one of the few clapboard houses still standing in Georgetown. Not much changed between the 1899 photograph above and the 1967 photograph at right. (Both, HABS.)

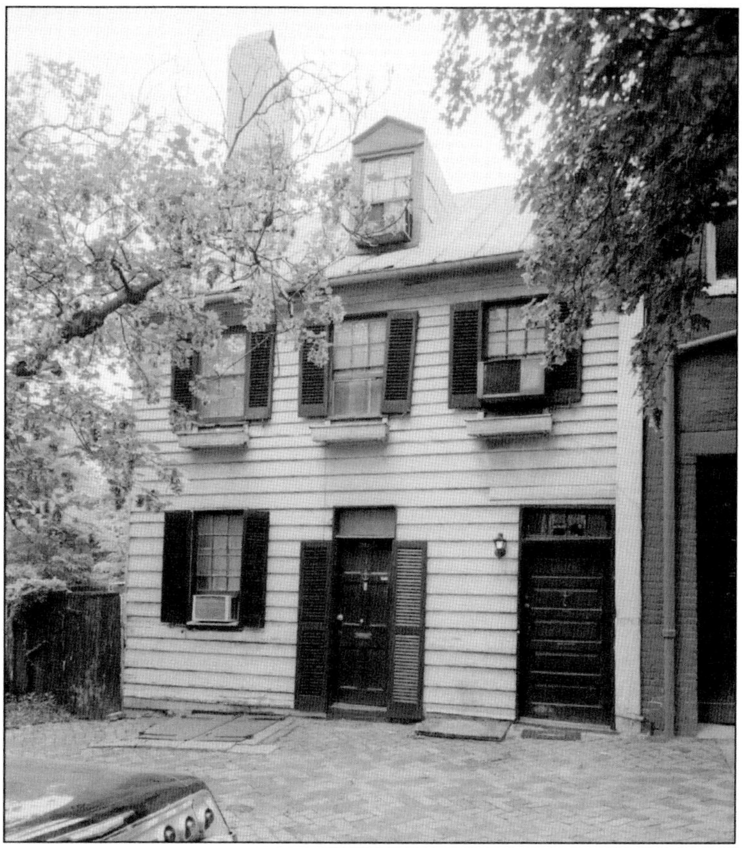

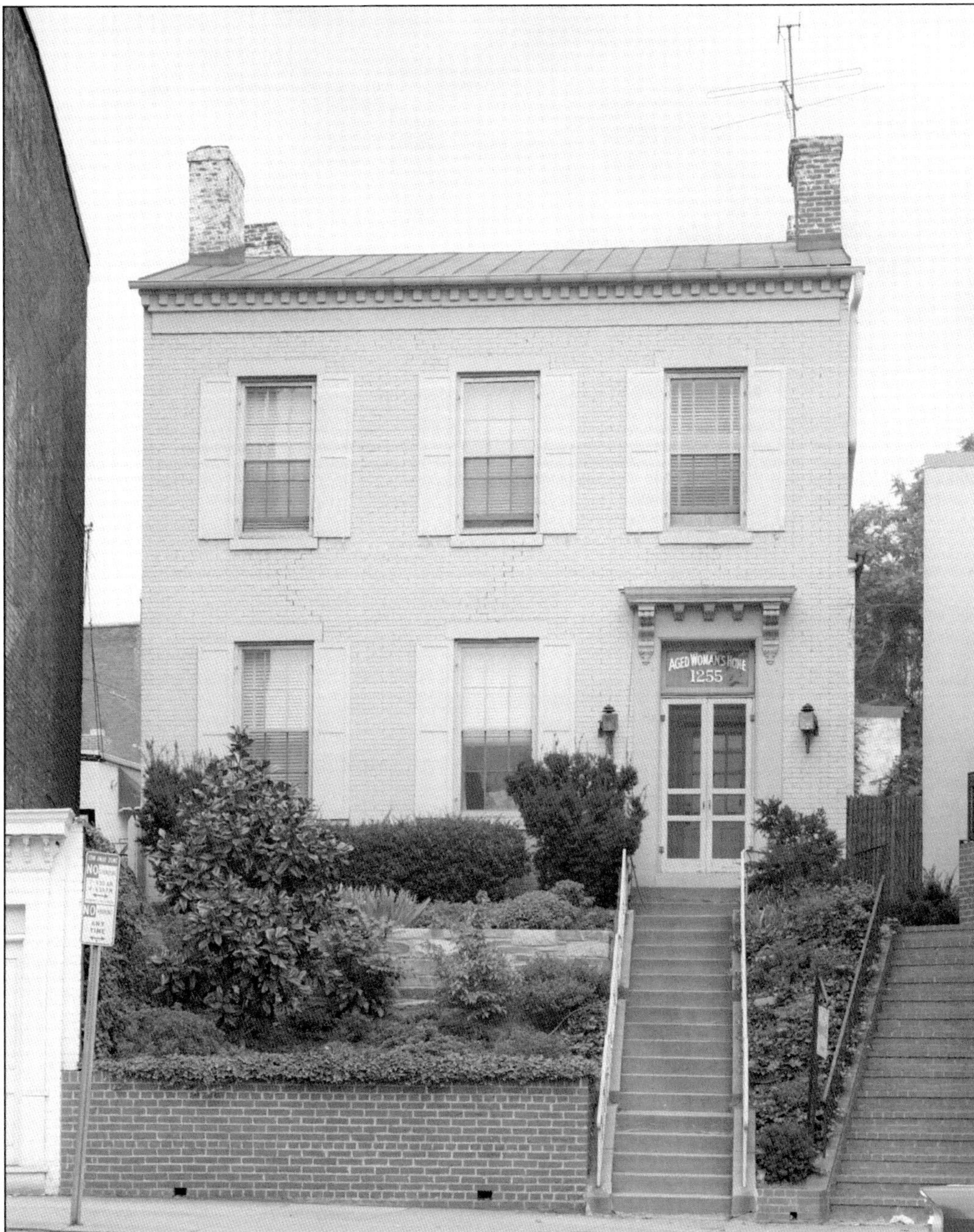

The oldest portion of this house is said to be from 1756, but most alterations and expansions were made from the 1840s to the 1870s. In 1804, it was purchased by John Lutz, the personal bodyguard to Gen. George Washington during the Revolutionary War. The Female Union Benevolent Society purchased it in 1868 as a refuge for aged women in Georgetown and Washington. The society was promoted through lectures by Mark Twain and a donation by W.W. Corcoran, who gave $15,000 on the condition that only the interest was used. He believed women could not possibly use the entire amount. It is still owned by the society today, but it is called the Aged Woman's Home of Georgetown. (HABS.)

These three homes were built explicitly for rental purposes and are still used in that capacity today. They were built in 1895 as simple frame houses by Mary Hardeny, who owned a liquor store on M Street with her husband. The year before Hardeny Row was condemned by the city, the rents were between $12 and $20 a month. After being sold to Georgetown College, they were renovated and used as rentals by the university. (HABS.)

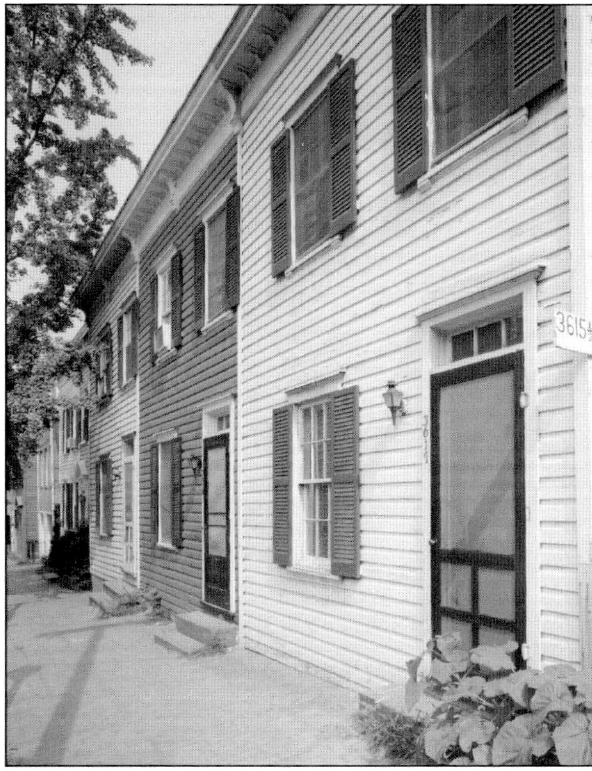

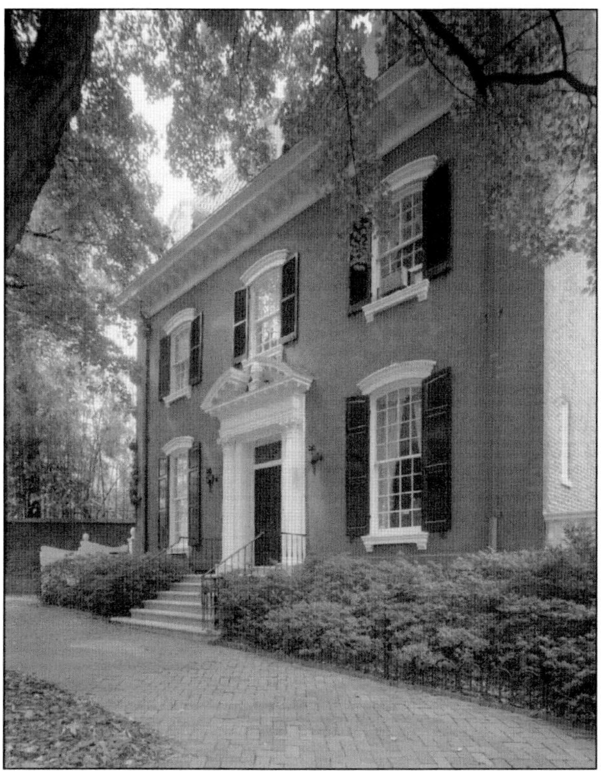

Unlike many of the historic homes in Georgetown, this house was built after the Civil War, in 1869. Though Georgetown is thought of as a place where successful men owned their homes, it was often the case that the homes were rented. This house at 3331 O Street NW was rented by Pres. Franklin D. Roosevelt's son James. In 1937, he applied for a permit for a ramp, presumably for use by his father. Robert Kennedy also lived in this house, a few blocks from his brother, in 1957. (HABS.)

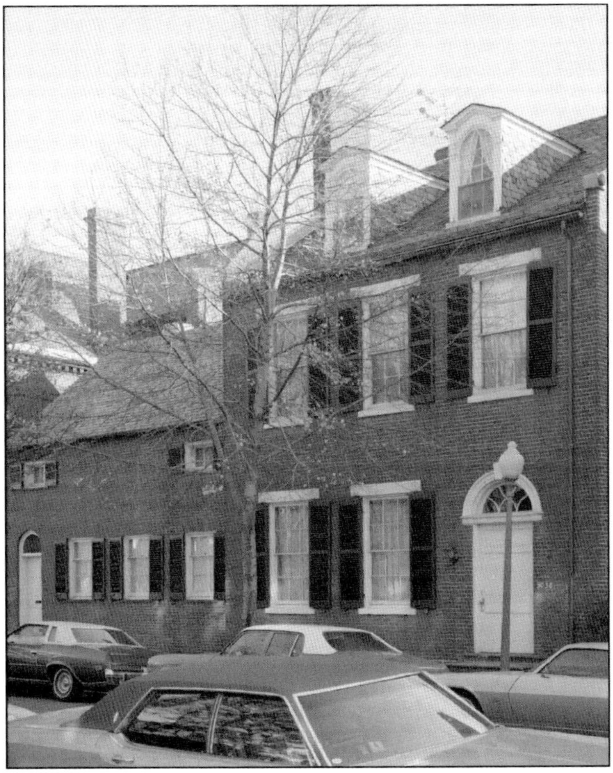

Considered part of the Kennedys' "Camelot," the Kennedy family lived in many homes in Georgetown. This one, however, was never lived in by John F. Kennedy himself. The Riggs-Riley House (c. 1812) was the temporary residence of Jackie Kennedy and the children after President Kennedy's assassination. (HABS.)

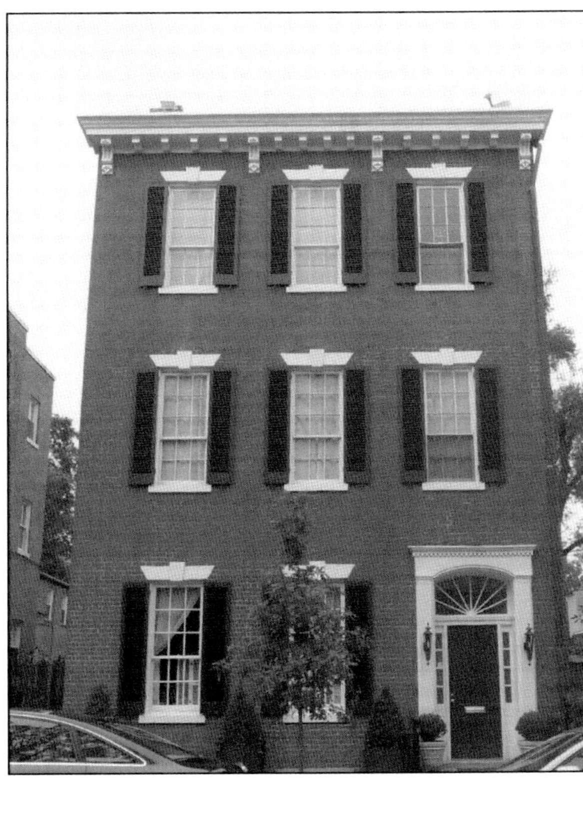

This house was the residence of William Marbury, of *Marbury v. Madison* fame. A simple redbrick house, it was the final private residence of John F. and Jackie Kennedy before they moved into the White House. The house across the street bears a plaque thanking the owner for her kindness on the long, cold nights when the press was covering the Kennedy campaign. She allowed the media to use her phone and offered them hot tea. (Author's collection.)

In the early 1800s, much of the land in Georgetown that was not already developed was bought on speculation, and it then traded hands between relatively few men. One of the wealthiest merchants in 1808, when this house was built, was Washington Bowie, who was bankrupt just a decade before and would be again shortly after. The owners in the early 1900s, the Seviers, wanted the house to become a historic house museum in memory of John Sevier, the first governor of Tennessee, but this was never realized. It is, however, still partially named for him, as the Bowie-Sevier House. (HABS.)

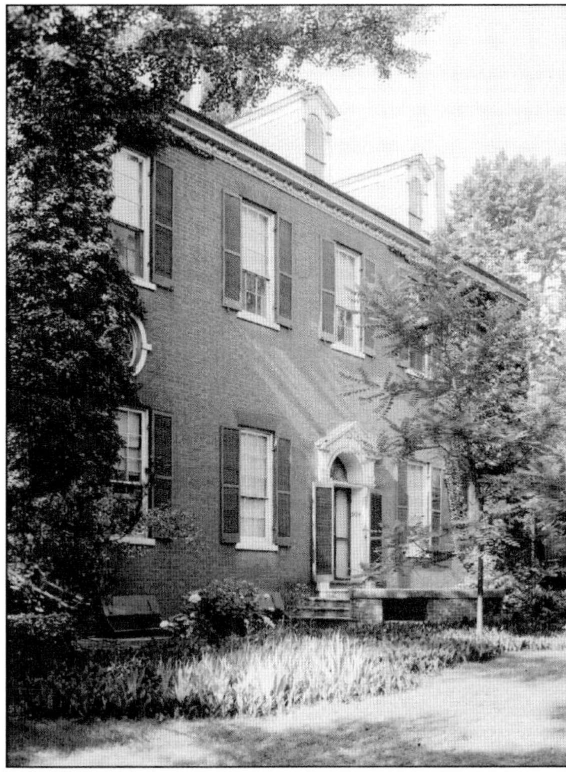

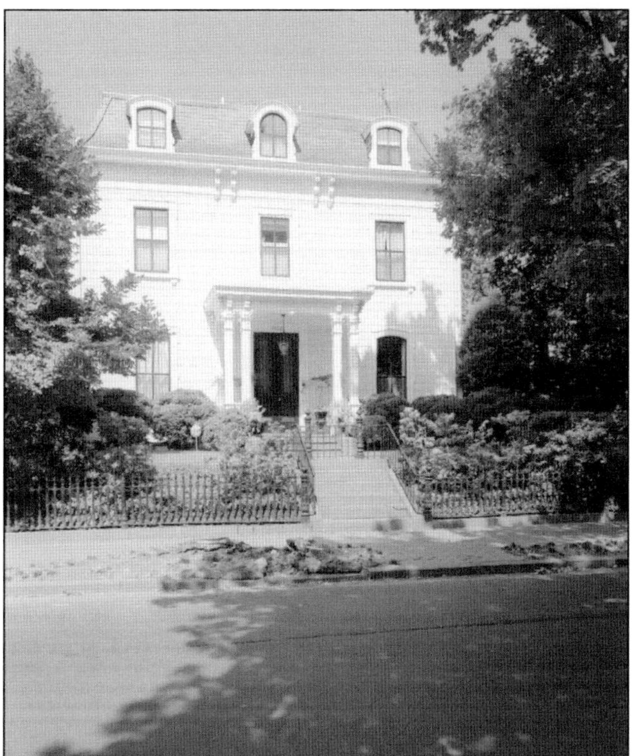

Though later research has proven the legend untrue, it still continues that this house was once made of brick. The legend goes that when a congressman from Maine who was involved in the shipping industry moved in, he had lumber from a shipyard in New England sent down to cover the house so his constituents would not be upset. That story is likely not true, however, and the house is not made of bricks, which in itself was rare for that time in Georgetown. Known as the Phillip T. Berry House, it was built in the 1870s. (HABS.)

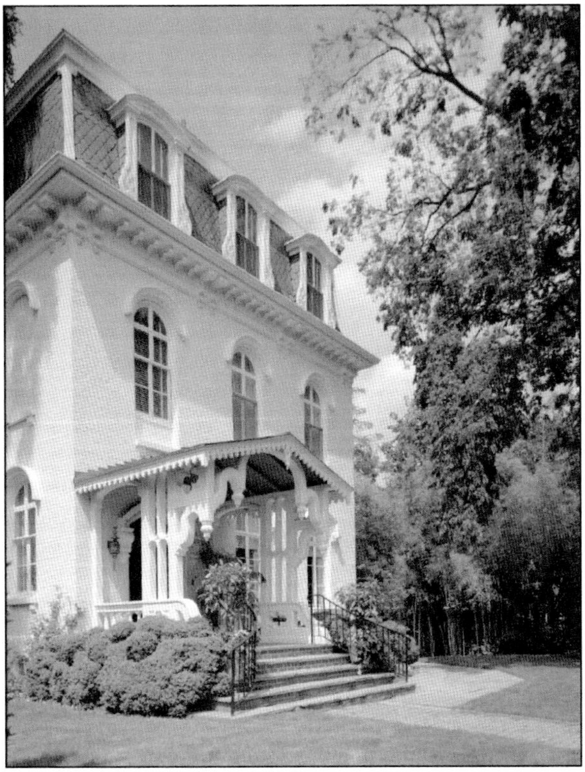

Situated on the heights between what was urban Georgetown and rural farmland, the Dougal House was built in the mid-19th-century for the Dougal family. It was actually on land owned by William Dougal's father-in-law, Morris Adler. Adler had the house built for his daughter Mary and her new husband. As an engraver, Dougal provided plates for the *Narrative of the U.S. Exploring Expedition*. (HABS.)

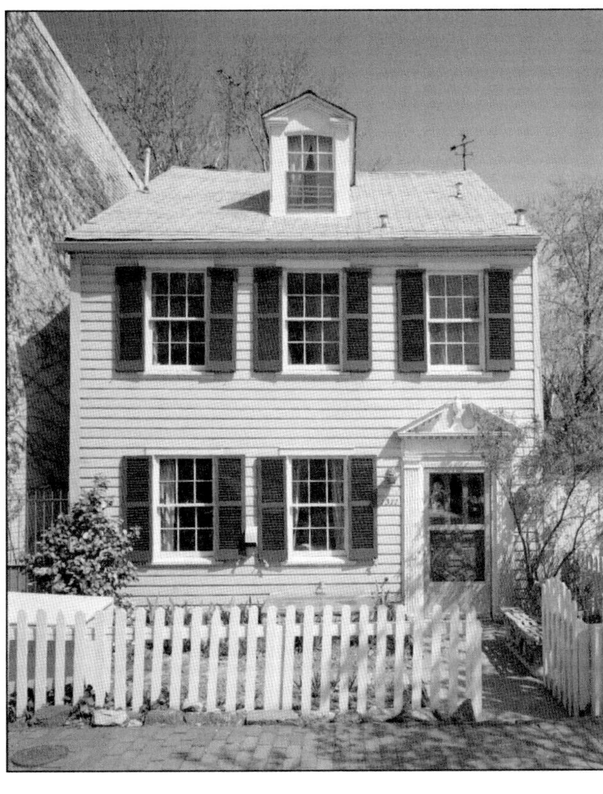

Smaller than the nearby mansions but larger than workers' cottages, the Bussard-Newman House is a mid-sized frame house that was built as a combination residence and shop from 1805 to 1808. It was owned or rented at different times by a butcher, a painter, a shoemaker, and a confectioner, who ran their shops out of one part and lived in the other. (HABS.)

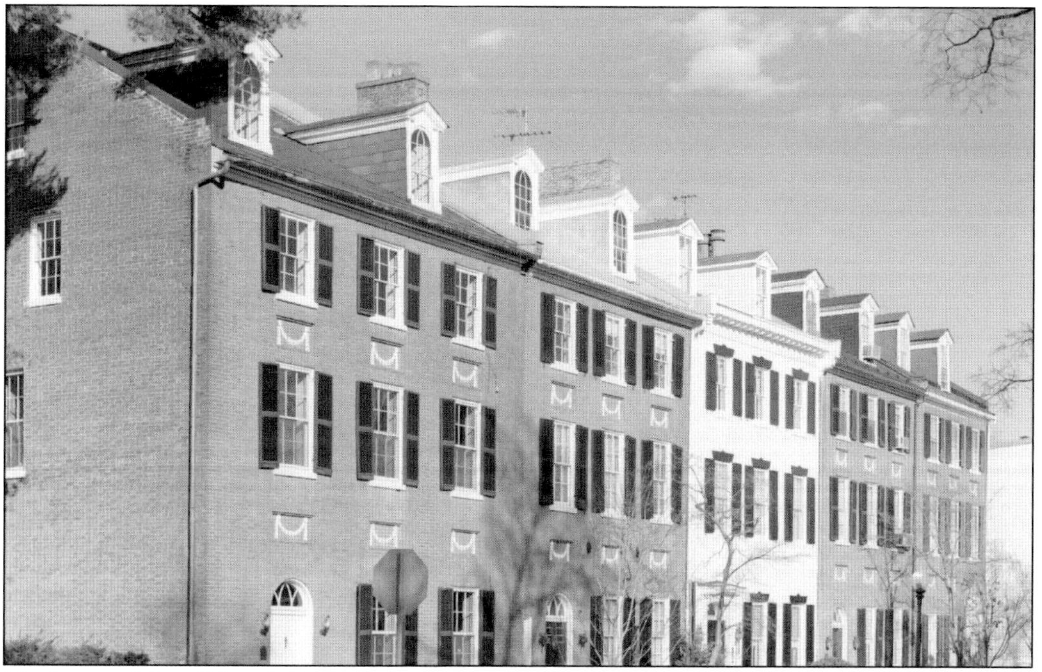

The home of Gen. John Cox, on the corner, gives the name to these 1817 Federal-style row houses: Cox Row. Cox was mayor of Georgetown from 1823 to 1845, after he took part in rearranging the city borders so he could run. Marquis de Lafayette lived here during his stay in Washington. This row of solid brick has had very little alteration since its construction. (HABS.)

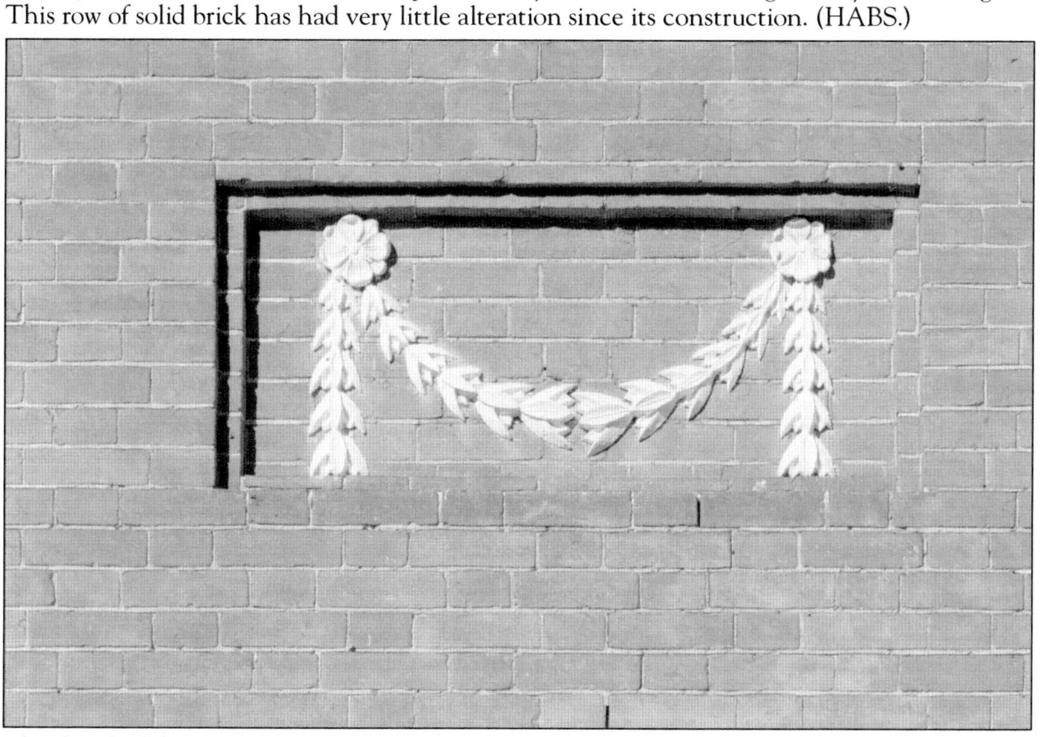

The detail of the swag above the windows on Cox Row is a staple of Federal-style architecture. These decorative embellishments are often found on mid-19th-century homes. (HABS.)

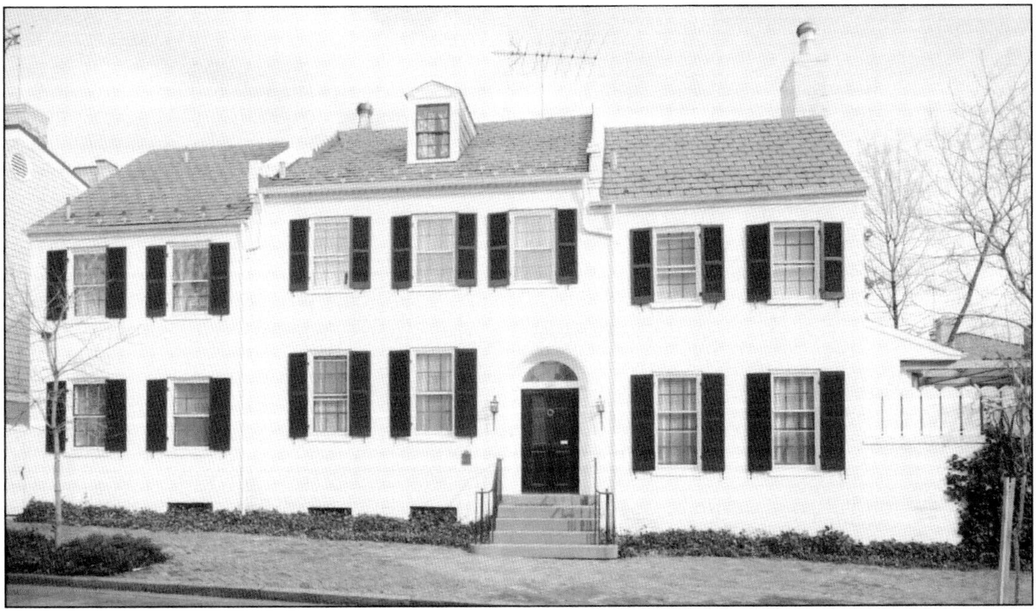

Since 1937, this has been a single house, but it was originally built in the late 18th century as three separate homes. In order to maintain the historic feel of the neighborhood, renovations were made to keep the original character in mind. This was done years before Georgetown became an official historic district, which legally required the historic feel be taken into consideration. It is named for the forward-thinking owner, Edward Burling, who was, fittingly, one of the original trustees for the National Trust for Historic Preservation. (HABS.)

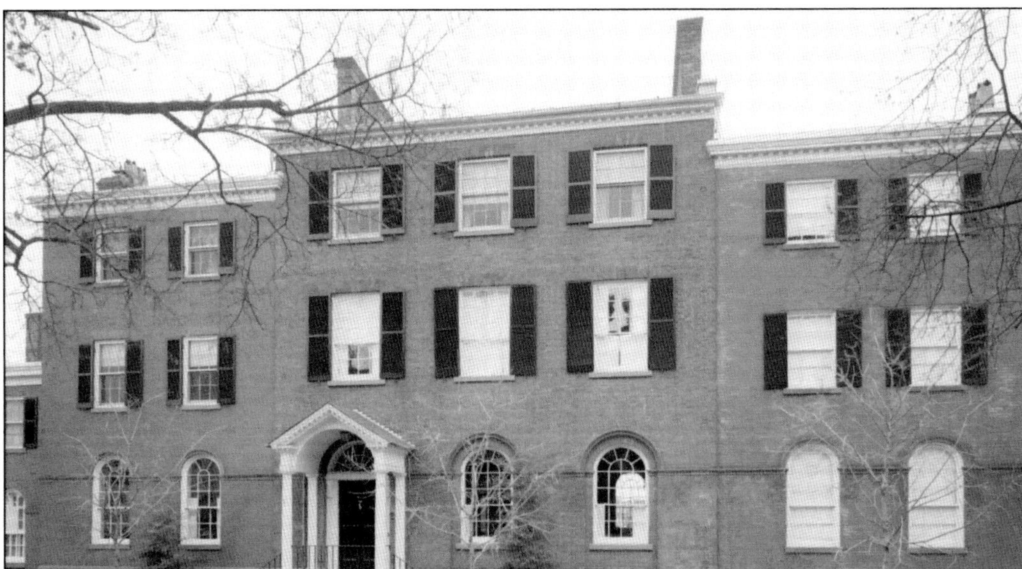

The only son of Abraham Lincoln to live past the age of 18, Robert Todd Lincoln, lived here. He purchased this 1790s Federal-style home in 1911 as a part-time residence. Robert Lincoln has the great misfortune of being present at or nearby three presidential assassinations, those of Lincoln, Garfield, and McKinley. The home was built by wealthy merchant John Laird and later inherited by his son-in-law Judge James Dunlop, giving the house its name: the Laird-Dunlop House. (HABS.)

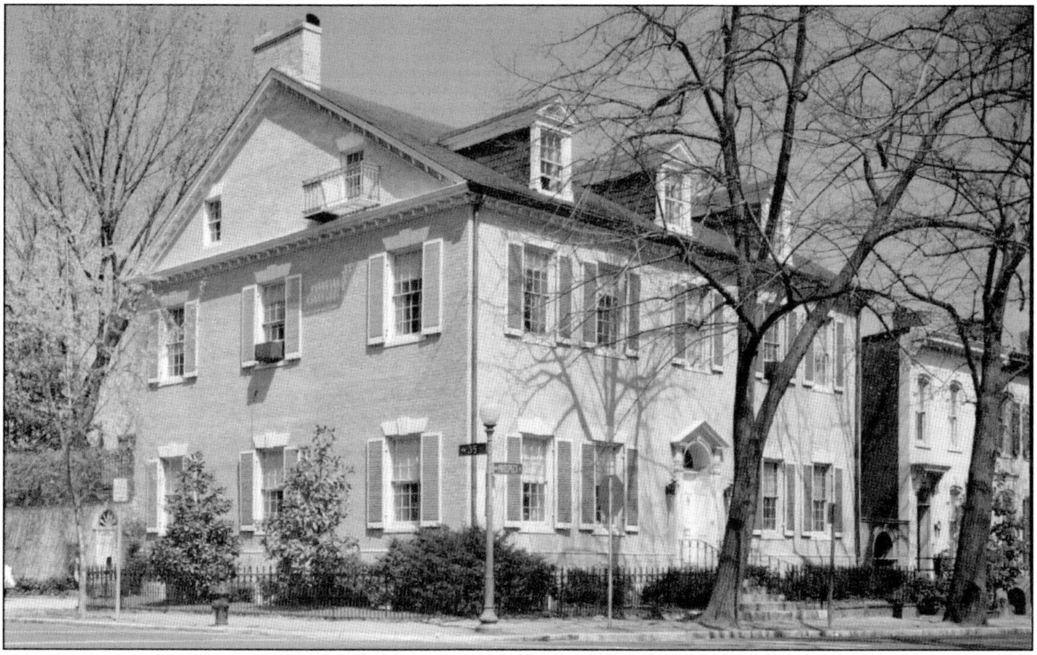

Owned by John Mason, for whom the island in the Potomac River was named, Quality Hill was built in 1797 and is one of the few remaining freestanding homes. While Mason was active in public affairs, he turned down many offers for political appointments, choosing instead to enjoy the social life that Georgetown encouraged. Of the many occurrences at the house, fellow Georgetown resident Thomas Jefferson once showed up so plainly clothed that he was turned away by a servant. (HABS.)

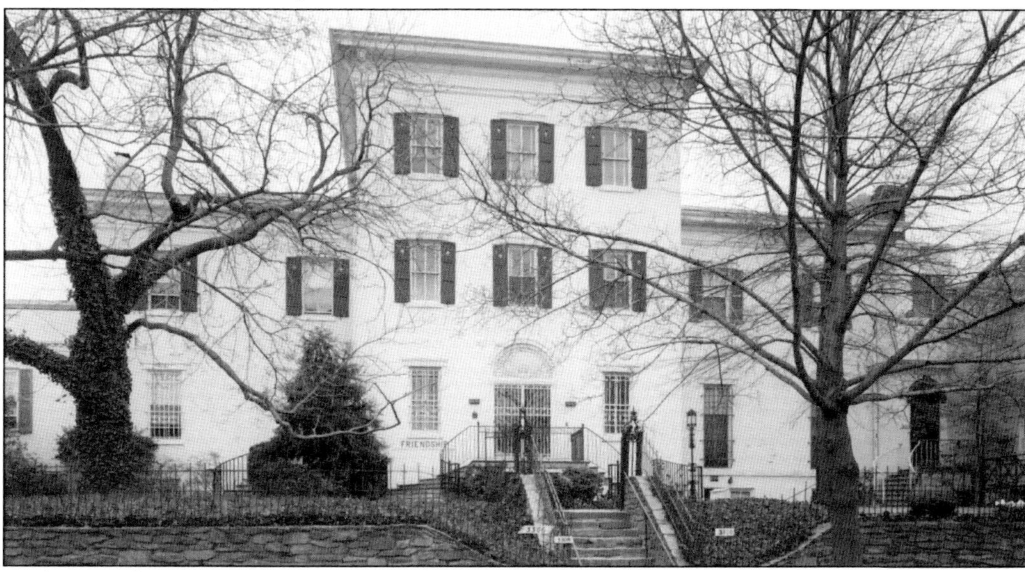

Built around 1830, Mount Hope is not known for its early residents, as influential as they were. It was built by an early mayor of Georgetown and named by a Virginia lawyer. It was then used as a social club with tennis courts until it was sold to the ambassador of Egypt, who added a swimming pool. In the 1940s, it was sold to Evelyn Walsh McLean and renamed Friendship, after her former estate. McLean was a DC socialite who was the last owner of the Hope Diamond. (HABS.)

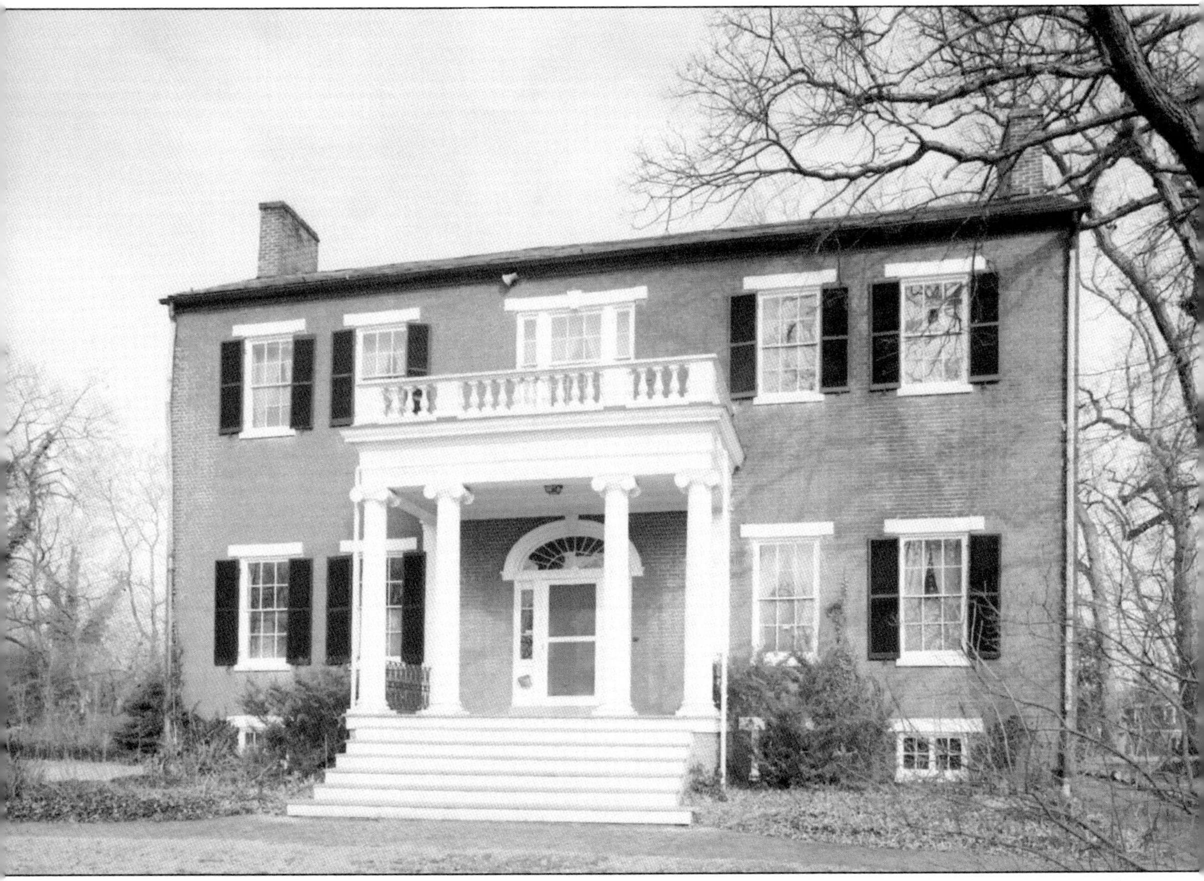

James Lingan had antiwar beliefs after being held as a Revolutionary War prisoner, so, when the War of 1812 began, he defended a Baltimore antiwar newspaper under the right of freedom of the press so staunchly that he was stoned to death by an angry mob. One lasting legacy, however, is his home, Prospect House, in Georgetown. It was built in 1788 and hosted John Adams and Gilbert du Motier, the Marquis de Lafayette, after the Revolutionary War. More than a century later, the house yet again hosted dignitaries, from the Shah of Iran to the French president, when Prospect House was rented by the State Department as a guesthouse for visiting officials while the Trumans stayed at the Blair-Lee House guesthouse in Lafayette Square during White House renovations. (HABS.)

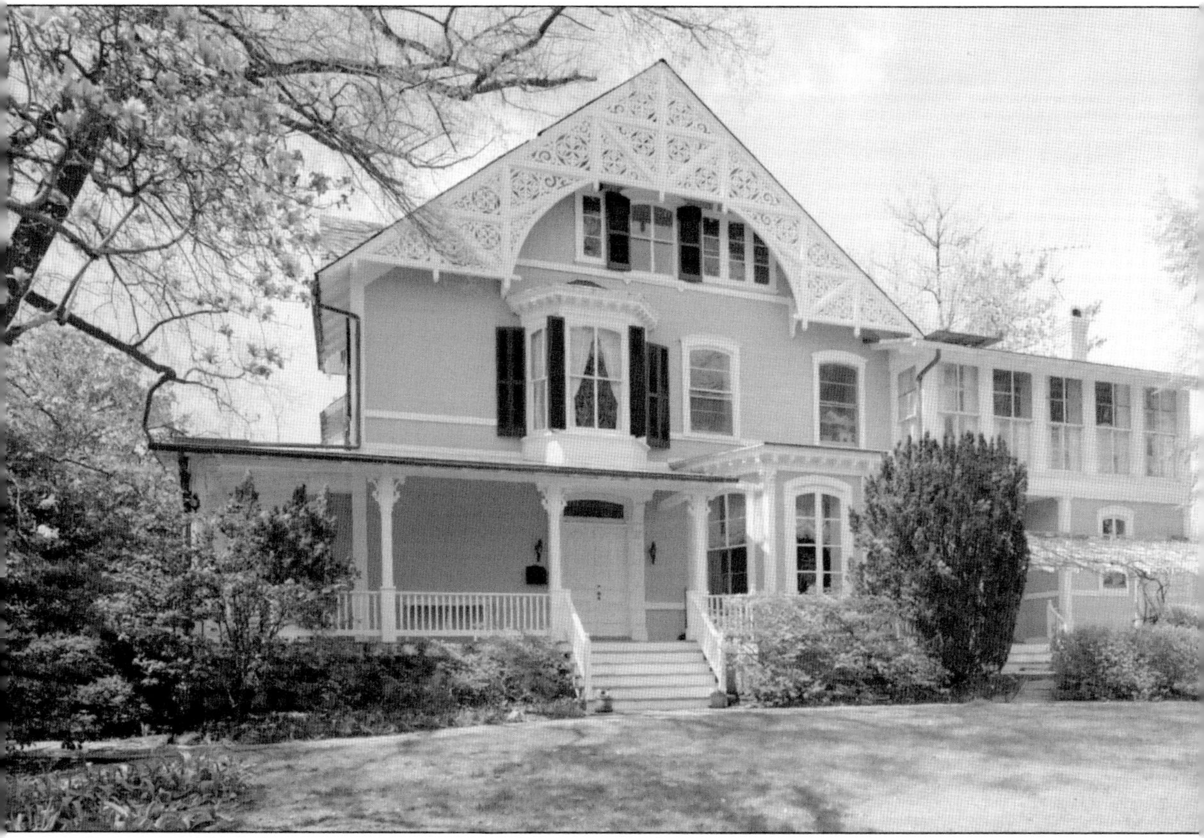

The original foundation of this house, on land bought by Jeremiah Williams, dates from around 1801, but the house itself, notably the lace-like roof overhang, is from the mid-19th century. It is possible that the entire house is from 1801, but frame houses such as this were exceedingly rare and that it is unlikely. The surrounding landscape was designed by landscape architect Rose Greely, the first female landscape architect licensed in DC. The property has two separate structures sharing a single staircase from the street, implying this house was once the larger family home and the small house was for servants. (HABS.)

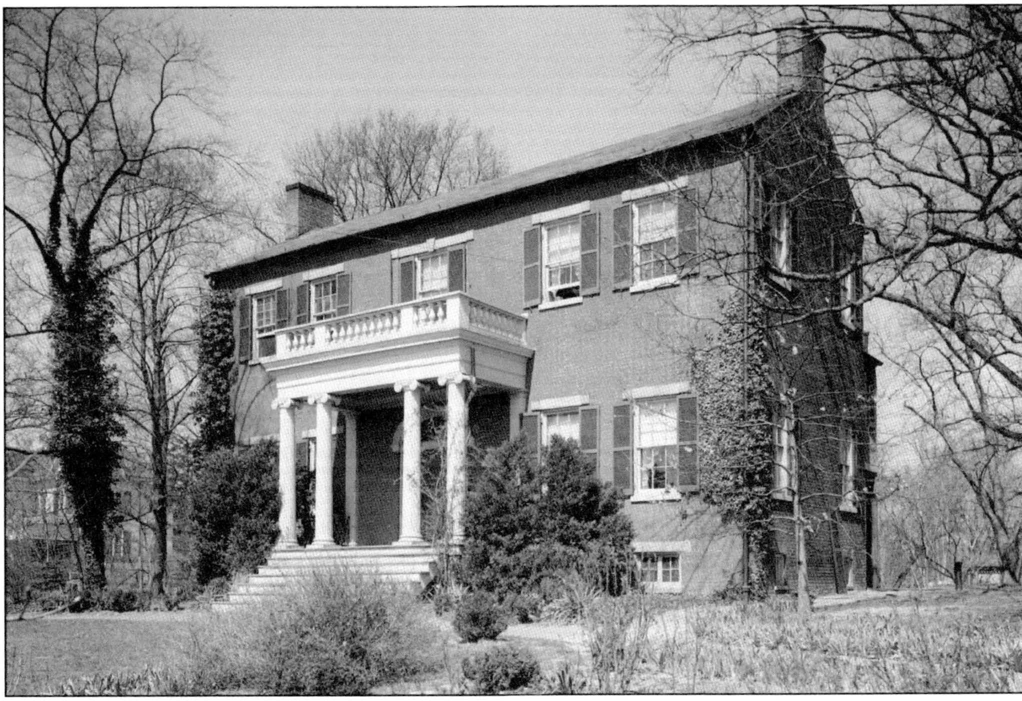

Mackall Square was the first place in the District of Columbia to be called a "square." The exact date of construction is contested, but increased land value suggests something was built in 1818, likely a two-story, wood-frame house. This larger brick house was built in 1839. Little is known about the current wooden structures in the back area of the house, but some say that they are from the mid-18th century and may have been a hunting lodge, which would make them the oldest structures in Georgetown. (Both, HABS.)

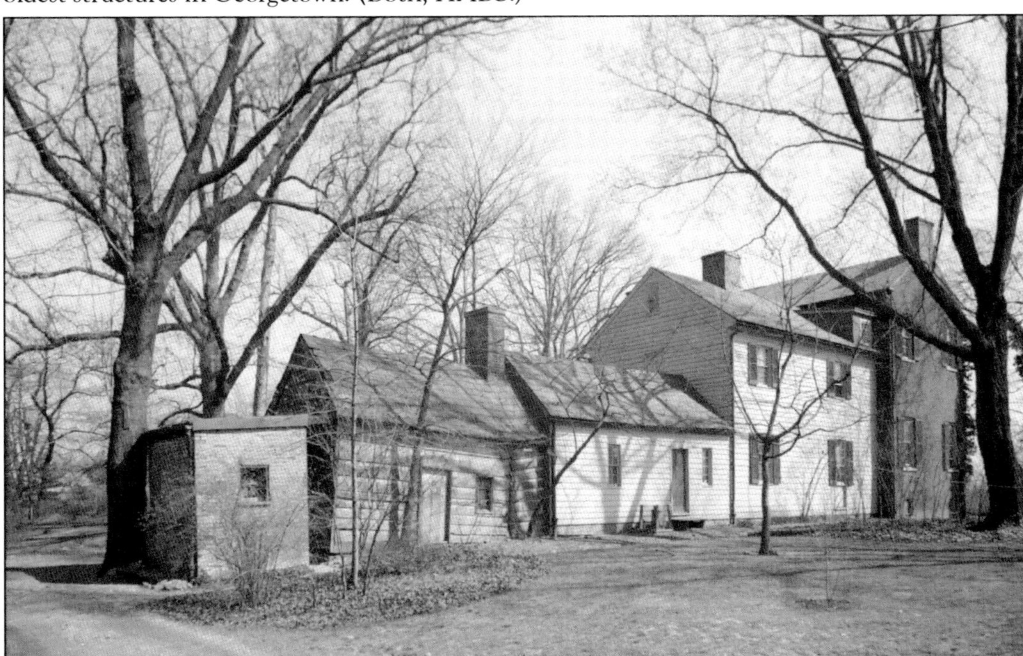

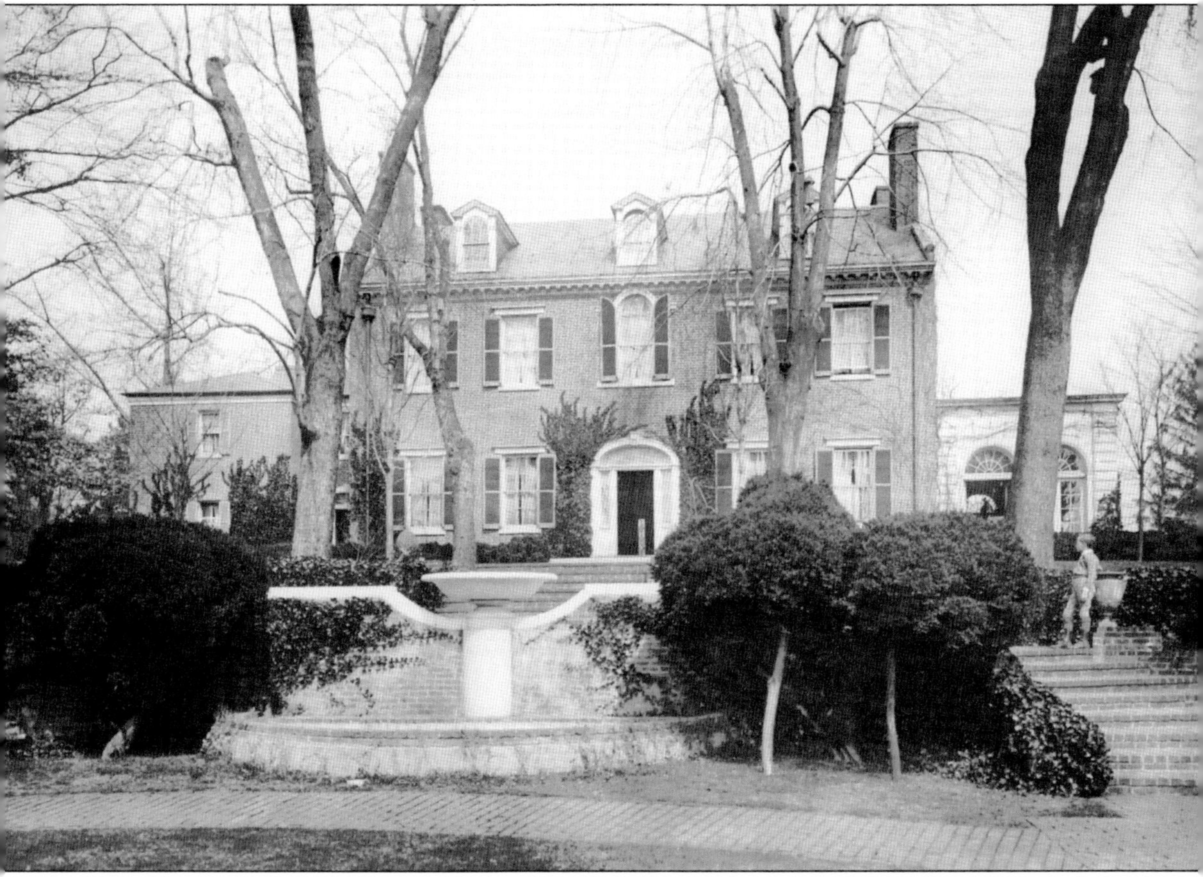

Built at the turn of the 19th century, Evermay was never lived in by its original owner. While it was being built, Samuel Davidson lived in town, but when he died, he had no children to inherit it, so he left Evermay to his nephew Lewis Grant on the condition that Grant change his surname to Davidson. Davidson was not a social man, as seen in a notice published in the newspaper warning "all parties to avoid Evermay as if a den of evils or rattlesnakes." (Historical Society of Washington, DC.)

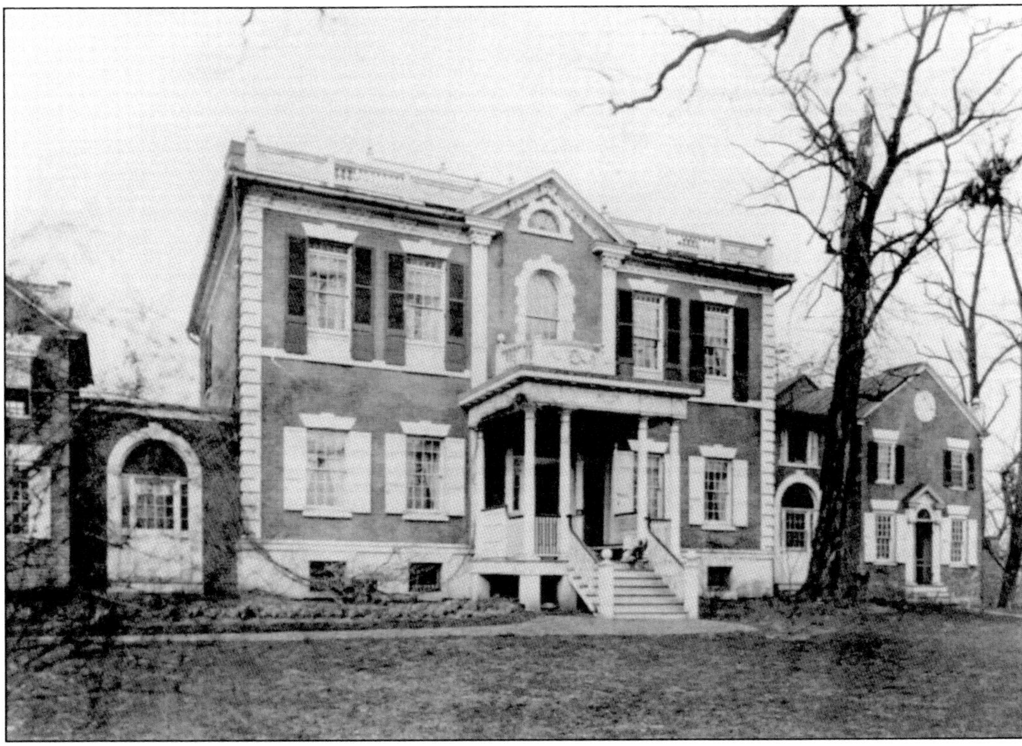

Dumbarton House is one of the finest examples of Federal-period architecture. For many years, historians debated what year the house was actually built, but it is generally accepted that it was around 1800. It was sold to Joseph Nourse, the first secretary of the treasury, in 1804. Both the front and rear views are seen here in the 1860s. (Both, Dumbarton House, the National Society of the Colonial Dames of America.)

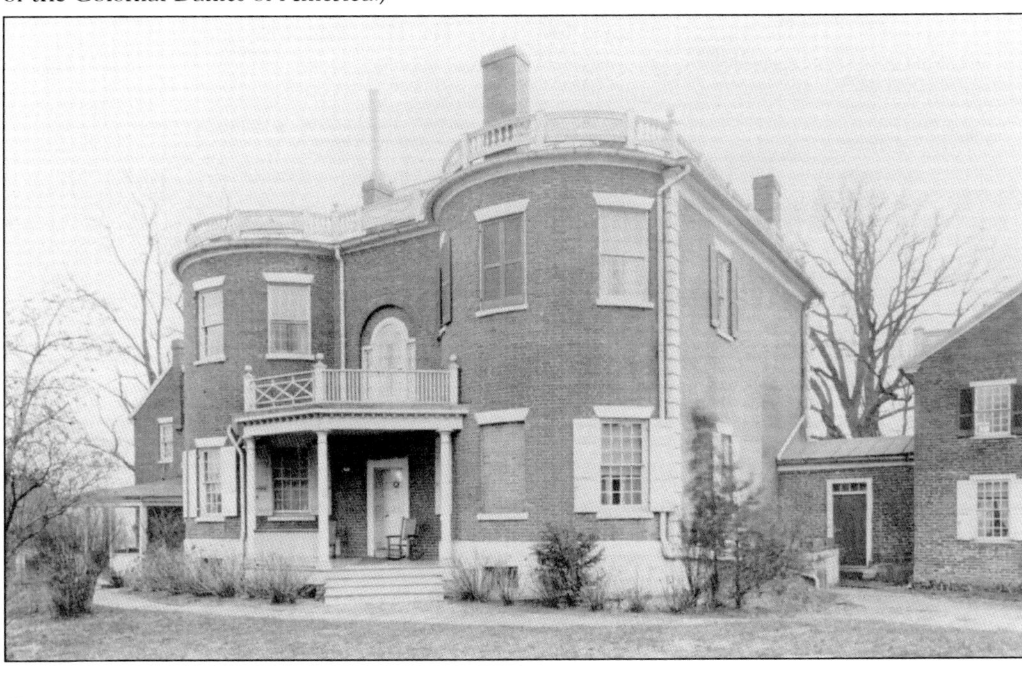

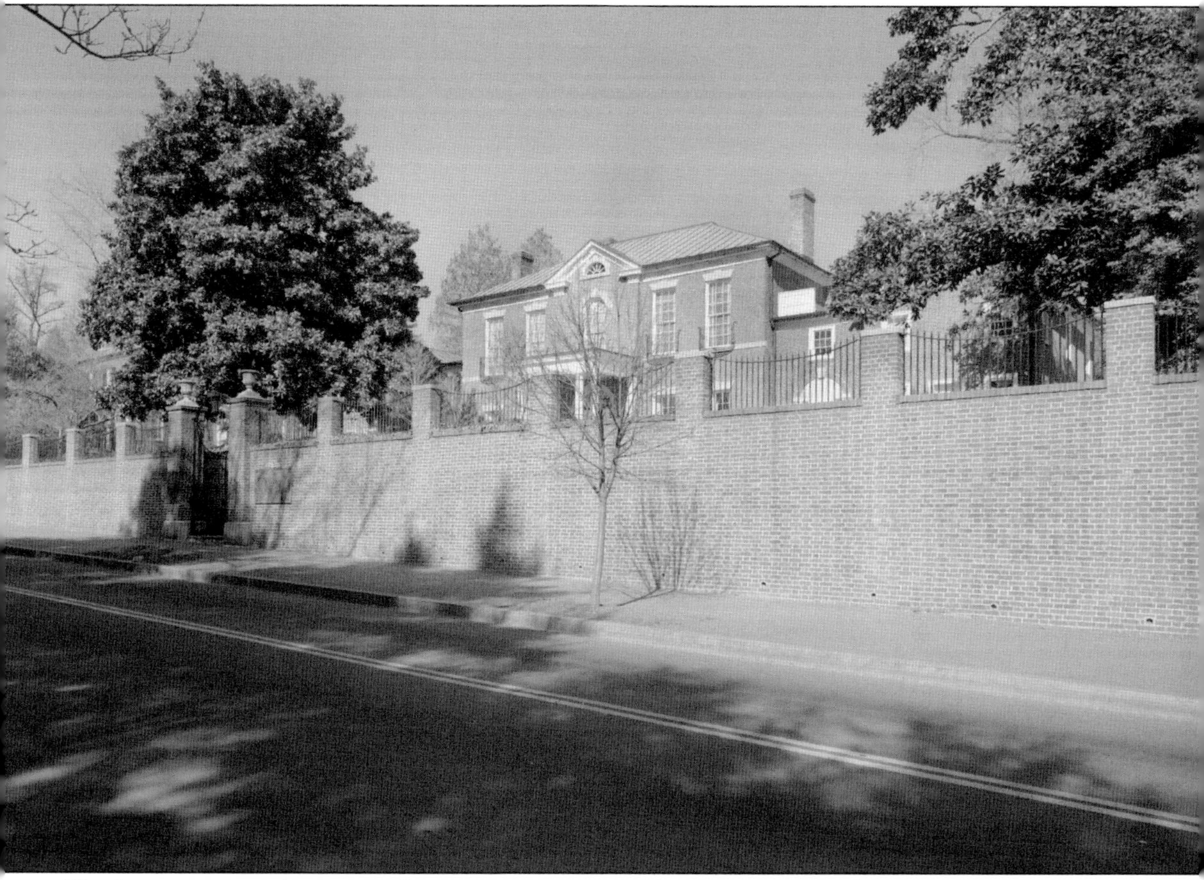

The house as it stands is original, just not in its original location. In 1915, the Q Street Bridge was built to add an additional throughway from Washington to Georgetown. In order to continue the street, it would have to go directly through Dumbarton House. To avoid demolishing the house, it was moved back 100 feet to the north, as seen here. (HABS.)

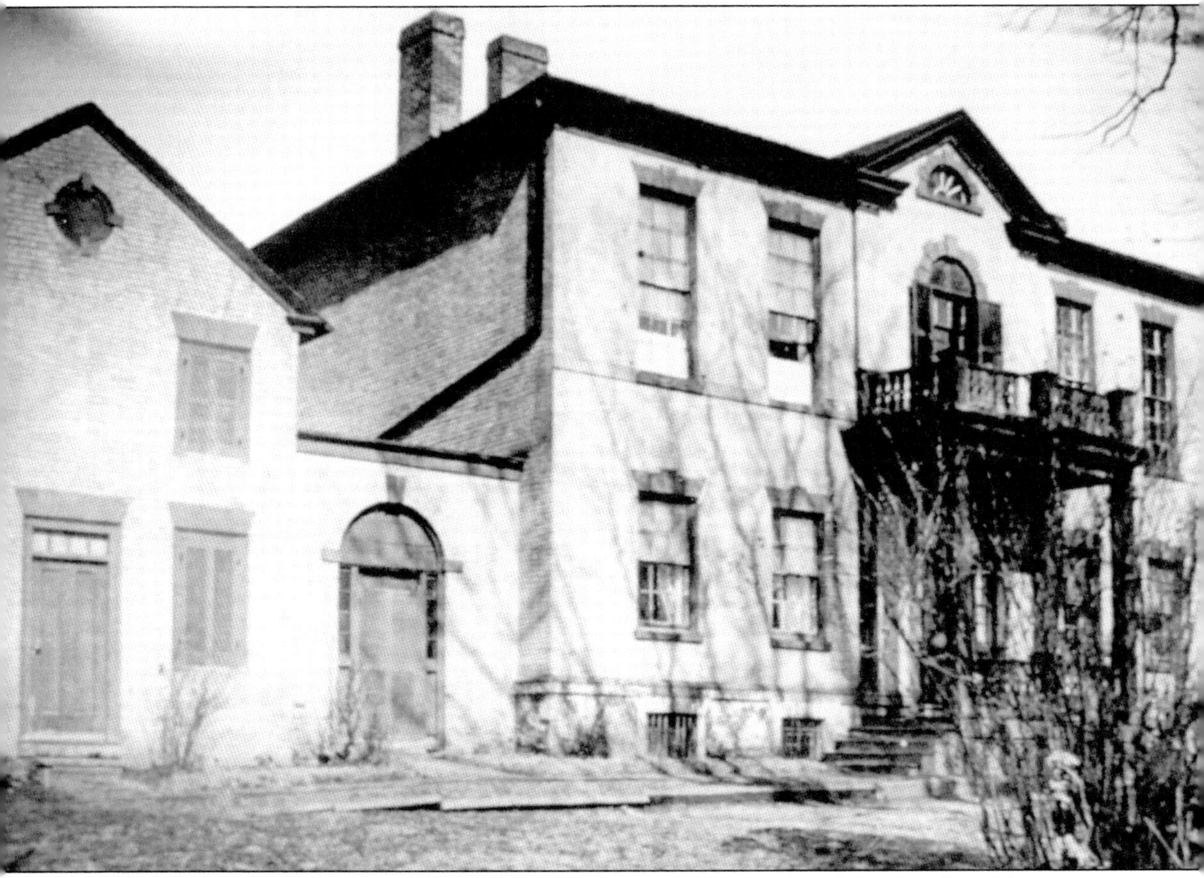

The land for Dumbarton House was given to Ninian Beall, considered the founder of Georgetown, in a land grant in 1703. He named it the Rock of Dumbarton, a nod to his native country of Scotland. With his beginnings here, many places are named after his original land title. However, for many years, this was called Bellevue. When the National Society of the Colonial Dames of America opened it as a house museum in 1932, it was named Dumbarton House. It is seen here in its original location between 1890 and 1910. (DH/NSCDA.)

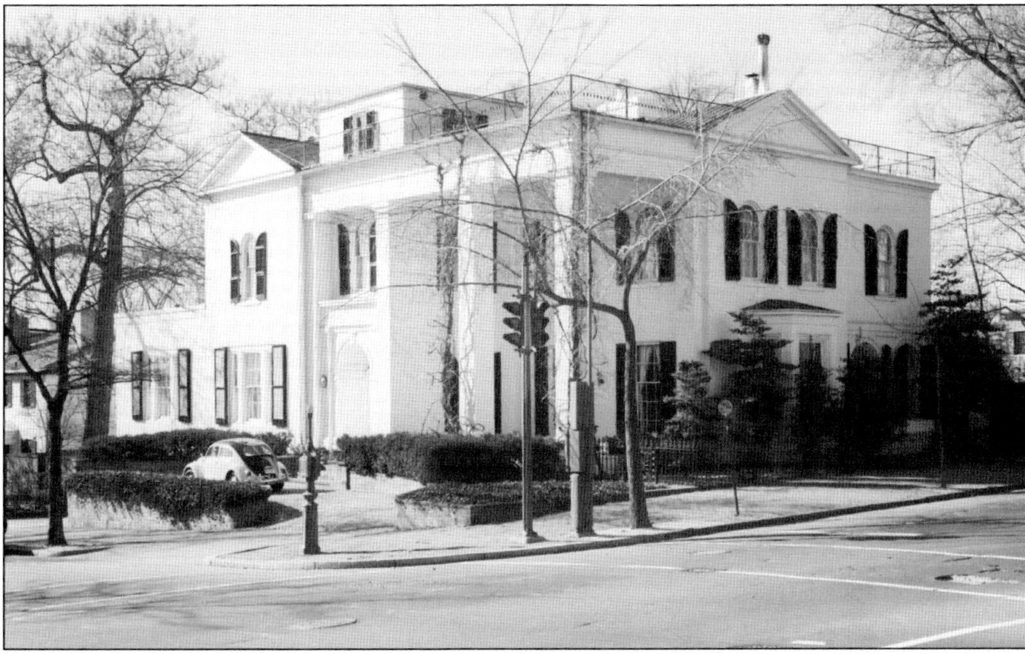

This Italian Villa–style home was one of the many Dodge houses in Georgetown. Completed in 1853, it was designed by Andrew Jackson Downing and Calvert Vaux in a popular style reminiscent of a suburban villa. This particular Dodge house was built for Robert P. Dodge, who was a successful businessman involved in the C&O Canal and the Columbia Flour Mill. (HABS.)

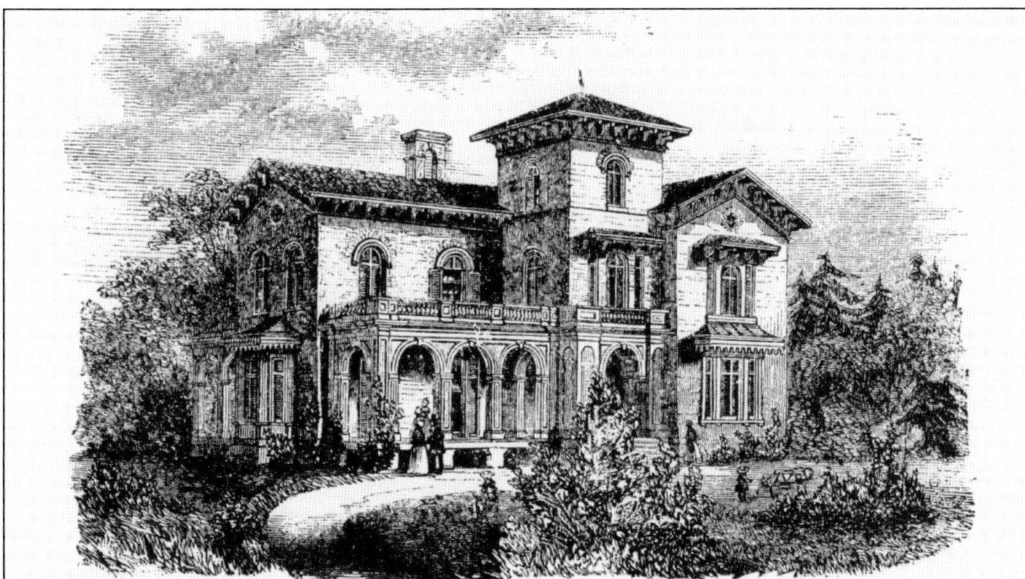

Downing and Vaux also designed this more decidedly Italianate home for Robert Dodge's brother Francis, around the corner. Francis apparently complained to Vaux about the $15,000 price tag for this house. The Dodge family was one of the wealthiest in Georgetown. They were mainly shipping merchants, and they owned many vessels and warehouses along the Potomac River. Their father, Francis Dodge Sr., had 11 children. The youngest four of the children were all married on the same day due to their father's failing health. (HABS.)

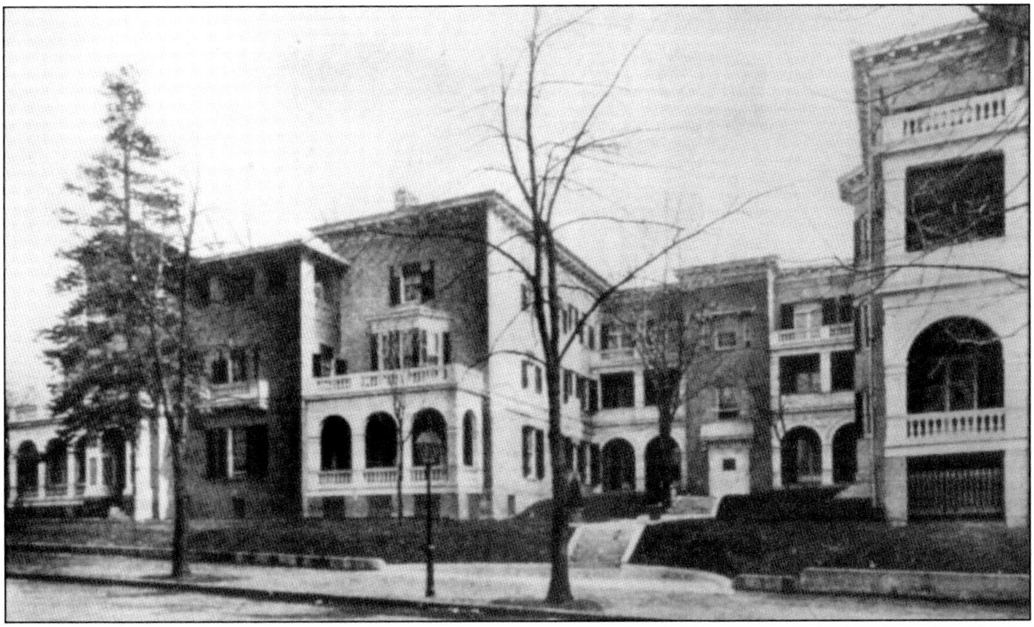

After Francis Dodge Jr. lost his wealth, Henry Cooke bought the house. Cooke had six daughters and wanted to keep them nearby, so he built homes around the corner. In the 1920s, the lot was expanded, but, in keeping with the character and feel of the historic house, the new condominiums look as if they are a part of the original home. (Historical Society of Washington, DC.)

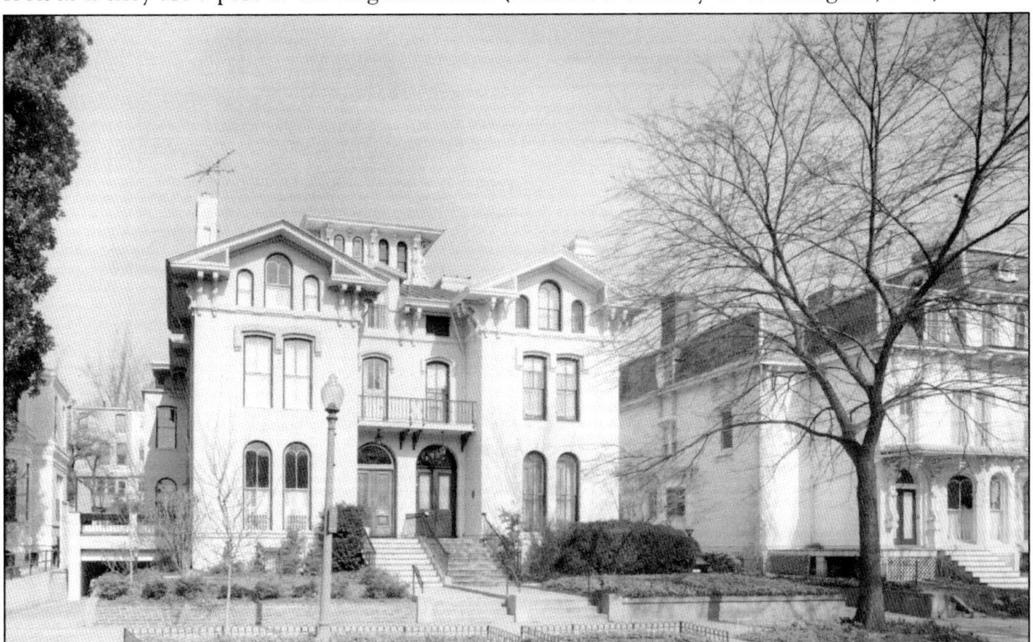

Cooke's Row was rumored to be built for the six daughters of Henry Cooke. Three stand-alone mansions with two homes in each, they were completed in the 1860s and were equipped with hot and cold running water in the kitchen and bathrooms, even on the second floor. Henry Cooke was the first territorial governor of the District of Columbia, a position that only existed for 36 years. (HABS.)

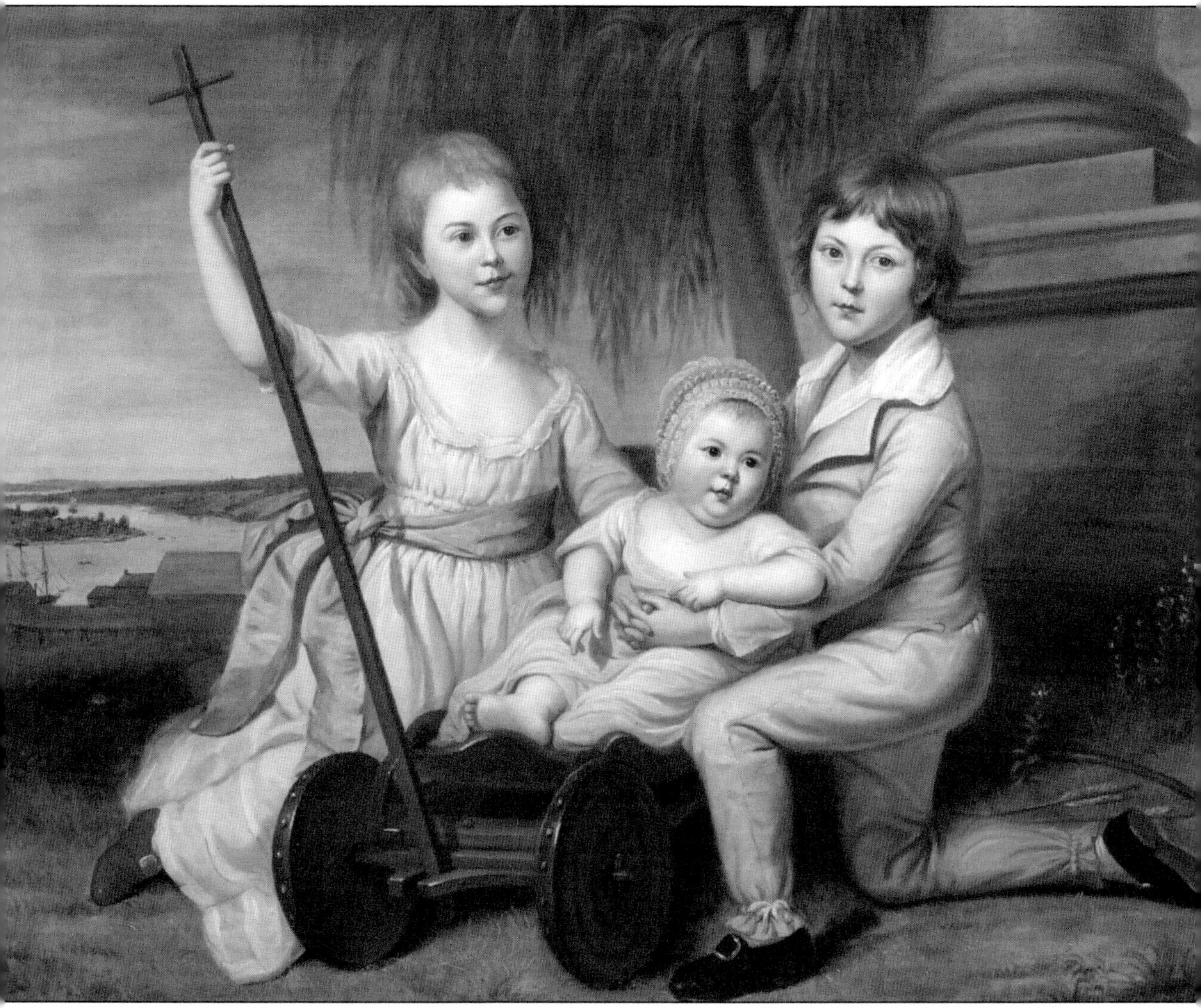

The first recorded image of the port town of George is seen in the background of this Charles Peele painting of the home of Benjamin Stoddert. These are the children of Stoddert, a prominent Georgetown resident who built Halcyon House. However, Halcyon House does not actually have any columns, so the classically themed front porch seen in this painting is just an artistic interpretation. The lack of development is evident in this 1789 oil painting. (DH/NSCDA.)

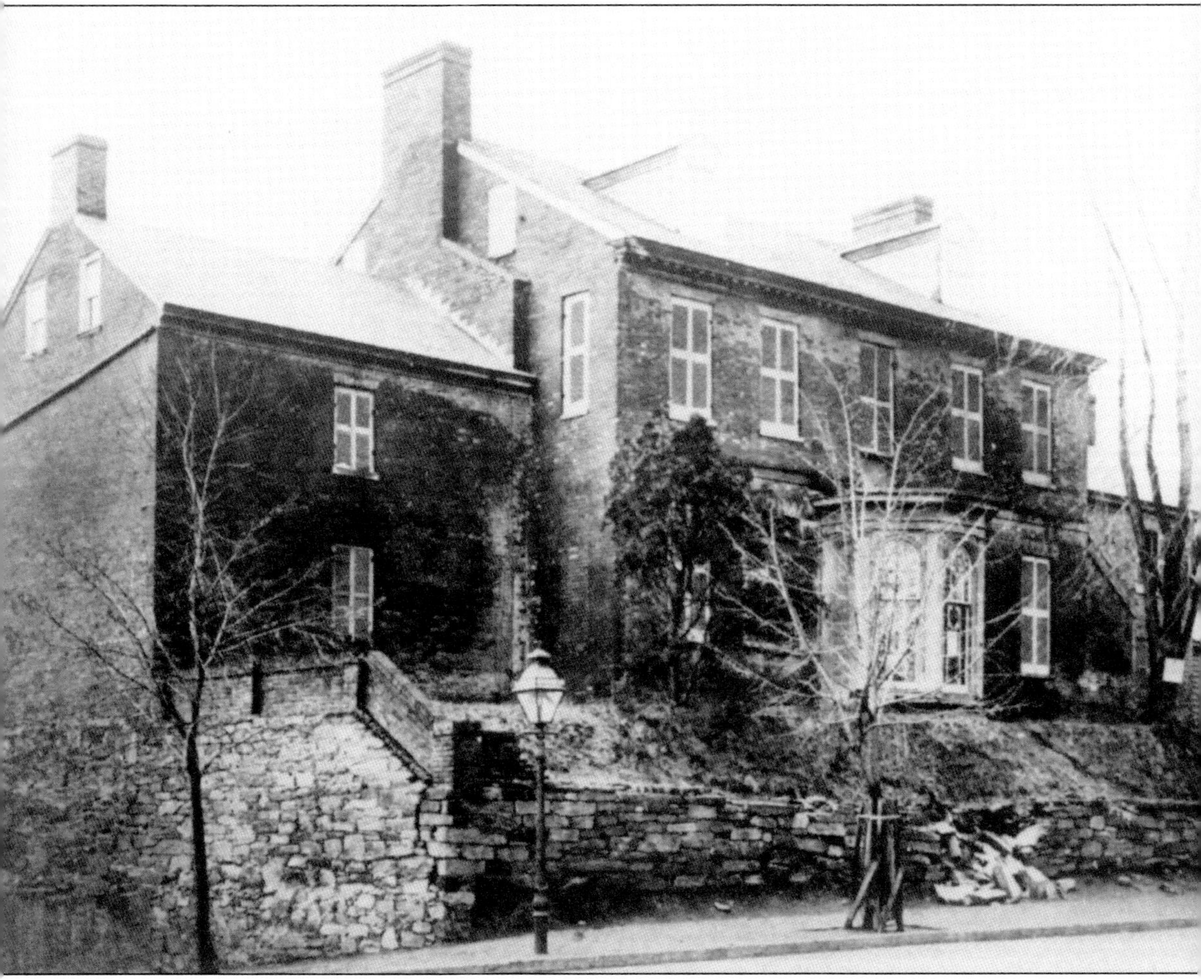

Halcyon House was built by Benjamin Stoddert, the first secretary of the Navy, in 1787 as his family home. Named for a bird who could charm the ocean winds, Halcyon House is a fitting name for a sailor. Stoddert helped convince President Washington that the new capital should be on the Potomac River. It is said that the grounds of Halcyon House were designed by Pierre L'Enfant, who also designed the layout of Washington, DC. (HABS.)

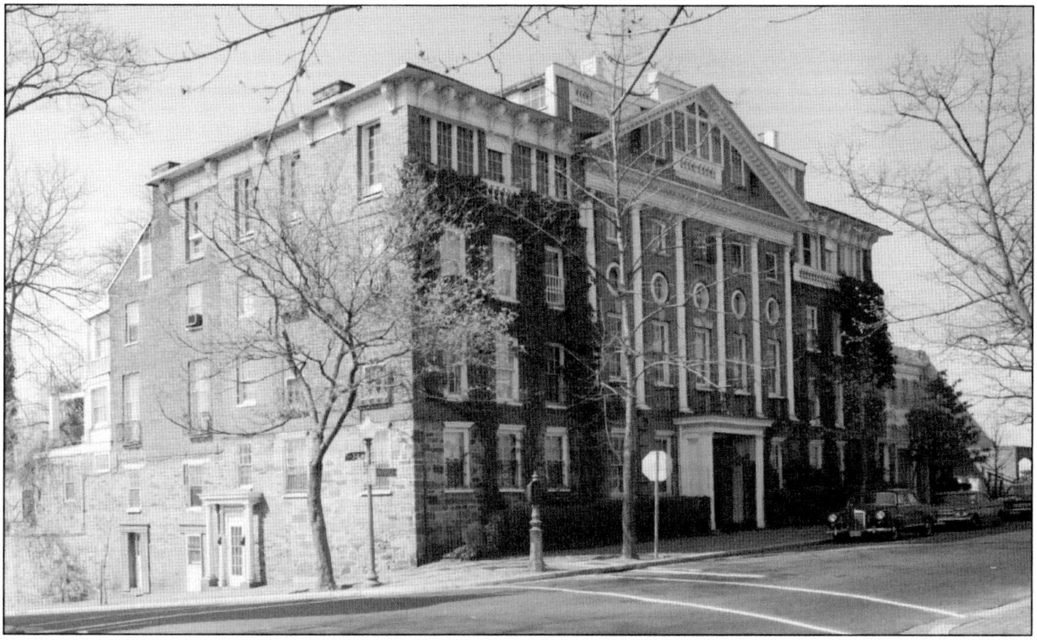

Halcyon House underwent many changes through the years, most extensively under the 1920s ownership of the eccentric Albert Clemens, who added rooms with no doors and stairs that led nowhere, as well as converting the carriage house to a crypt. He buried two mummies in the backyard to represent the loss of his youth and his figure. In order to pay for the carpenter that he had move into the house to complete his requests, Clemens rented out rooms under a few conditions: no electricity would be added, and, each year, the tenant had to move to the other side of the building to keep it from tilting to one side. The house was purchased by Georgetown University in 1951 and remodeled into dorms, though it is back under private ownership today. (Both, HABS.)

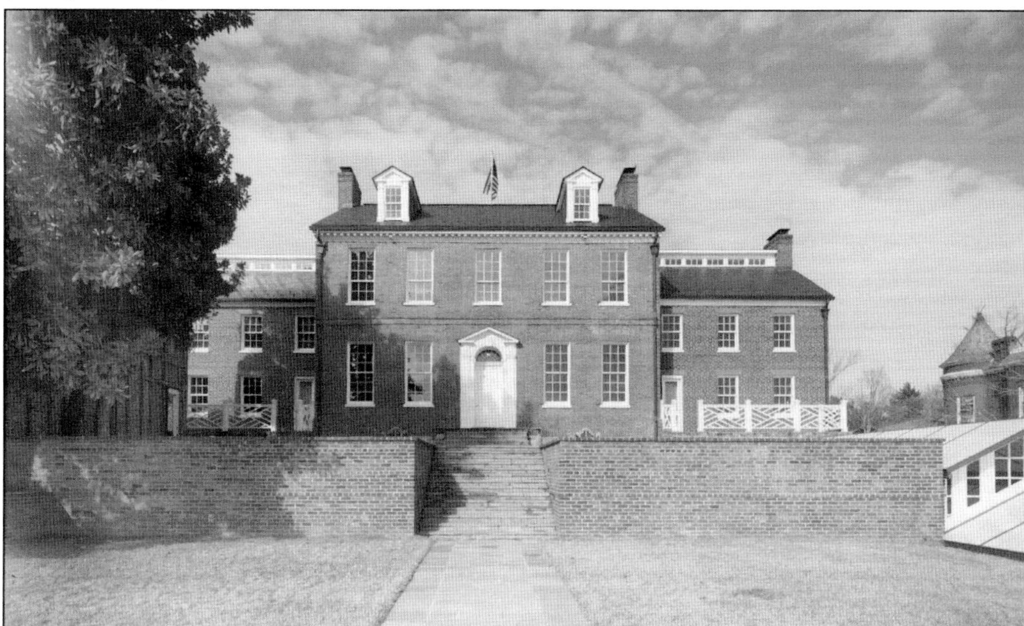

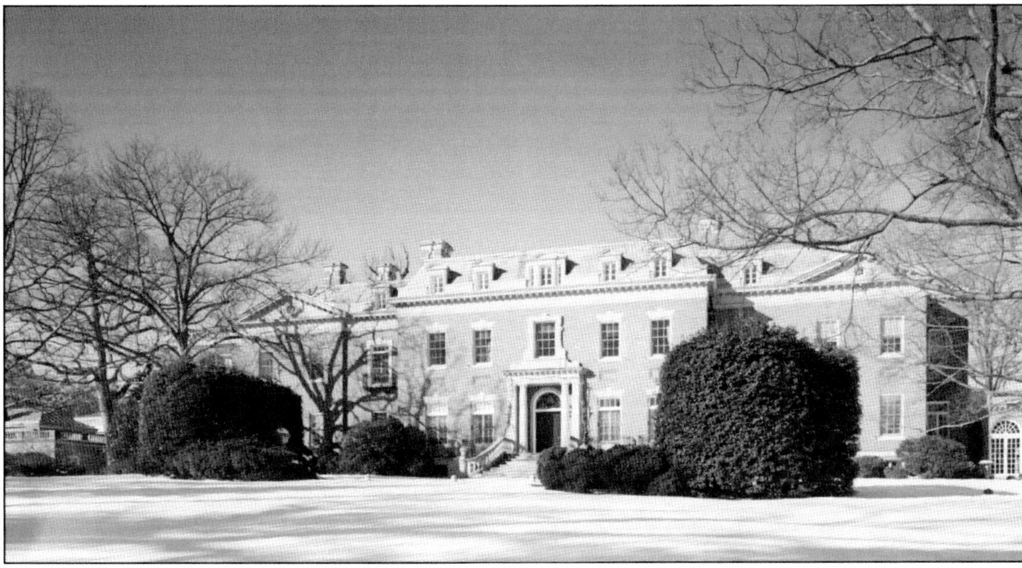

The construction of Dumbarton Oaks began in 1800, but there have been expansions and alterations through the years. The name Dumbarton Oaks combines the historic nomenclature of Ninian Beall's land grant, the Rock of Dumbarton, with The Oaks or Oakley, as the house was called by the Calhoun family, who lived there in the 1820s. John C. Calhoun would become secretary of war and, eventually, vice president. (HABS.)

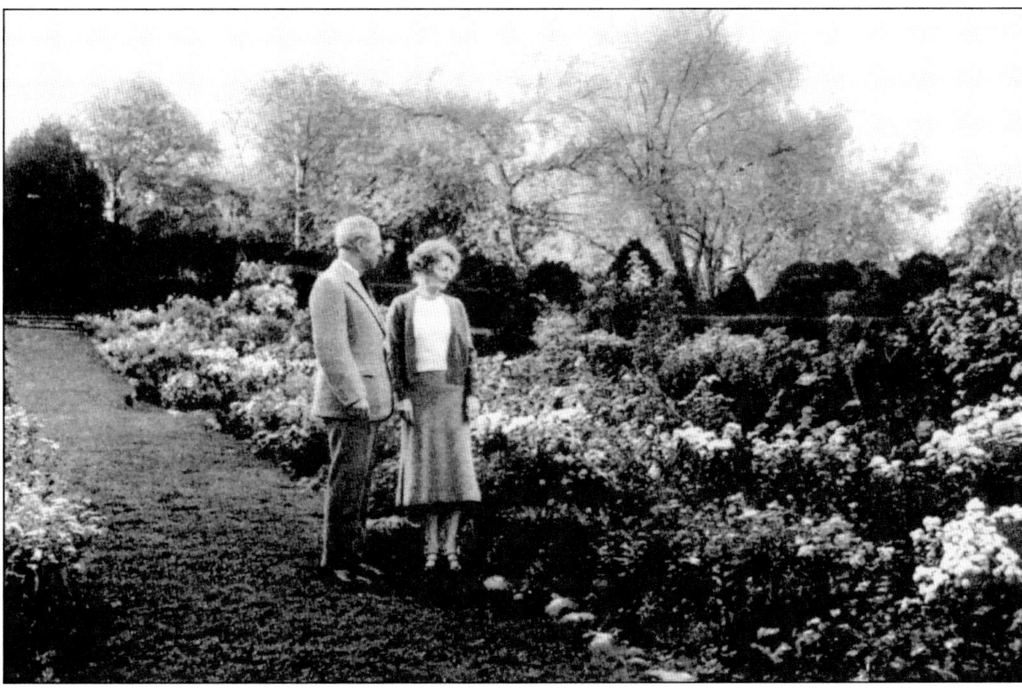

The last private owners of Dumbarton Oaks were the Blisses, a diplomat couple who arrived with a large pre-Columbian and Byzantine art collection that is still on display now, although under the ownership of Harvard University. Robert and Mildred Bliss brought greatness to Dumbarton Oaks. For their 30th wedding anniversary, they commissioned Igor Stravinsky to write a celebratory piece, called the "Dumbarton Concerto." (Dumbarton Oaks Archives.)

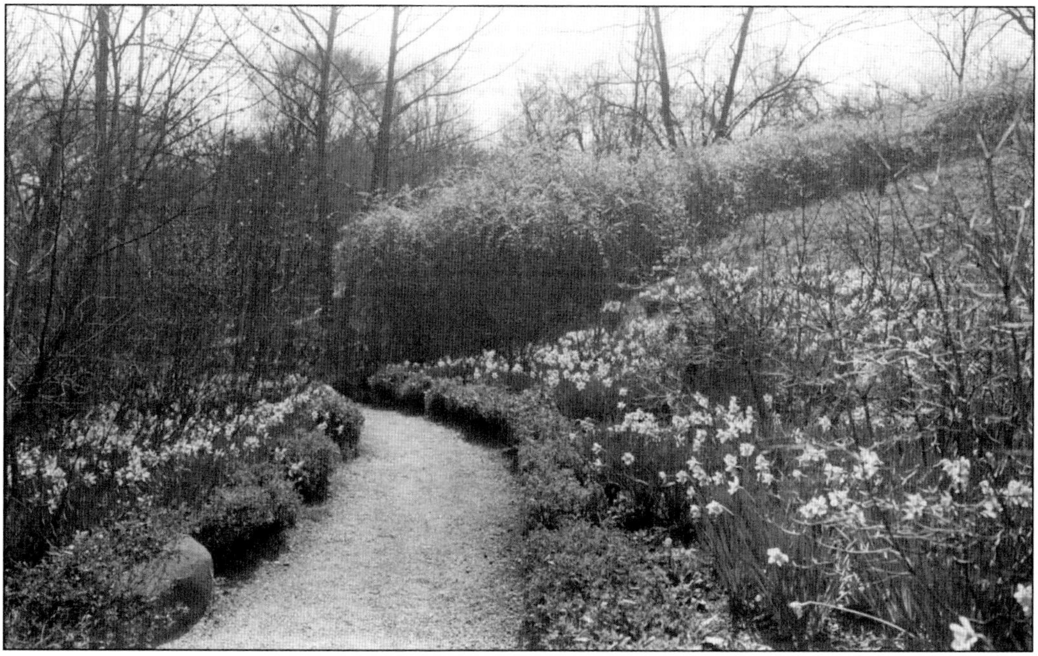

Mildred Bliss worked closely with Beatrix Farrand to design the gardens surrounding Dumbarton Oaks. Farrand was the only woman of the 11 founding members of the American Society of Landscape Architects. Since the two women corresponded mostly by letters, there is written documentation of the design of the gardens. (Dumbarton Oaks Archives.)

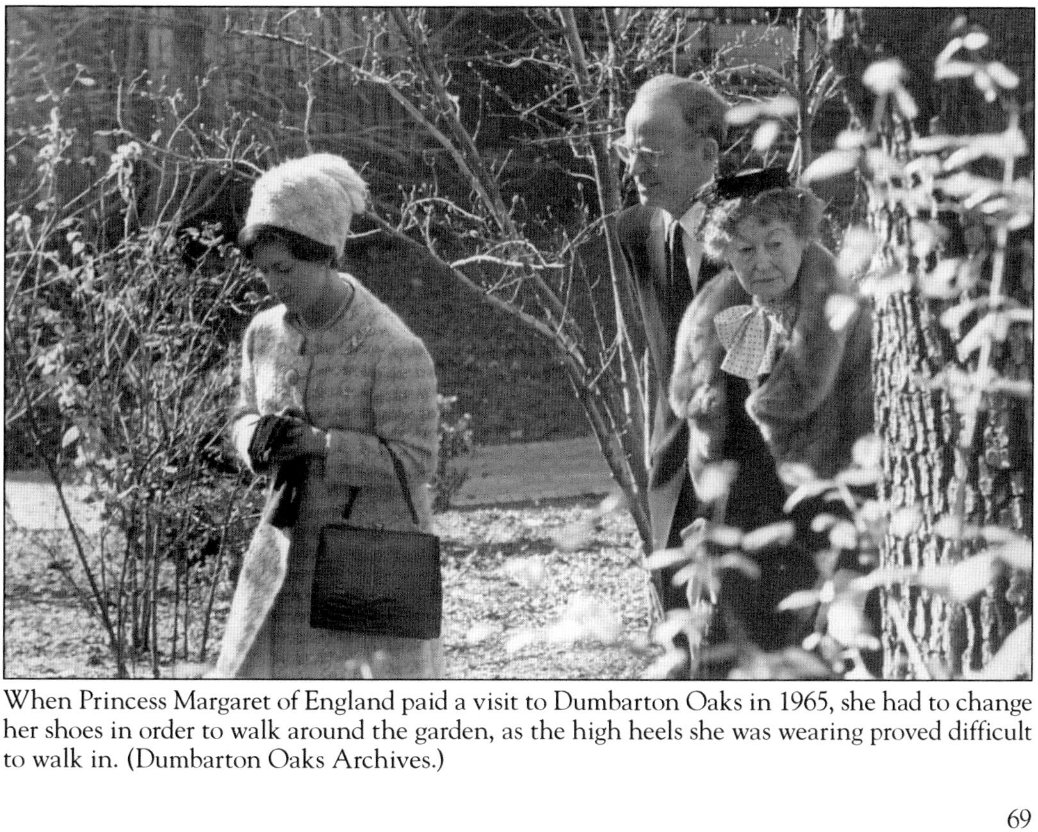

When Princess Margaret of England paid a visit to Dumbarton Oaks in 1965, she had to change her shoes in order to walk around the garden, as the high heels she was wearing proved difficult to walk in. (Dumbarton Oaks Archives.)

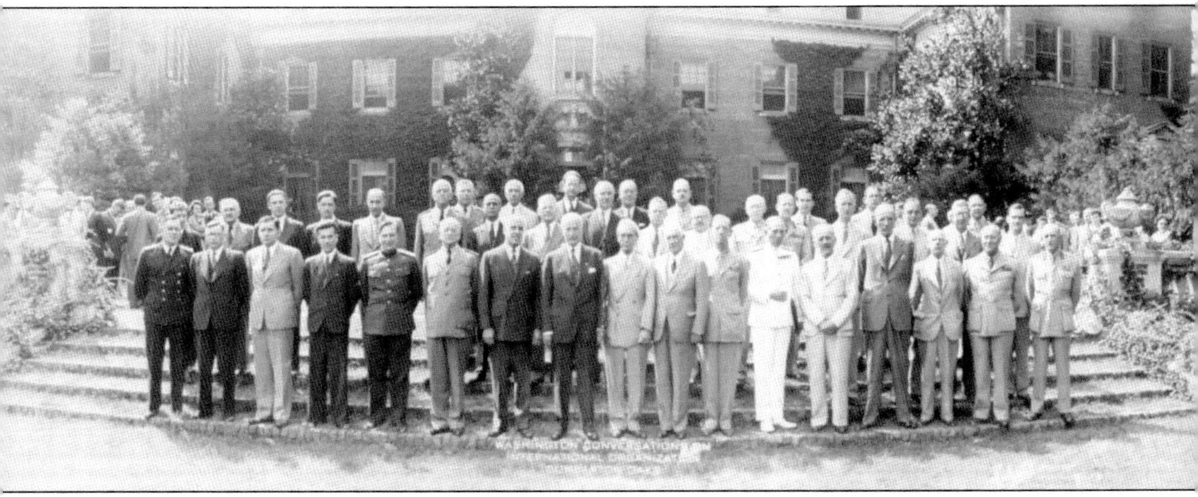

Held at Dumbarton Oaks in Georgetown, the Washington Conversations on International Peace and Security Organization, in 1944, were a series of meetings between the Soviet Union, Chinese, United Kingdom, and United States delegations for a peacekeeping and security force. They had to meet two separate times because the Soviet Union and China refused to have direct talks. The delegates were the British permanent undersecretary of state for foreign affairs, Sir Alexander Cadogan; the Soviet ambassador to the United States, Andrei Gromyko; the Chinese ambassador to the United Kingdom, Wellington Koo; and the US undersecretary of state, Edward Reilly Stettinius Jr. This photograph shows the American, British, and Soviet delegates. (Schutz Group Photographers.)

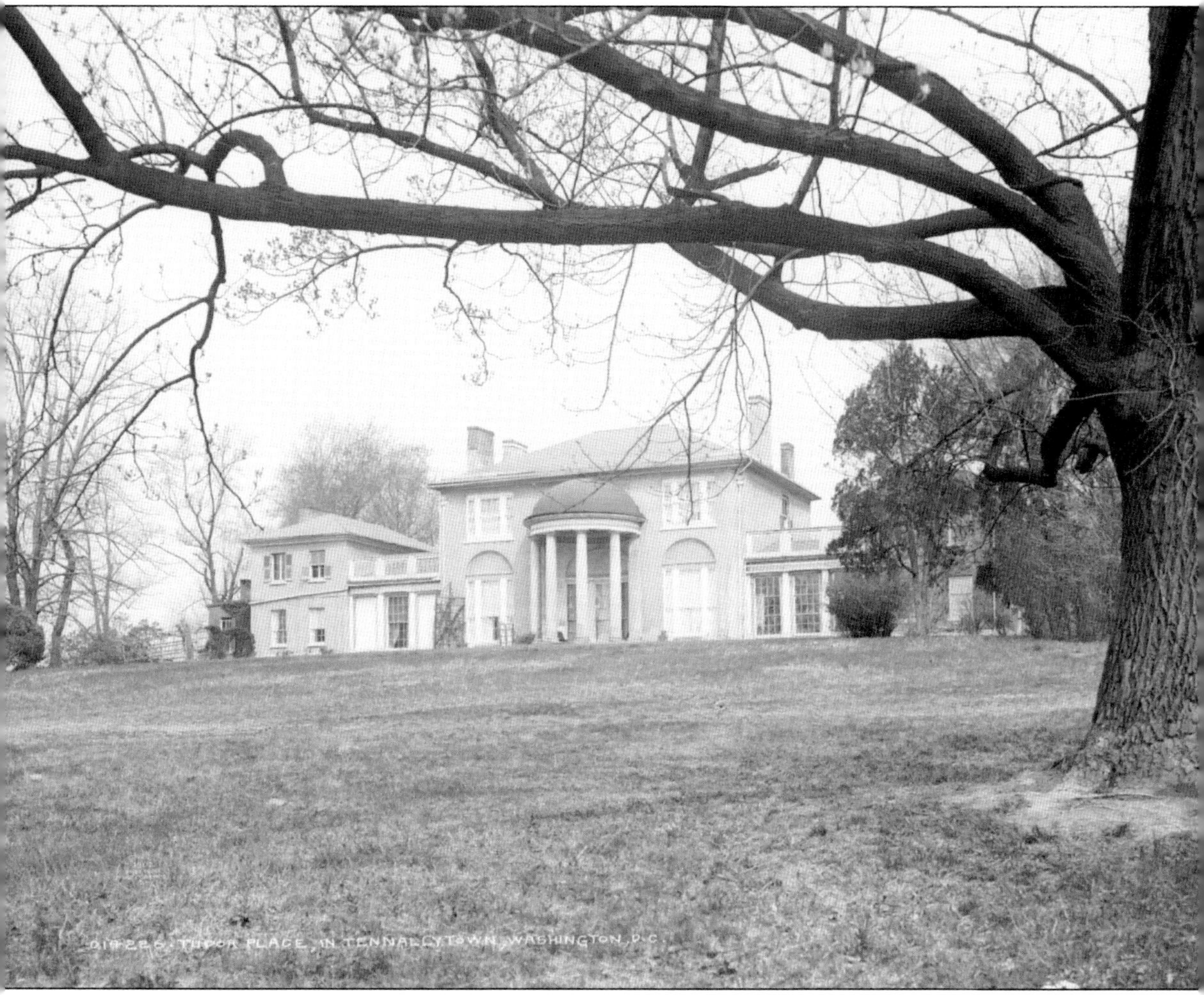

Tudor Place was purchased with the inheritance received from George Washington by his step-granddaughter Martha and her husband, Thomas Peter, in 1805. It remained in the Peter family until 1983, when it was donated by its last resident, Armistead Peter III, as a historic house museum. The house was designed by William Thornton, a friend of the family who also designed the Capitol. (HABS.)

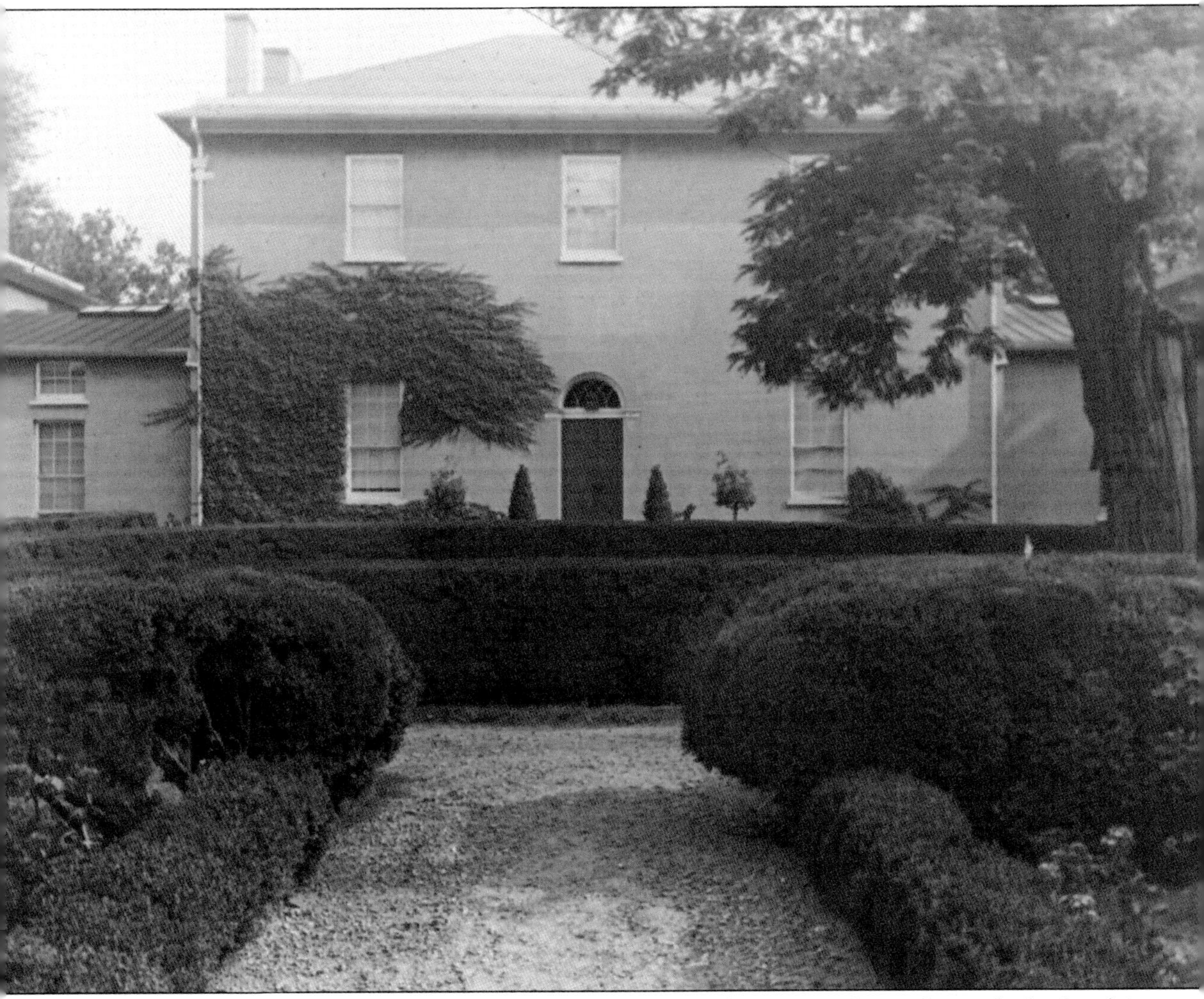

The descendants of Martha and Thomas Peter maintained a strong relationship with the family's Washington heritage and extensively cataloged the artifacts from Mount Vernon. The Lees of Virginia and the Peters of Georgetown were cousins, so when the Civil War broke out, the Peter family left until rumor reached them that Union forces were taking over these large residences as hospitals. To avoid having the home commandeered and the Washington artifacts compromised, Britannia Peter Kennon returned to rent out the home as a boardinghouse for Union officers. (Frances Benjamin Johnston, Library of Congress.)

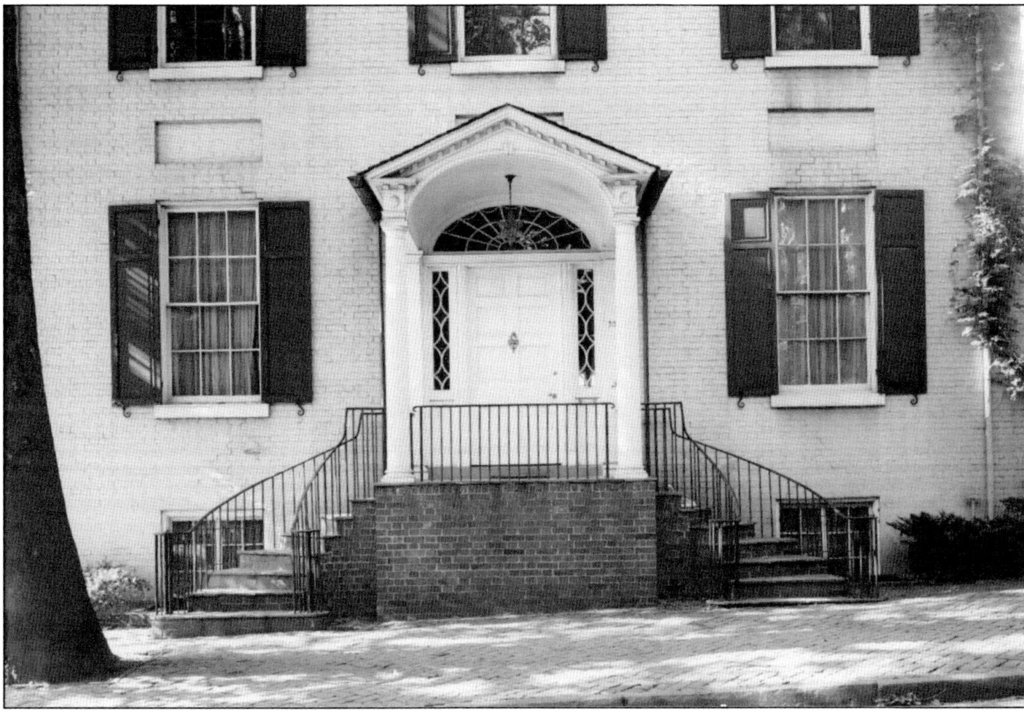

The Bodisco House was originally constructed in 1818 but is named for later owner Baron Alexandre Bodisco. An older man of either 44 or 64, depending on the source, he fell in love with a local schoolgirl of 16, Harriet Beall Williams. The couple was known as "Beauty and the Beast" to locals, but their wedding and marriage were anything but scandalous. The ceremony was attended by the president and his cabinet, with ambassadors from England and Texas as groomsmen. (HABS.)

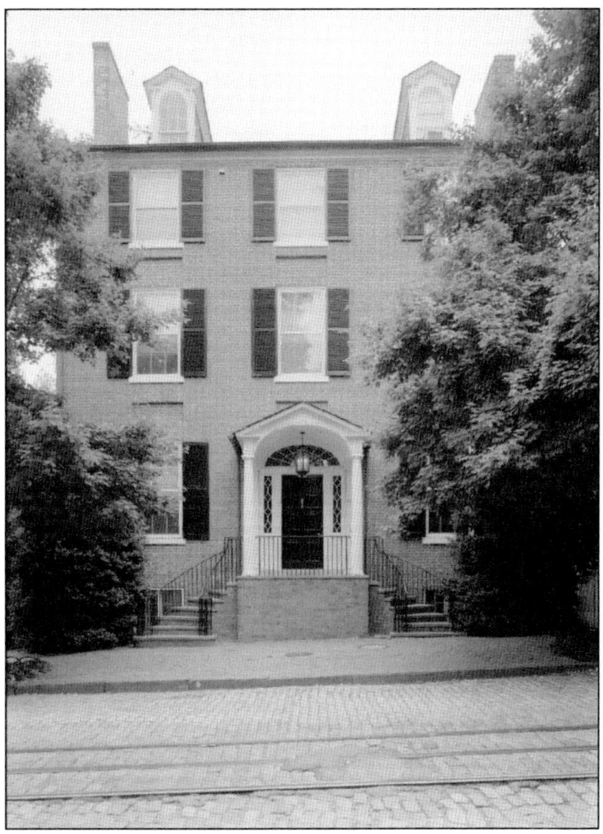

Baron Bodisco purchased the house as a wedding gift for his young bride. They were happily married for 14 years and had seven children. It is the current local residence of former senator and current secretary of state John Kerry. (HABS.)

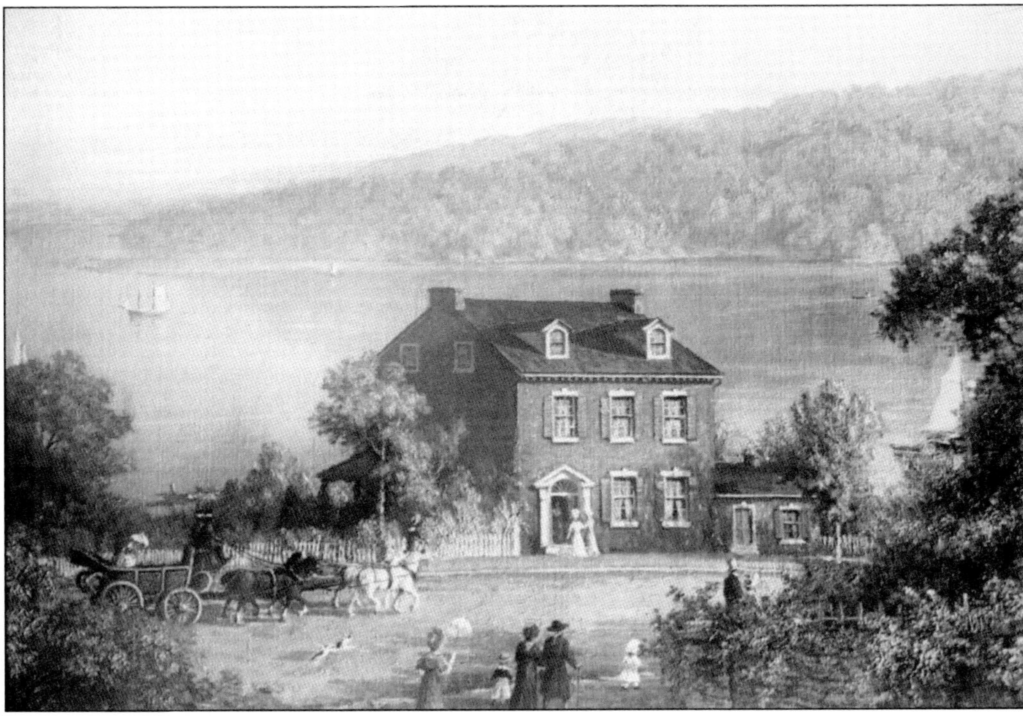

A simple house built in 1795, this drawing shows Francis Scott Key's home from 1805 to 1830. He left here to go to Baltimore during the War of 1812 to negotiate the release of his friend, but he was kept on a British ship after overhearing their plans to attack Fort McHenry. It was on this ship he saw bombs bursting in air and awoke to find that the flag was still there. His poem "In Defense of Ft. McHenry" was later set to the tune of a British drinking song and became "The Star-Spangled Banner," the American national anthem. (National Photo Company.)

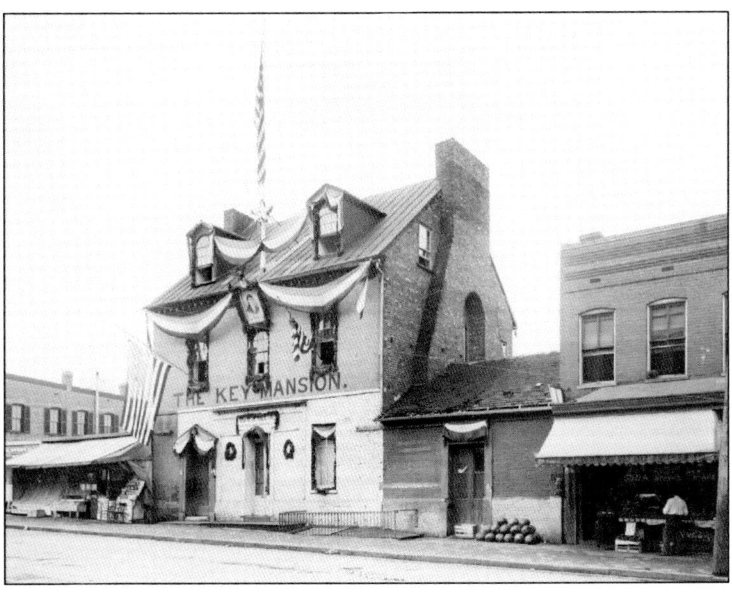

A 1908 photograph of the historic Key Mansion shows it draped with American flags and a photograph of its namesake. When Key's great-grandson heard word that the house was to be torn down, he rushed to save it. It opened as a museum but was unsuccessful. The house was eventually torn down but the bricks were numbered so it could be rebuilt elsewhere. That is until the bricks were lost. (HABS.)

Four

Working Town

Shops, Factories, and the C&O Canal

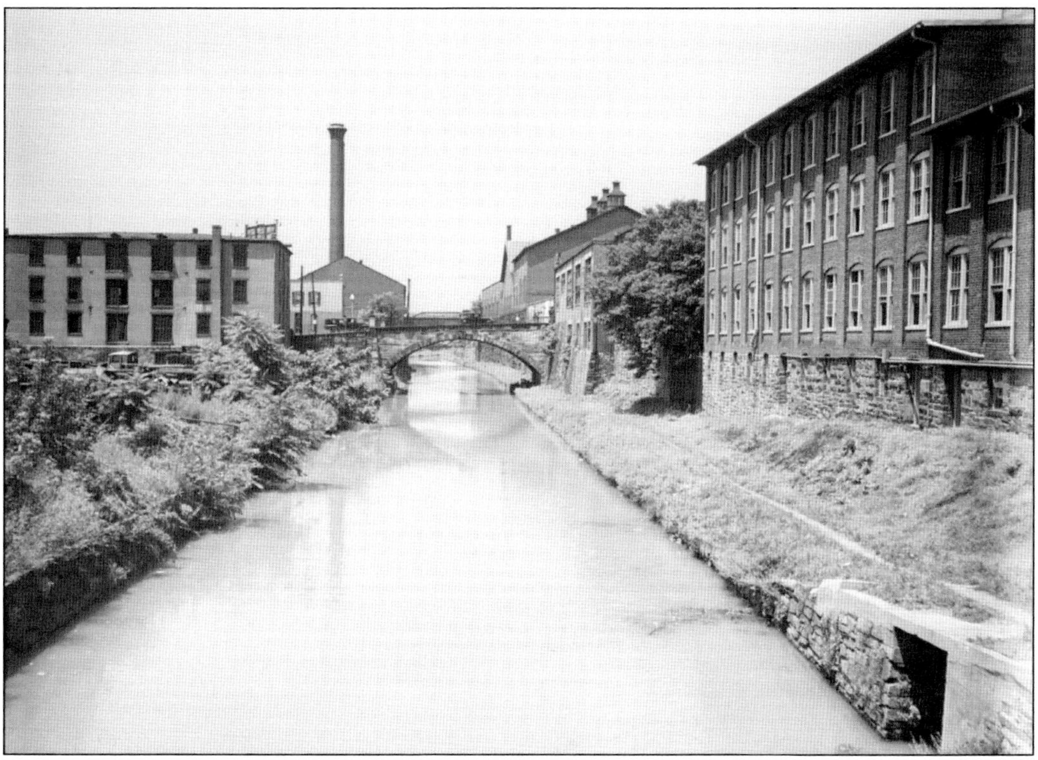

The Chesapeake and Ohio (C&O) Canal runs from Georgetown to Cumberland, Maryland, a length of more than 184 miles. It operated as part of the industrial trade from 1831 to 1924 and remains as a national park today. The canal was not just used for trade; many families who worked on it also lived on houseboats on the end. Children would play and fish in the waters just as they would in a lake. (Harris Ewing Photography.)

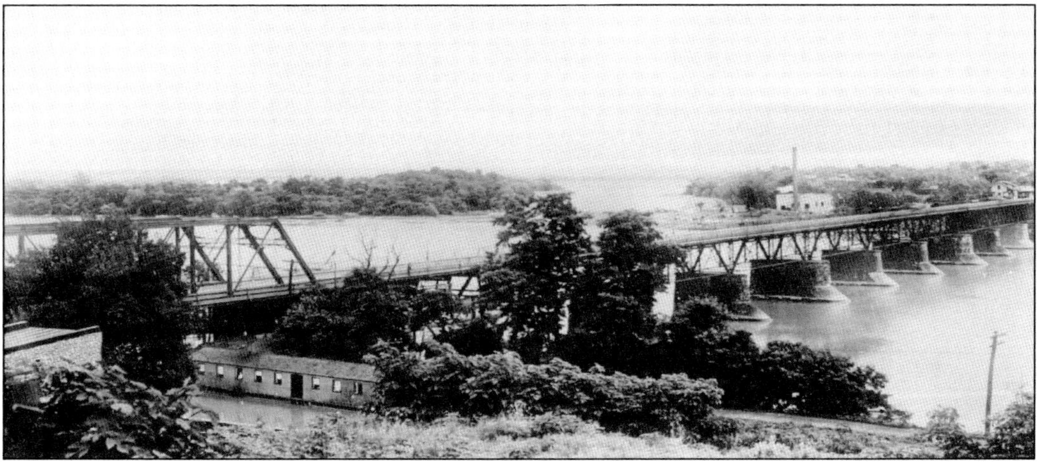

With the development of the C&O Canal in Georgetown, rival port town Alexandria feared losses in its own trade business. To combat this, the Aqueduct Bridge was built in the decade after 1833 to allow canal barges to continue across the Potomac River to Virginia from the terminus of the canal. Heralded as a triumph of engineering at the time, the bridge was built on solid stone foundations. The photograph above, from 1910, shows the bridge renovations when a light iron truss was added to the existing stone piers. The bridge was in use, running alongside the newer Key Bridge, until 1933, when the structure was removed, leaving only the piers, as seen in the photograph below from the 1940s. The stones were considered a nuisance and removed in 1962. (Both, HABS.)

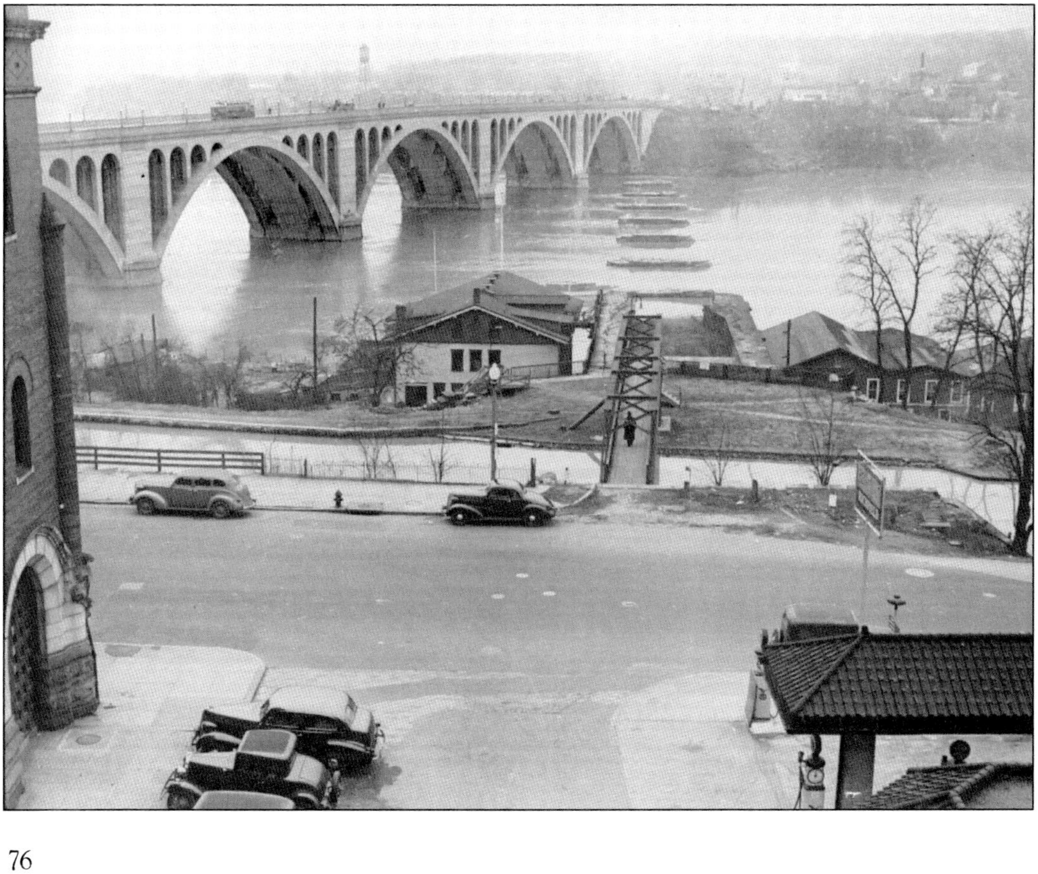

Through Georgetown, four locks were used to help raise the canal from sea level. It took 22 years to build the canal in its entirety. By the time it was finished in 1850, railroads were becoming a more prevalent mode of transporting goods. It took 5–7 days, working 18 hours a day, to traverse the entire canal. (National Photo Company.)

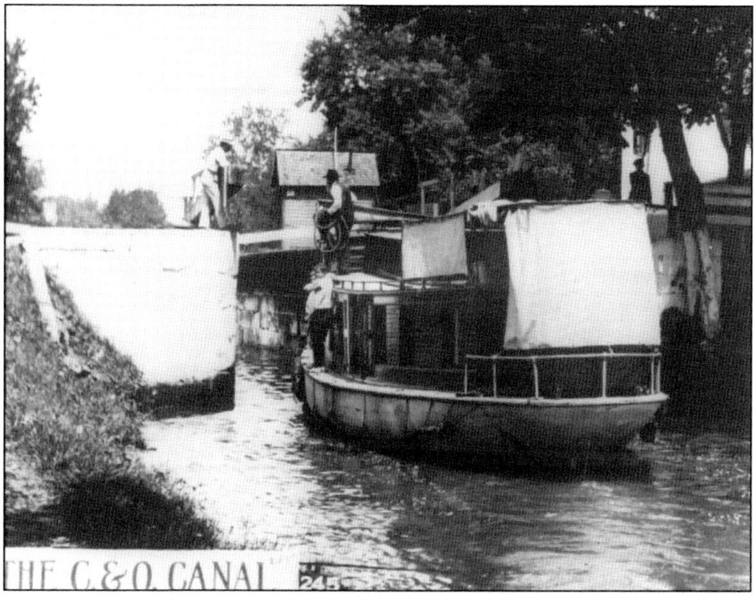

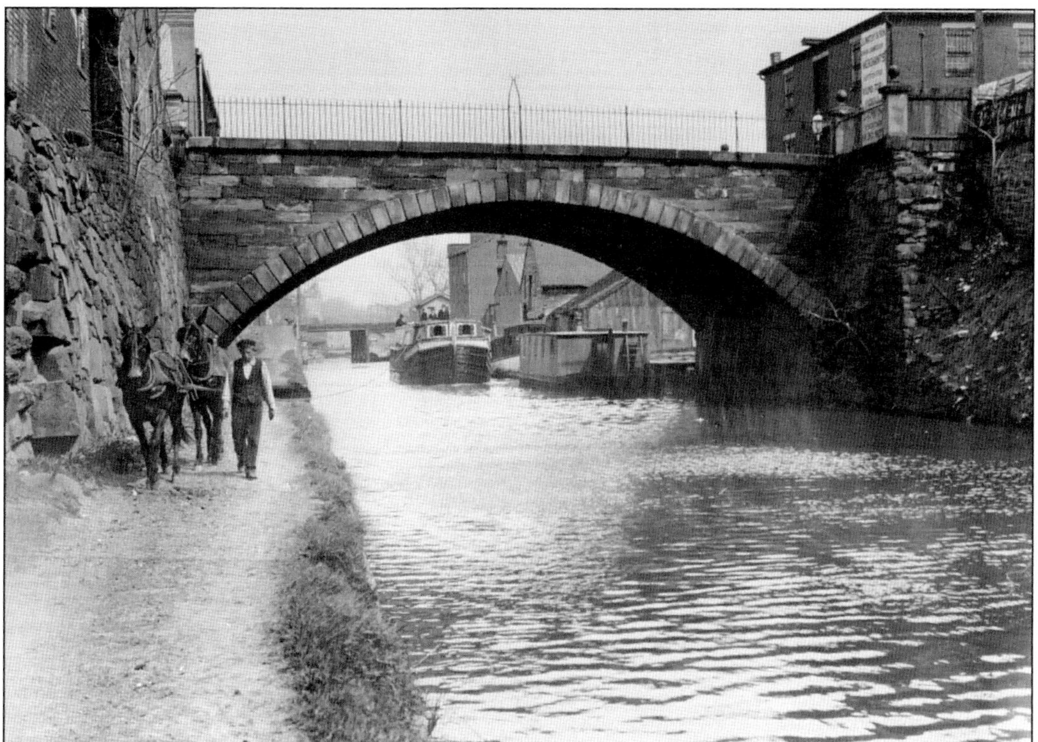

In the front cabin of the canal boats, one would often find a small mule stable. Mules were the preferred pack animal for pulling the canal boats through the C&O because they were less expensive, sturdier, more intelligent, and surer-footed than horses. The mules were often treated as pets and sometimes even given names and taken care of by the children. The mules would walk along the towpath and pull the canal boat behind them. (Detroit Publishing Company.)

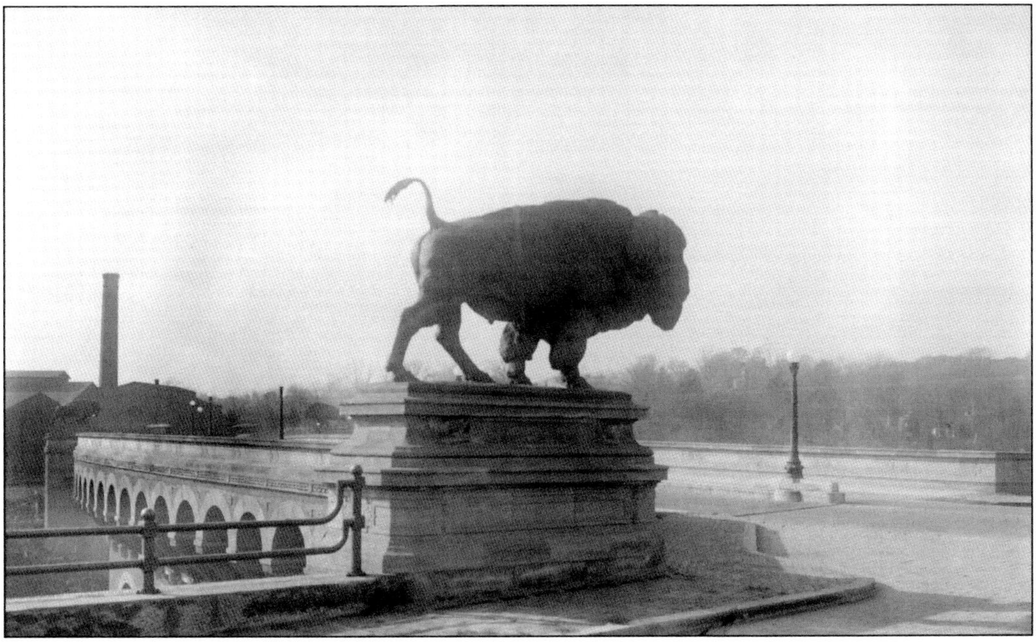

A bridge by many names, the Dumbarton or Q Street or Buffalo Bridge was built in 1914 to connect Dupont Circle with Georgetown. Because the Georgetown streets were not built on the same grid, the two Q Streets did not match up, thus the bridge is slightly curved. The four corners of the bridge are adorned with large bronze sculptures of buffaloes, giving the bridge its nickname. They are the largest statues ever cast in one piece of bronze. (HABS.)

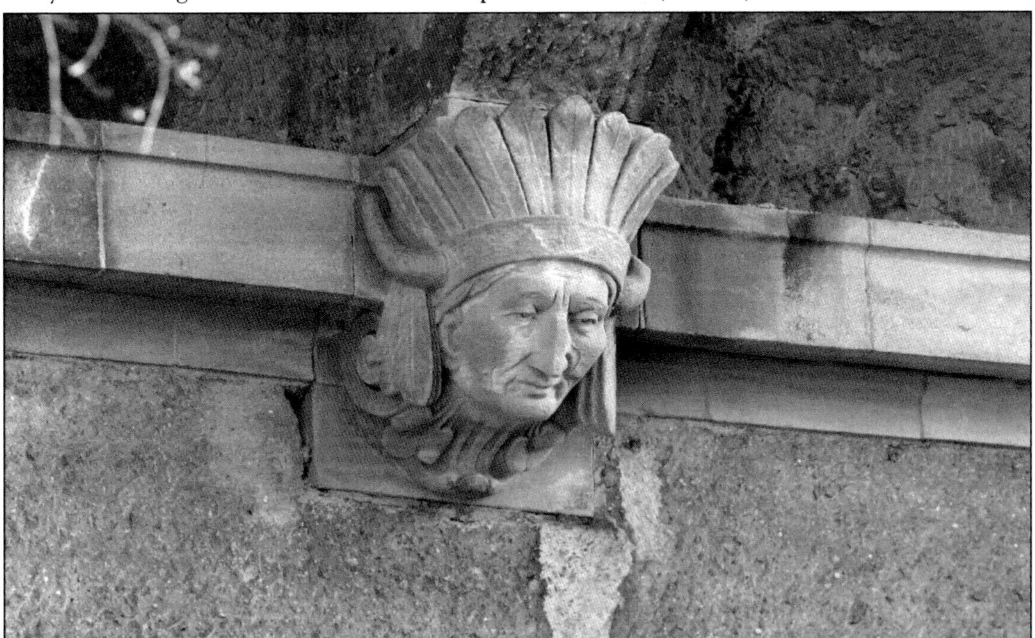

The life mask of Sioux chief Kicking Bear was used to create the Native American heads along the side of the bridge. It was done in homage to Native Americans but also partially out of fear that there would be no indigenous people in the future. (HABS.)

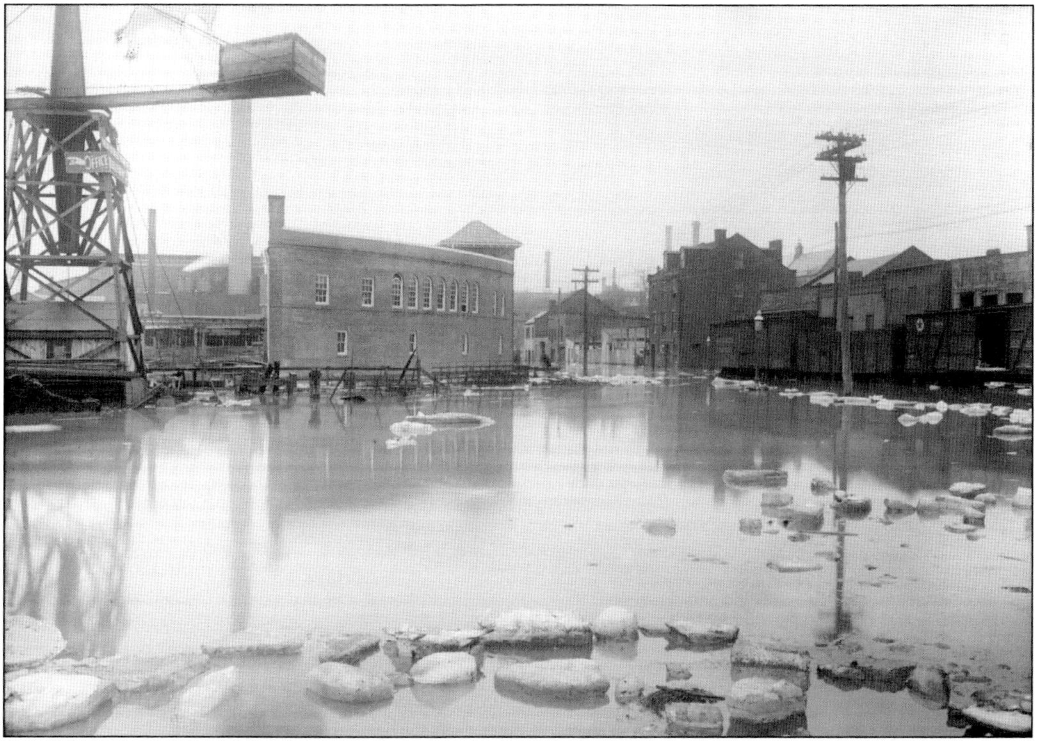

February 1918 saw the waterfront of Georgetown become an extension of the Potomac River. A historic flood damaged many of the boathouses and businesses along the river. If the water was a few feet higher, newspapers reported that the local utilities would have been compromised. The water reached 15 feet above normal levels and carried with it heavy blocks of ice. (Both, National Photo Company.)

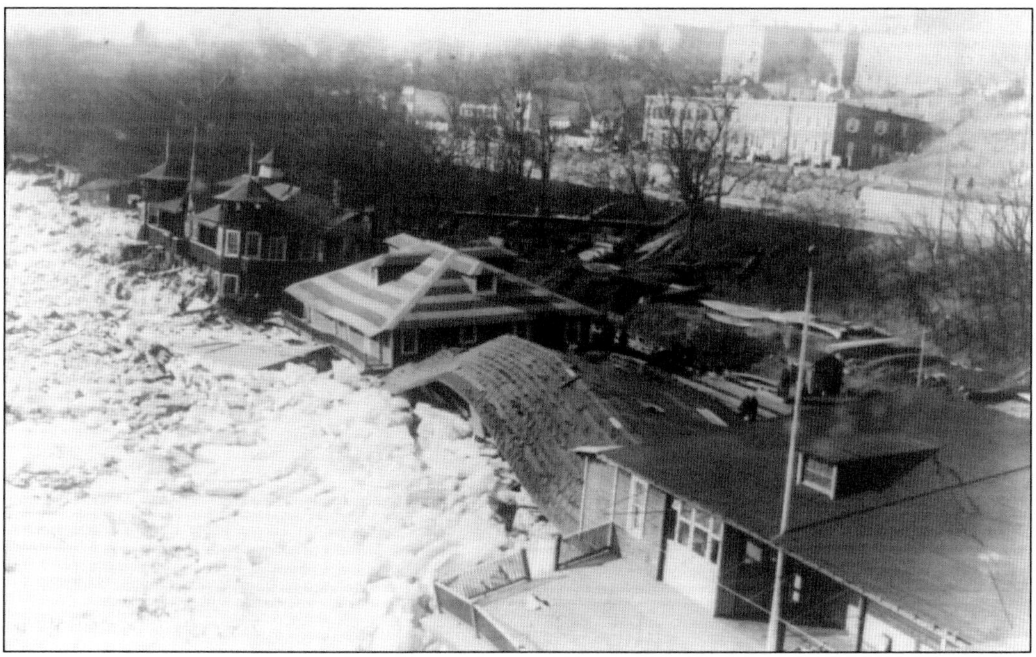

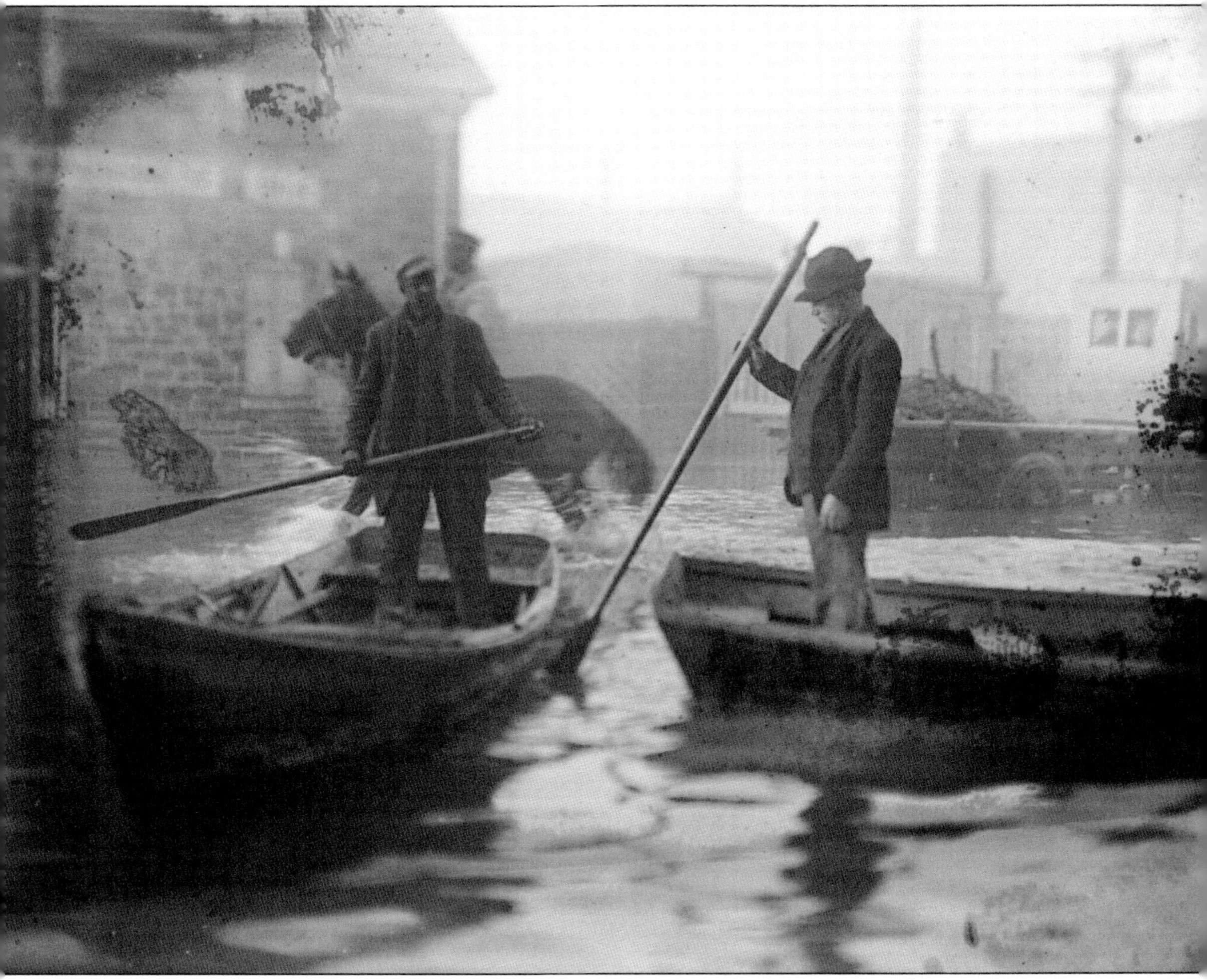

With K Street NW in Georgetown flooded, residents traversed the streets like canals. Arguments erupted when regular rules of right-of-way were not acknowledged. (National Photo Company.)

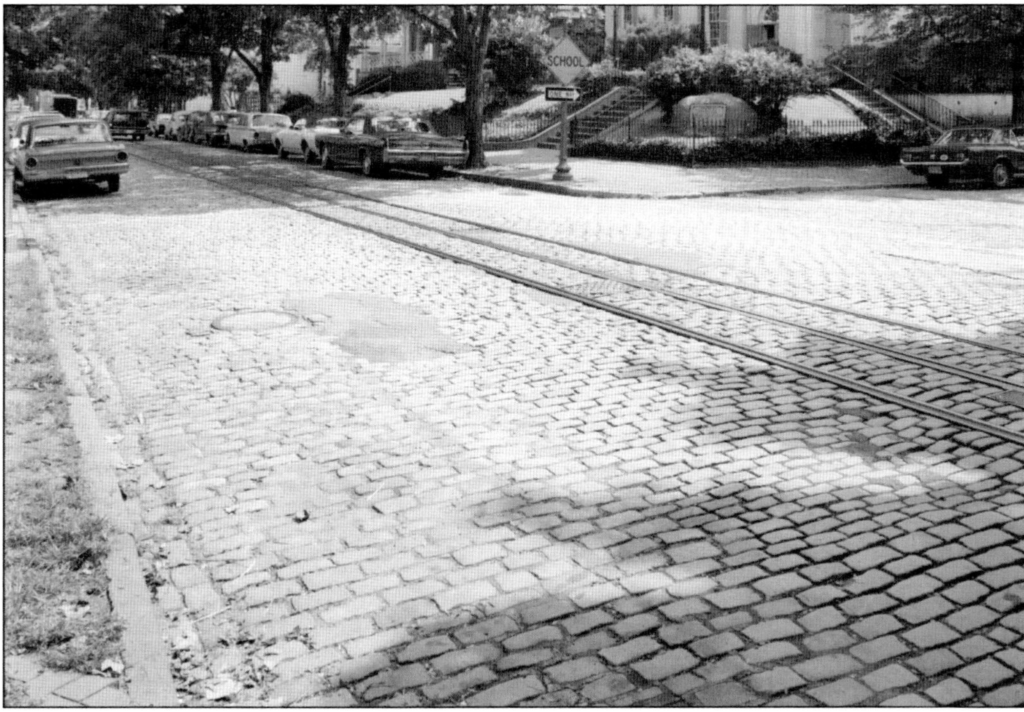

Georgetown is set apart from Washington, DC, both physically by Rock Creek and because of the lack of public transportation. Few remnants remain of the trolley tracks that ran through the cobblestone streets and were used by many to travel through town, but a visible reminder of what the roads used to look like can still be found on O and P Streets NW. When Congress banned overhead wires, these underground conduit systems provided electric power to streetcars. (HABS.)

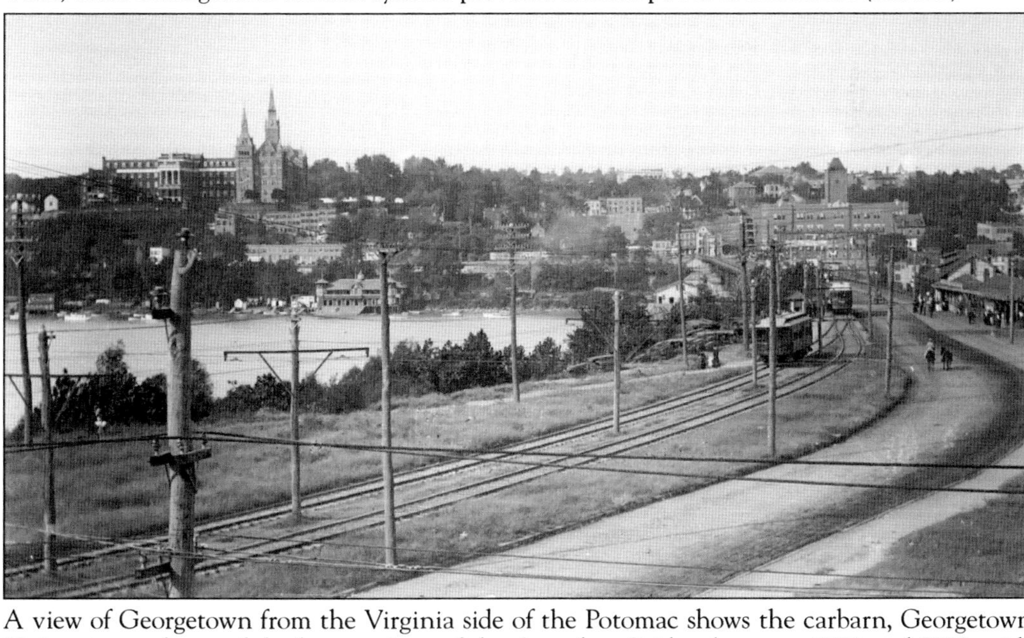

A view of Georgetown from the Virginia side of the Potomac shows the carbarn, Georgetown University, and one of the last versions of the Aqueduct Bridge, between 1909 and 1920, with the trolley tracks that ran down the center. (National Photo Company.)

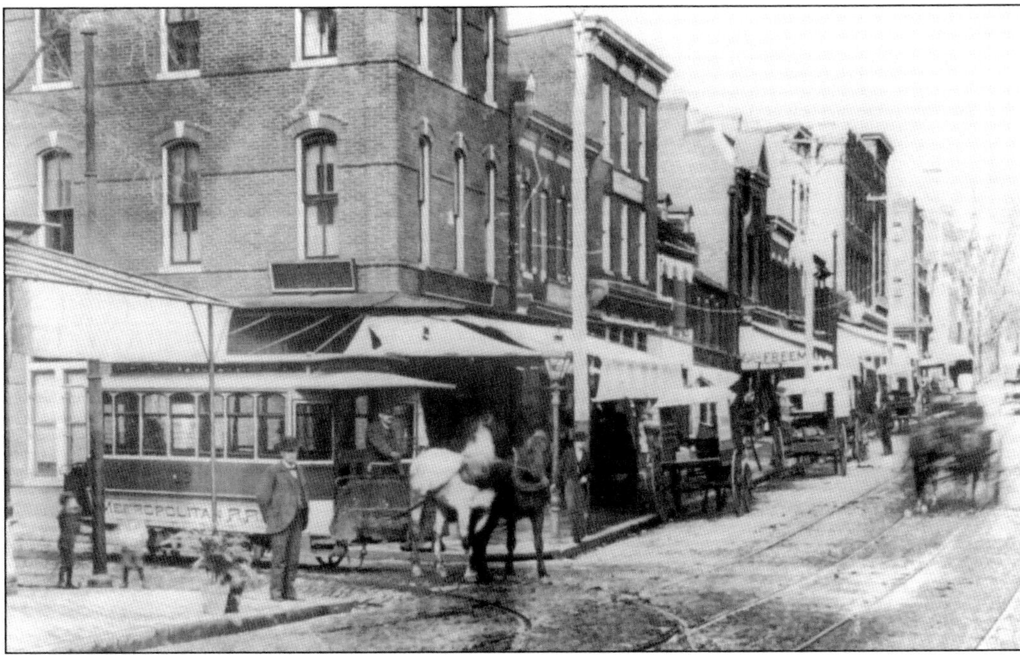

Taken in 1893, this photograph shows the intersection of O Street NW and Wisconsin Avenue, with a horse-drawn trolley from the Metropolitan Railroad. The Metropolitan was founded in 1864 but did not expand to Georgetown until 1872, when it crossed the P Street Bridge. The railroad switched to electric cars in the 1890s. (Library of Congress.)

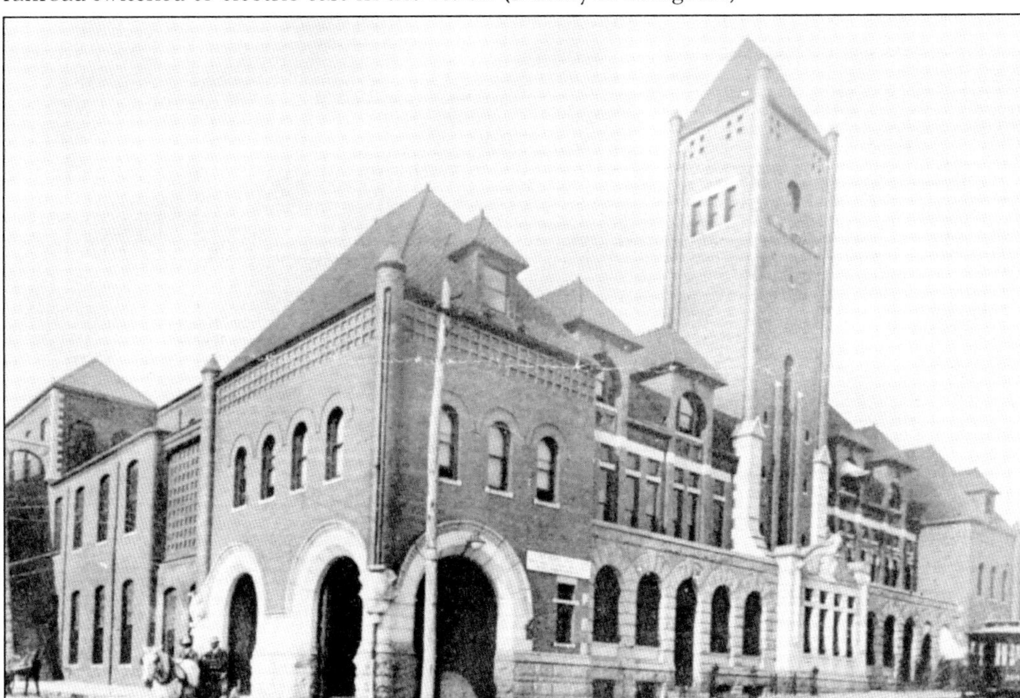

The current site of the Georgetown Car Barn, seen here, used to be the home of one of the original tobacco warehouses, built in 1761. (HABS.)

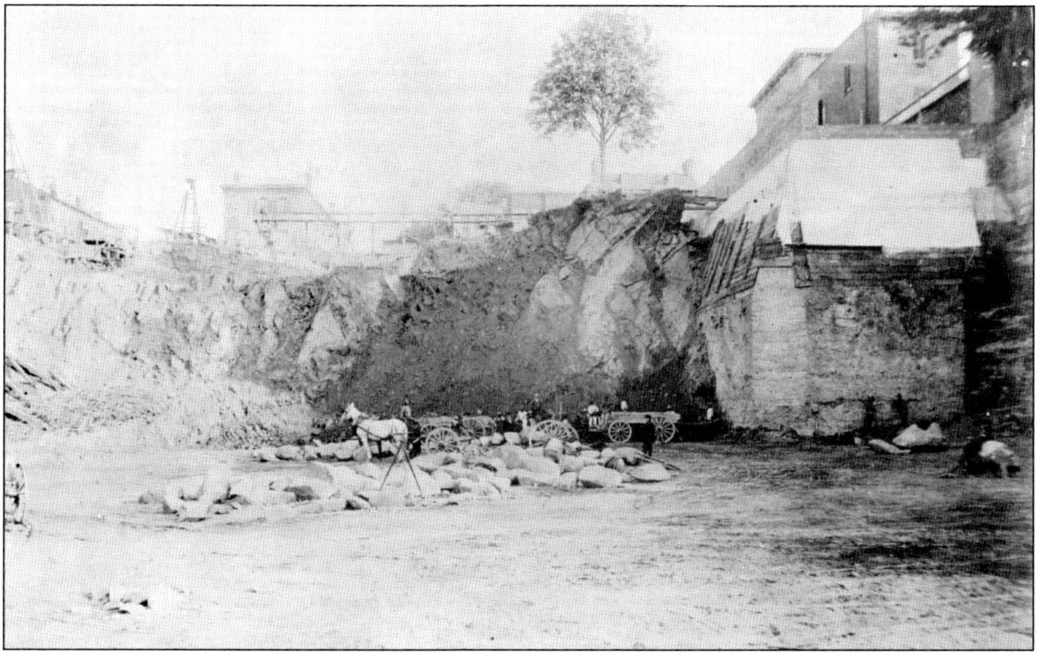

This 1894 photograph shows the evacuation of the Capitol Traction Company Union Station, at Thirty-sixth and M Streets NW. (HABS.)

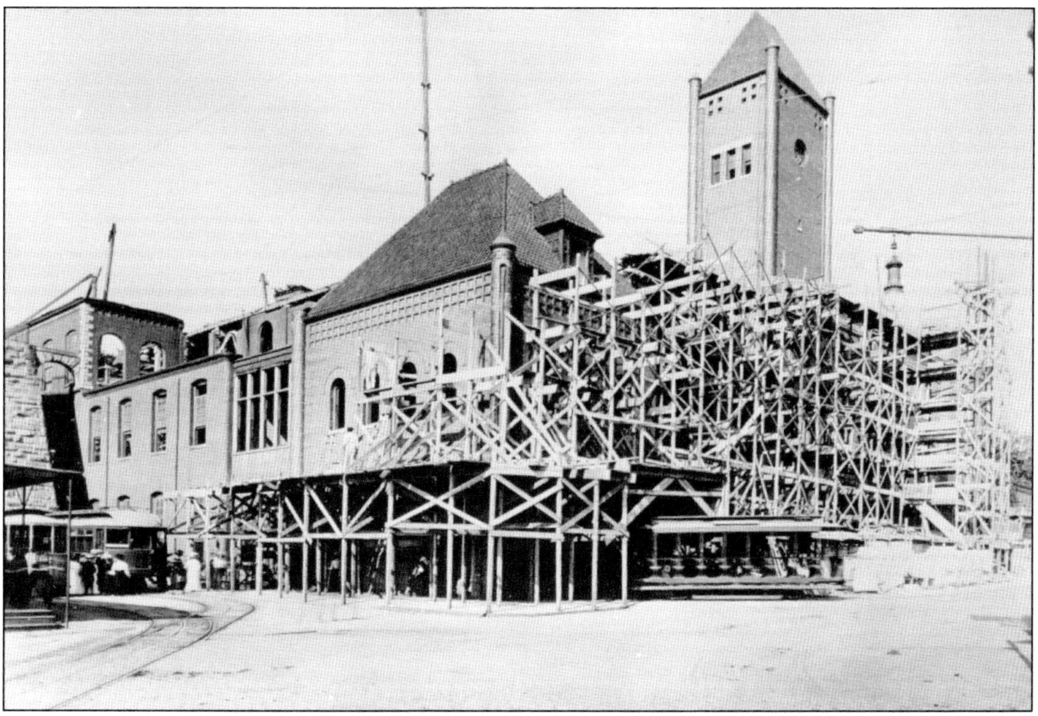

The station was built in 1897, with a later expansion shown in this 1911 photograph. It was originally a carbarn for Capitol Traction Company's streetcars, but it also had trolley tracks, passenger stations, and offices. After the loss of the streetcars, it became a part of Georgetown University. (HABS.)

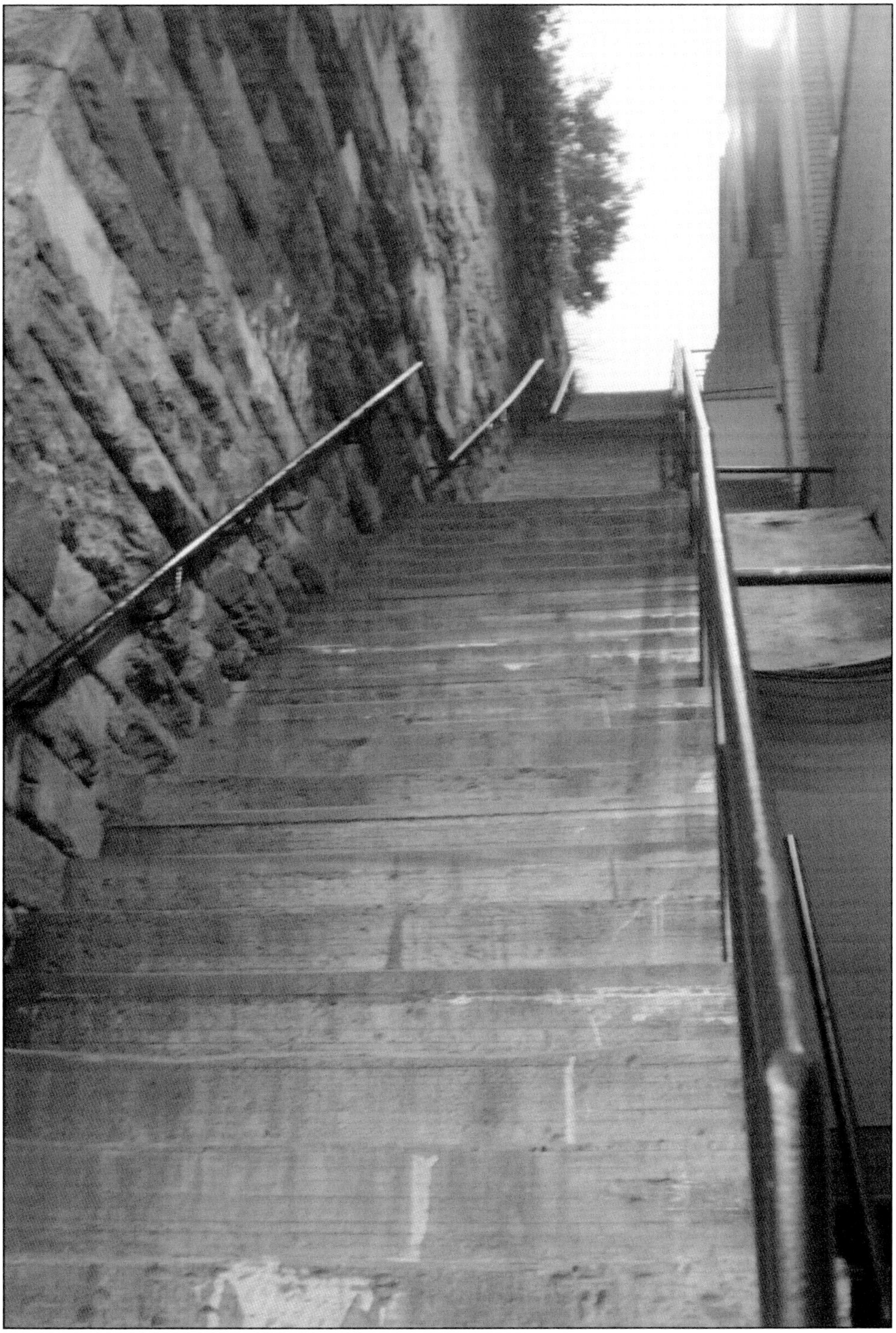

Thirty-sixth Street NW used to run down the hill continuously until it reached the Aqueduct Bridge. Eventually, the road was closed and a large stone retaining wall was built in order to give M Street more flat land. In order to keep pedestrian access, a long set of 75 steps was built. They were made famous by the 1970 film *The Exorcist*. (Author's collection.)

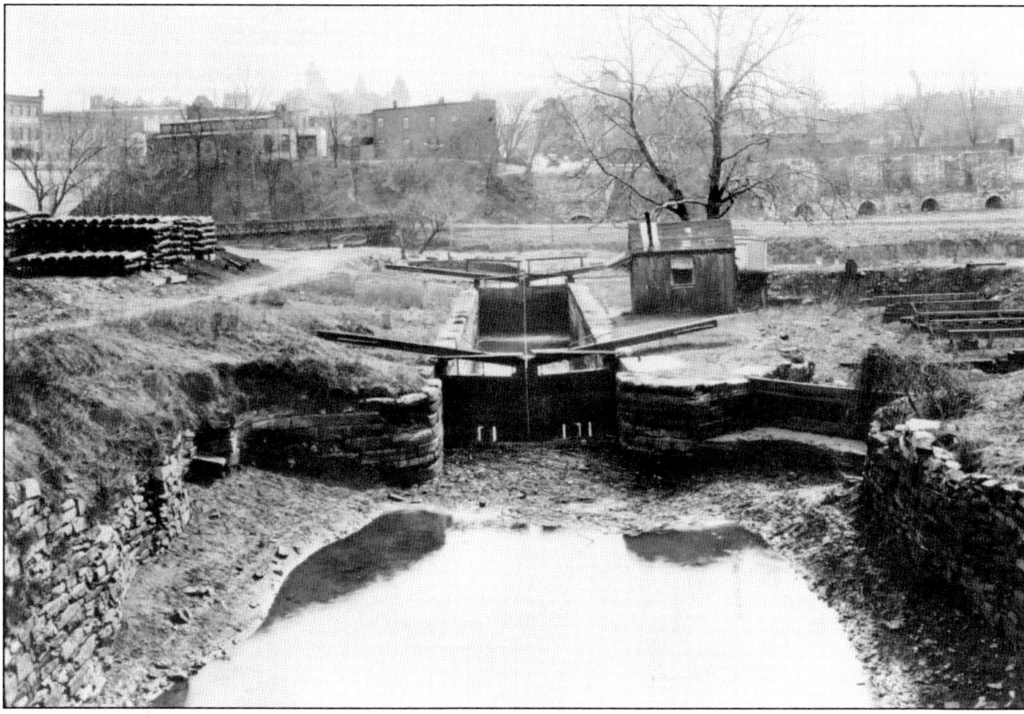

At the far east end of Georgetown, at the terminus of the C&O Canal, are the ruins of the Godey Lime Kiln. William Godey built a kiln using limestone to make lime and plaster in 1864. The business remained here until 1908, run by his family after his death in 1873. (HABS.)

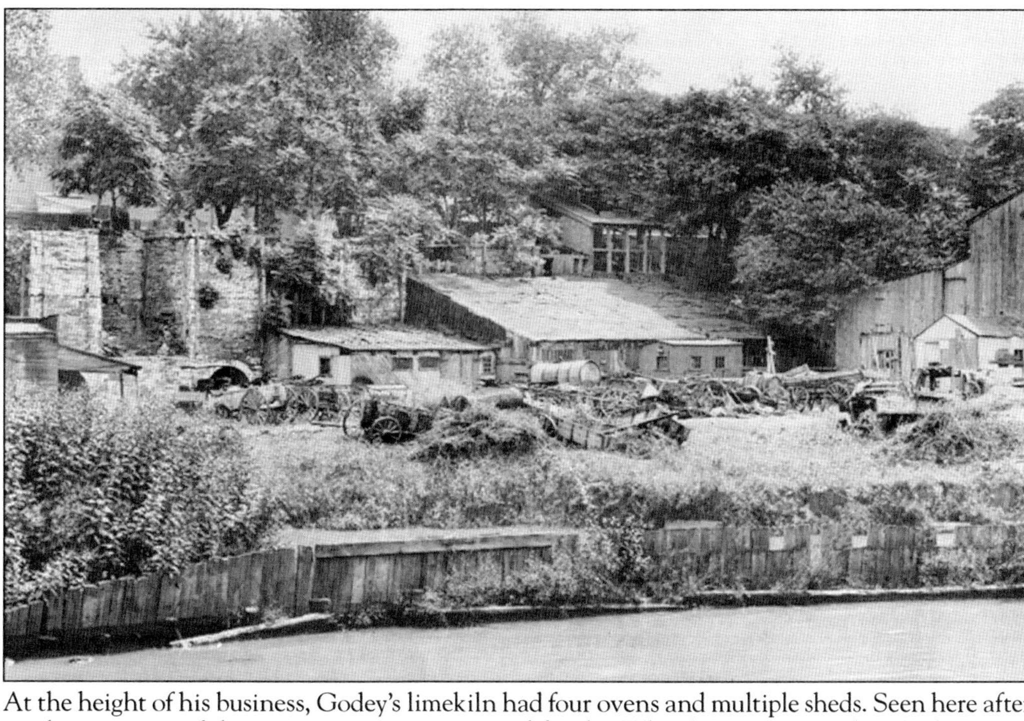

At the height of his business, Godey's limekiln had four ovens and multiple sheds. Seen here after its closure, most of these remnants were removed for the Whitehurst Freeway. (HABS.)

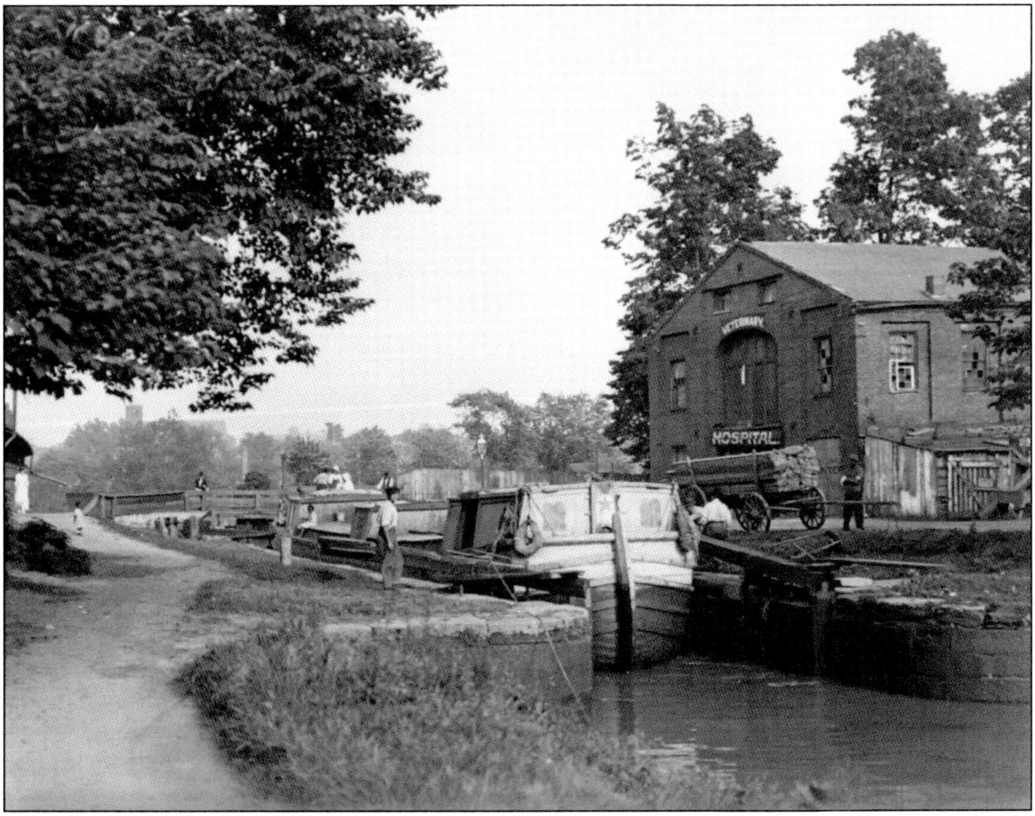

The idea for a national foundry located in Georgetown began in 1836. With the C&O Canal, the B&O Railroad, and the Potomac River, it would easy to bring in raw materials and ship out weapons. William Duvall opened his foundry in 1856 and made muskets during the Civil War. By 1903, it had become a veterinary hospital, as seen in this 1914 photograph. (HABS.)

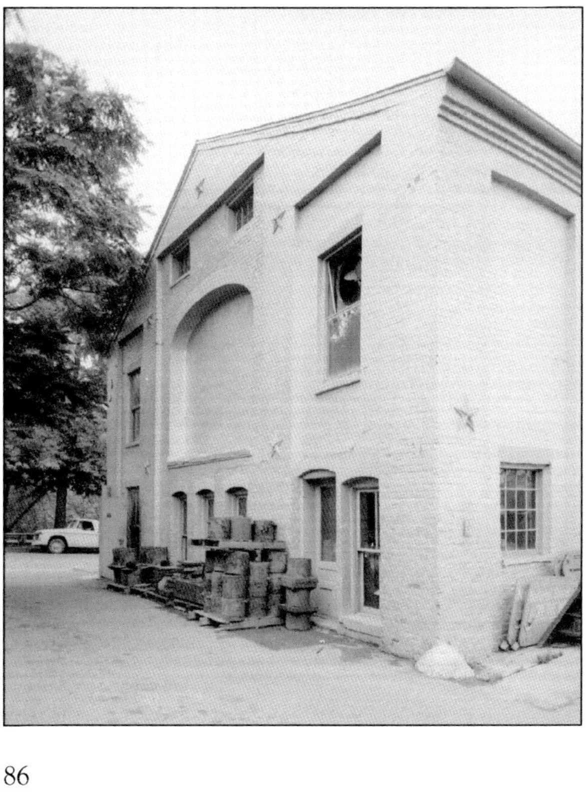

This 1967 photograph of the Duvall Foundry shows how little the building has changed but also the extensive difference in the surrounding grounds. In this photograph, the building was used as storage and as a welding school for the Washington Gas Light Company. (HABS.)

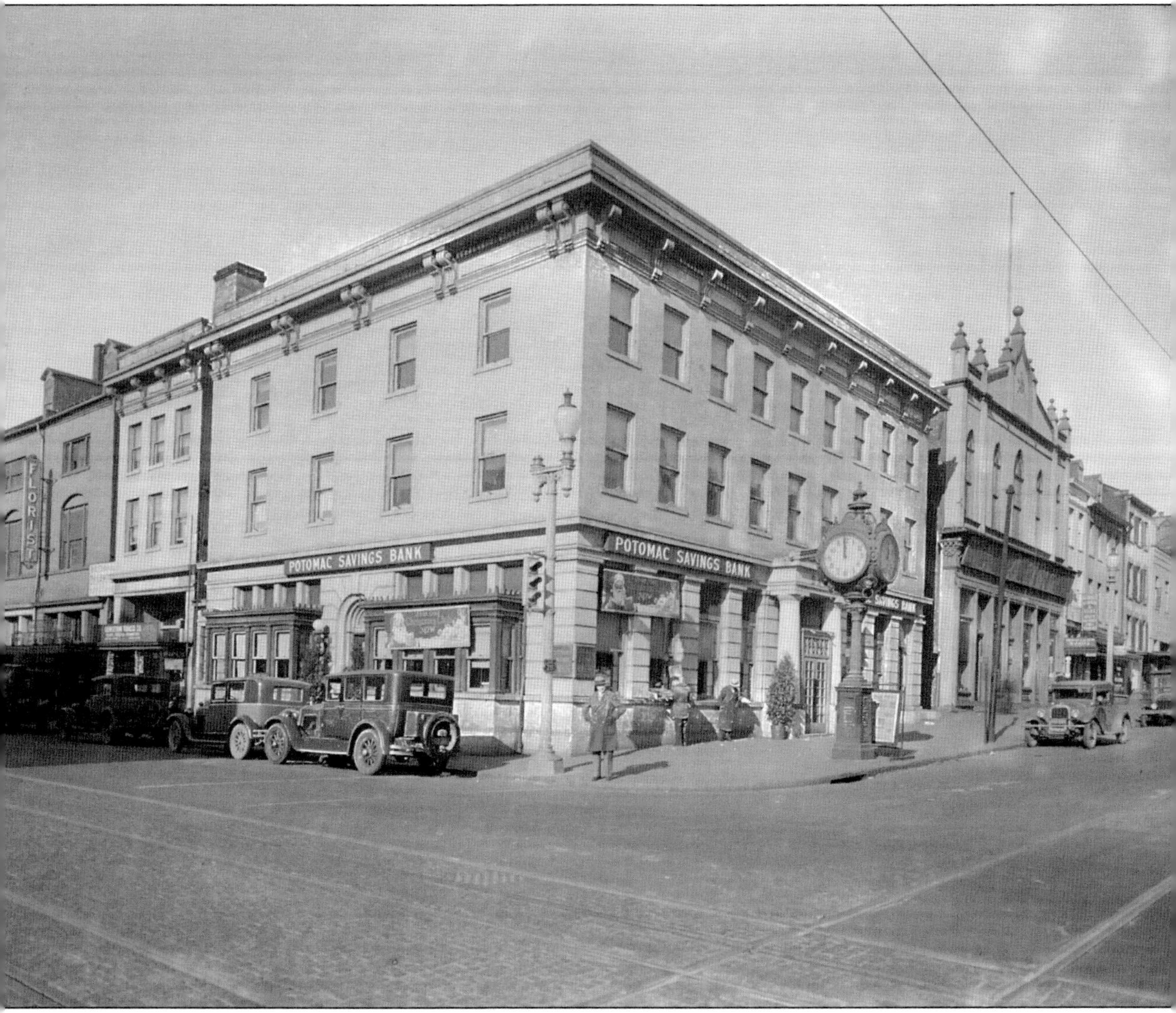

The Potomac Bank was established in 1903 and moved to this location at the corner of Wisconsin Avenue and M Street NW the following year. The building that stands now replaced one that burned down in 1909. The Potomac Savings Bank, seen here in the 1920s, was in business until 1933, when the Hamilton National Bank occupied this building. In 1954, Hamilton merged with the National Bank of Washington and this became its Georgetown branch until the bank collapsed in 1990. (HABS.)

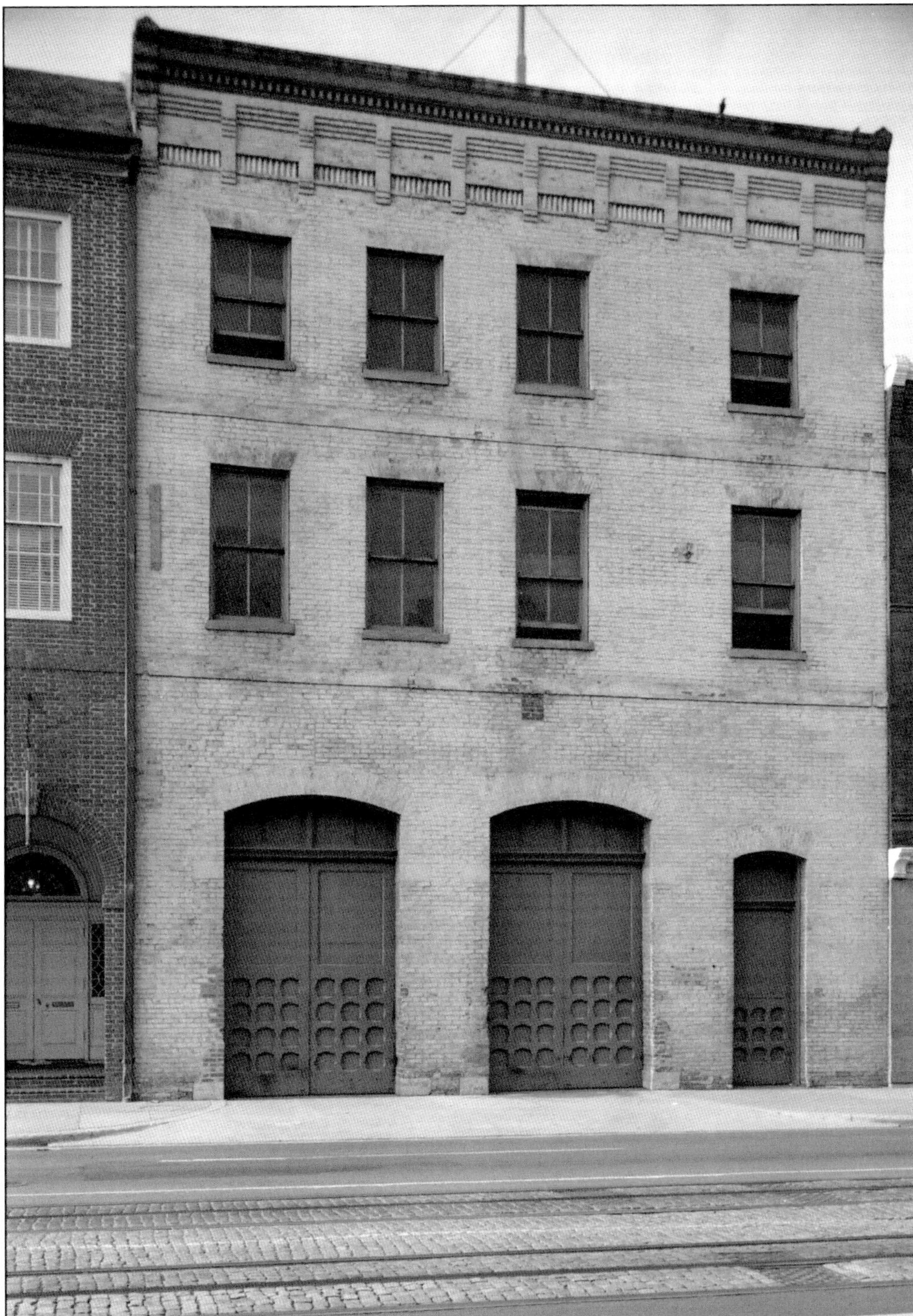

The Bank of Columbia branch on M Street NW was built in 1796 and served as a bank for the next 10 years. When the bank moved, the Bureau of Indian Trade settled into the premises. Starting in 1823, it was essentially Georgetown's city hall, with offices for the mayor and council and storage for the records. It remained as such until the city was dissolved in 1871, and the building then became District of Columbia property. The city used it as Fire Station No. 5 until 1940 and then as part of the sanitation department. (HABS.)

People's Drug Store No. 9 was located at M Street NW and Thirty-first Street NW in Georgetown. The once-ubiquitous pharmacy had more than 500 stores along the East Coast. The first was opened in downtown DC in 1905, and the company continued to expand until it became the largest chain in the area. In the 1990s, People's was merged into CVS Pharmacy. (National Photo Company.)

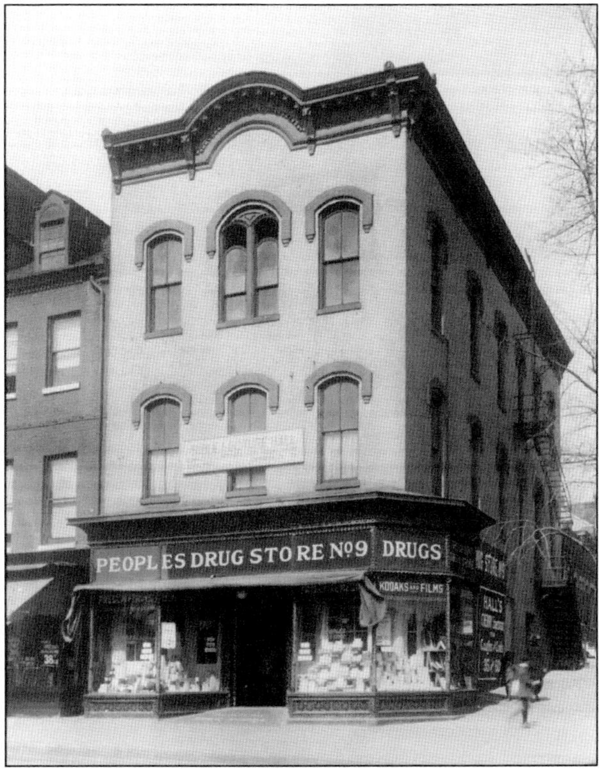

Taken between 1909 and 1932, this interior shot of the same People's Drug Store shows that it sold an egg and tar shampoo for 59¢, as well as other beauty products. (National Photo Company.)

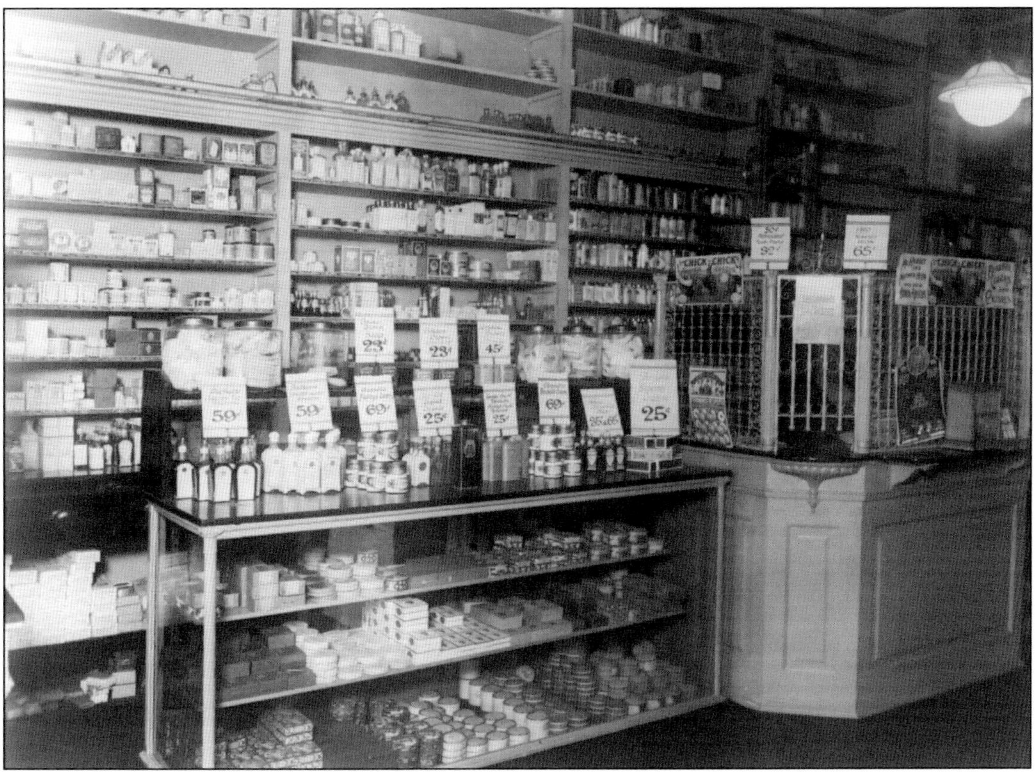

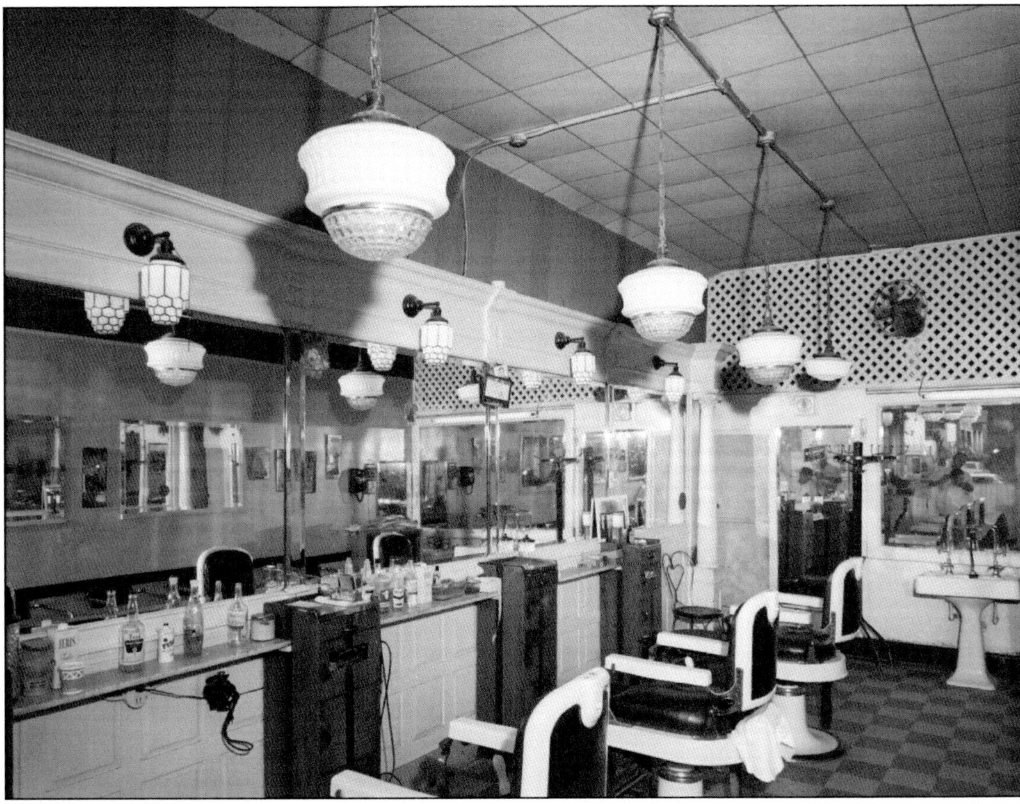

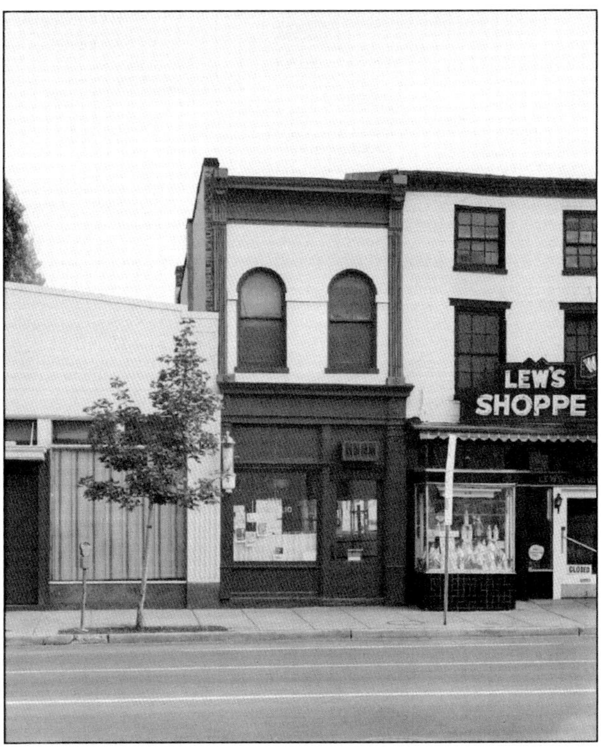

This commercial building on M Street NW was likely built between 1877 and 1890. It was a barbershop from 1913 until the 1970s, run by Frank Coniglio and, later, his son. Coniglio emigrated from Sicily in 1911 to Georgetown. His son Phillip learned the trade in the shop growing up and, when the elder Coniglio died in 1948, took over. For its final decade, it was run by James Randolph, until the building was sold. It is still a commercial establishment today. (Both, HABS.)

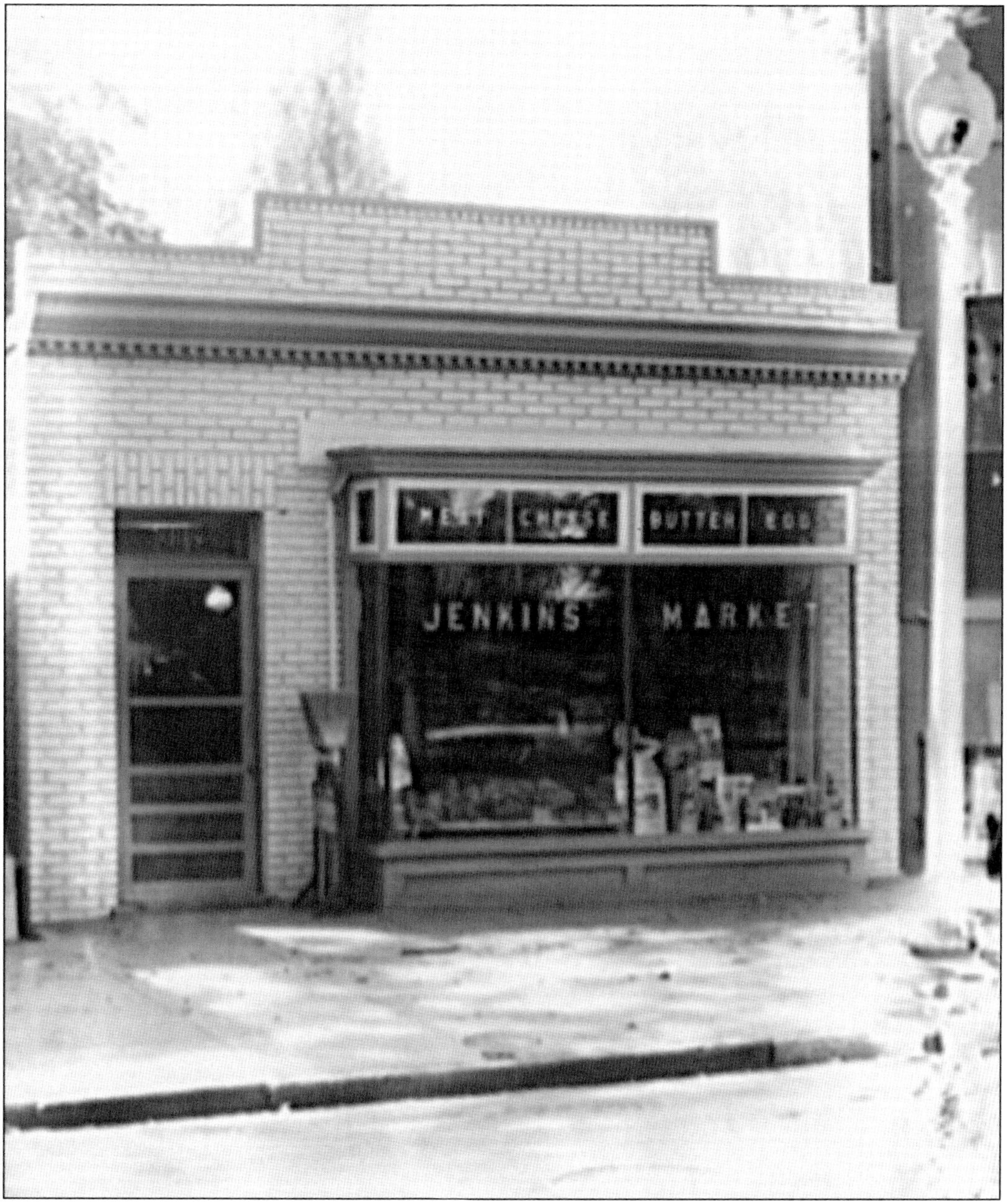

A small commercial building was transferred to John Jenkins in 1919 for $10. Jenkins Market was a local grocery until 1952. Jenkins had already been a grocer for 21 years in Georgetown when he purchased this property, on Q Street NW. (Theodor Horydczak.)

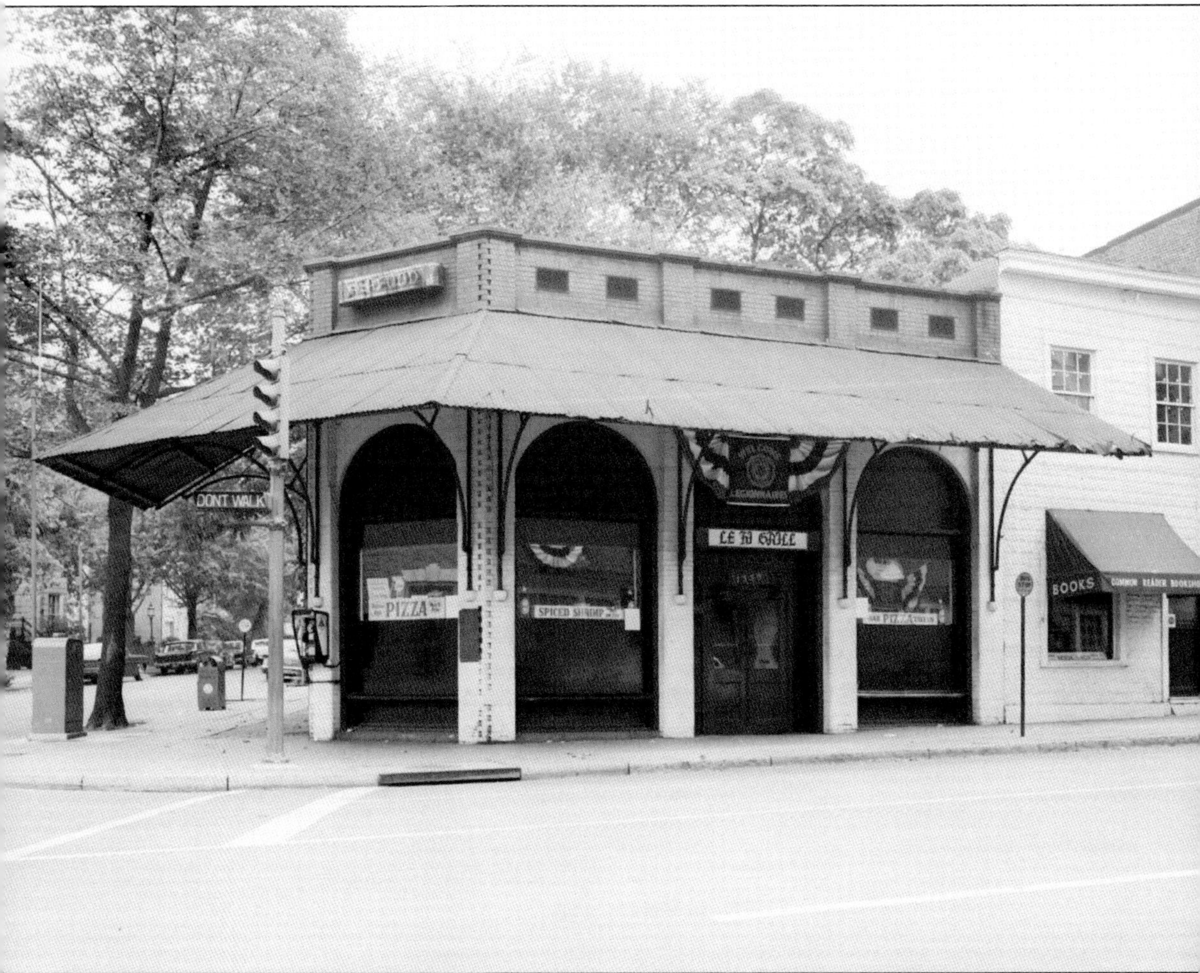

A one-story commercial building without living quarters, this may have been a meat market in 1890. At the very least, it was documented as a grocer in 1900. It has been a restaurant since the 1930s. In the 1980s, it was an Au Pied Du Cochen, and it was here that KGB defector Vitaly Yurchenko left his CIA handler and returned to the KGB via the Soviet Embassy in DC. (HABS.)

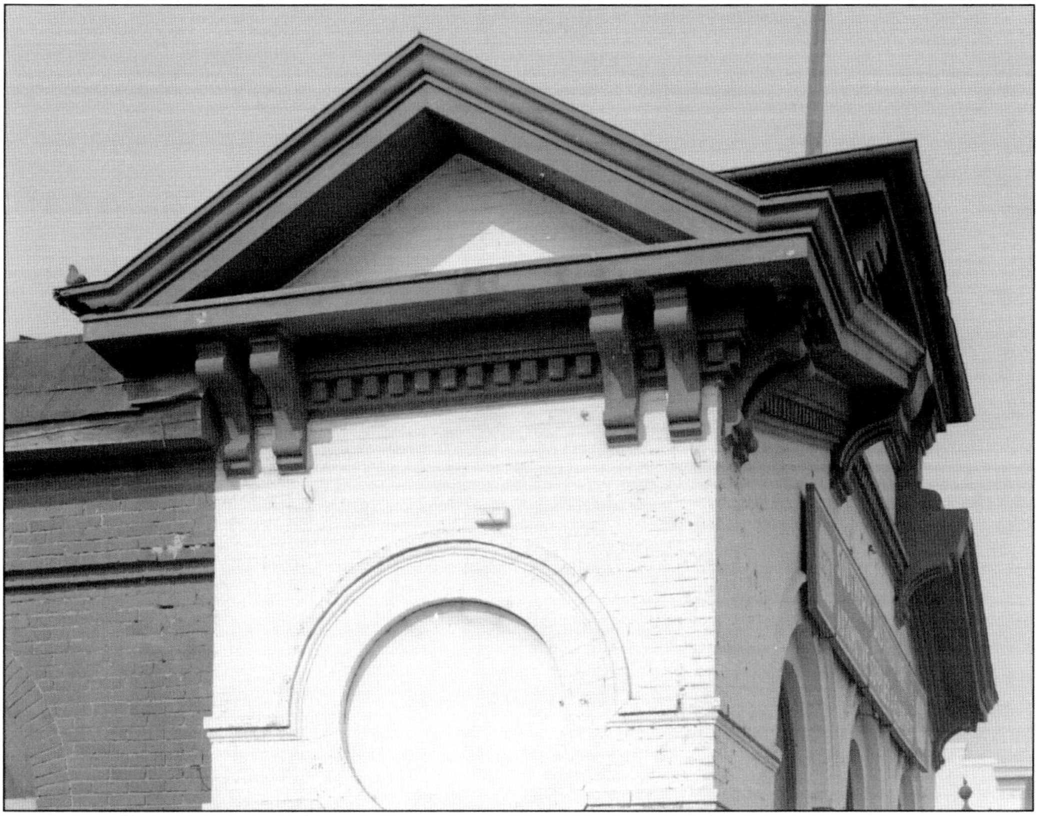

The original Georgetown Market was built in 1796 at this location, though this building dates to 1865. The original land deed stipulated that it be "for the use of the market aforesaid forever, and for no other use, interest or purpose whatsoever." Of course, it is not a market anymore. It took congressional action in the 1920s to lease the land to an automobile wholesaler. Today, it is a historic landmark, part of which is owned by the National Park Service and the rest of which operates as a Dean & Deluca, an upscale food store, which, in some ways, is a market. (Both, National Photo Company.)

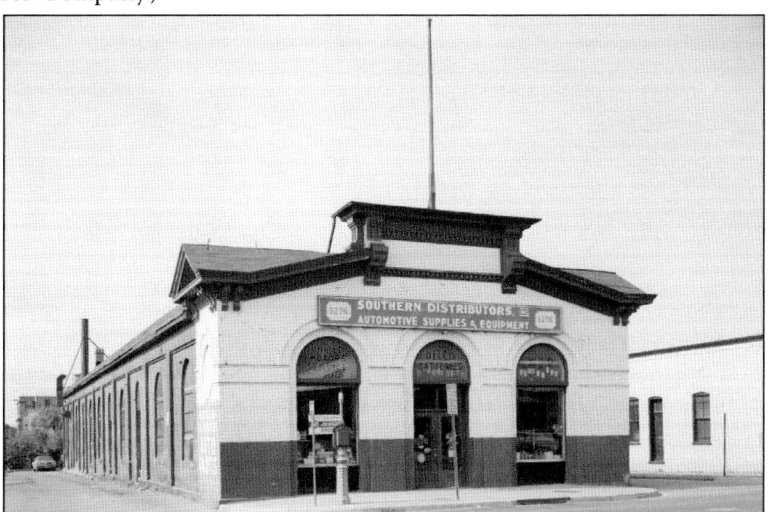

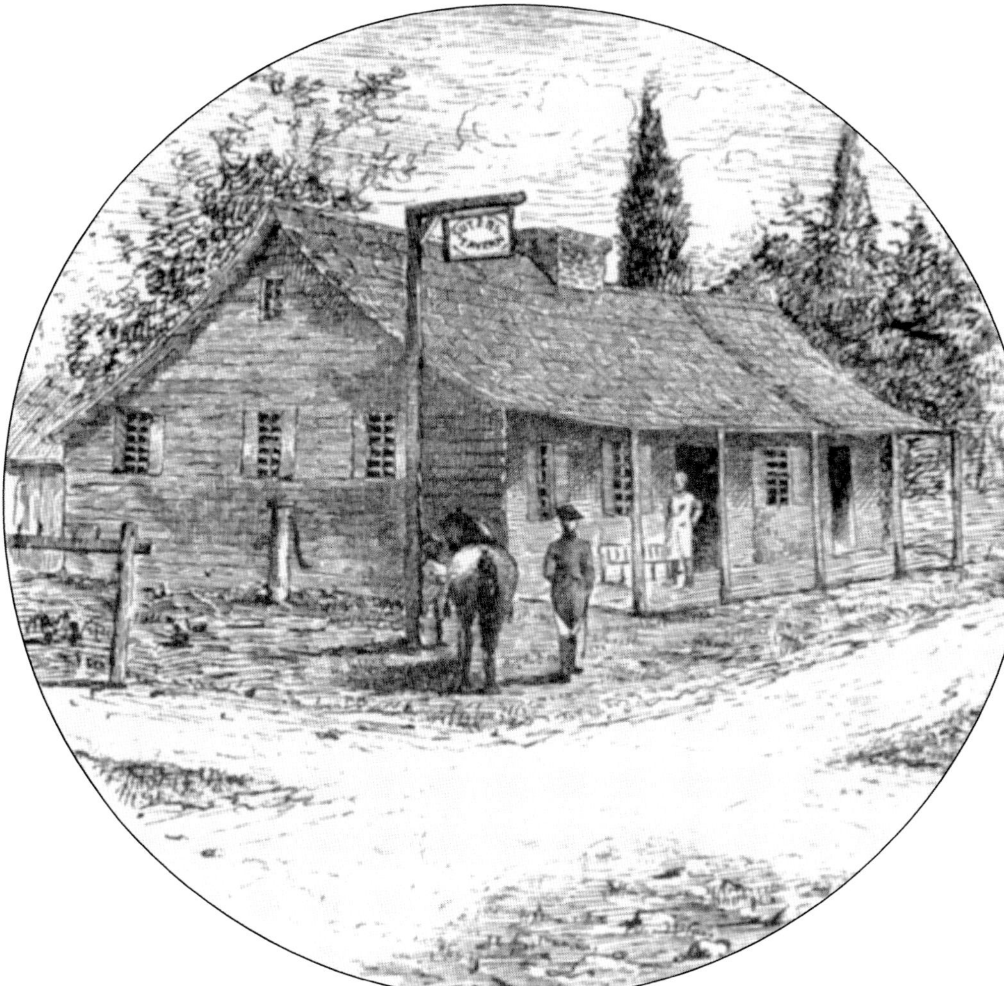

Suter's Tavern remains a mysterious site in Georgetown history. George Washington met with landowners, commissioners, and city planner Pierre L'Enfant in Georgetown in 1791 at the Fountain Inn, locally known as Suter's Tavern, after its owner, John Suter. Because there is no written documentation of an address—not that it would matter, as the road names have changed—and firsthand knowledge has long since passed, the exact location of Suter's Tavern has been forgotten. (*Perley's Reminiscences of Sixty Years in the National Metropolis*, 1886.)

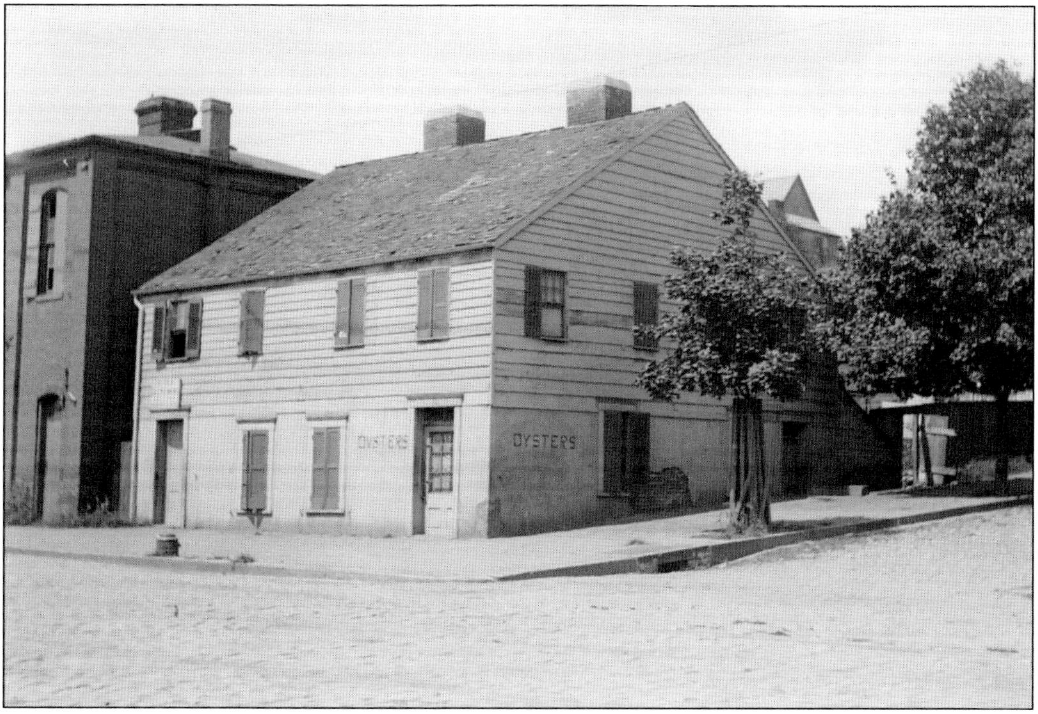

Through the years Suter's Tavern has been "rediscovered" in many locations, from the Old Stone House to as far up Wisconsin Avenue as the Georgetown Club. This old photograph in the Library of Congress, labeled as a building at Thirty-first and K Streets NW, was discovered with "Suter's" written on the back. Though for years it was considered fact that Suter's Tavern was at that corner, that claim has since been proven false. Perhaps this photograph is not of the corner of Thirty-first and K Streets NW, or maybe it is just not Suter's. (National Photo Company.)

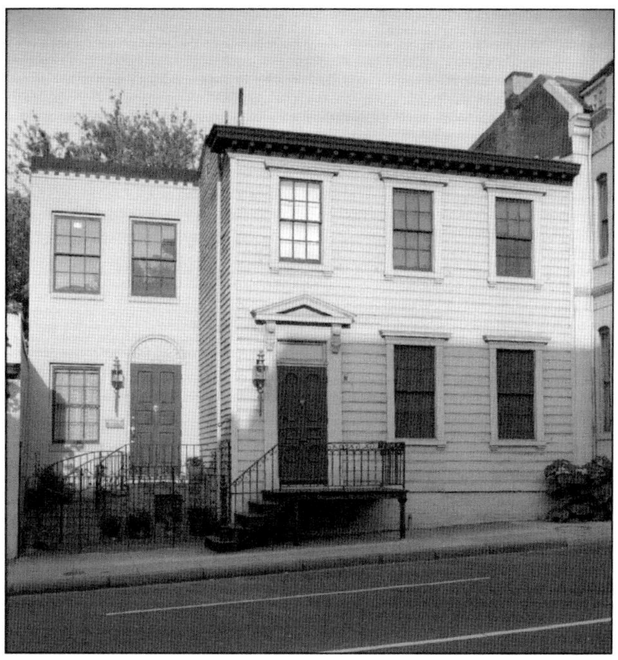

The current occupant of this building, the Georgetown Club, claims that the frame house was constructed in the 1780s and was the famed Suter's Tavern. Research of the deeds does not support this theory, however. (HABS.)

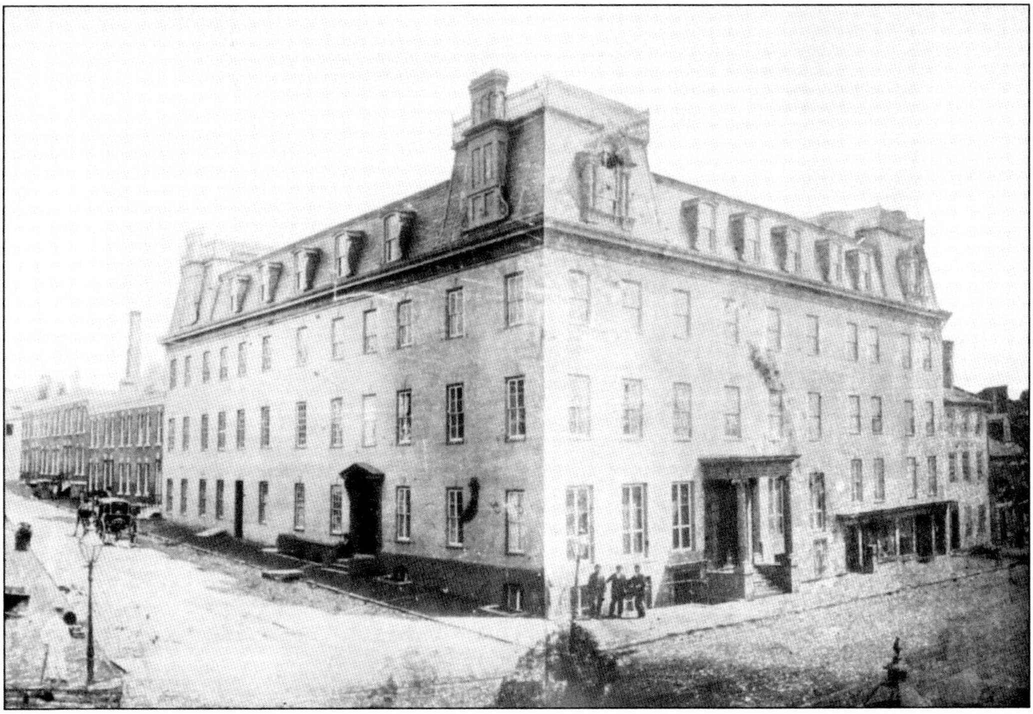

One of many hotels in Georgetown no longer standing, the Union Hotel and Tavern was built in 1796. It was a successful business until the Civil War, when the Union government notified the proprietor that it would be turned into a hospital. As the boarders and staff left, they took everything, including the chamber pots, with them. This photograph was taken after the government returned the hotel and it went through substantial renovations, including the addition of a mansard roof. (National Photo Company.)

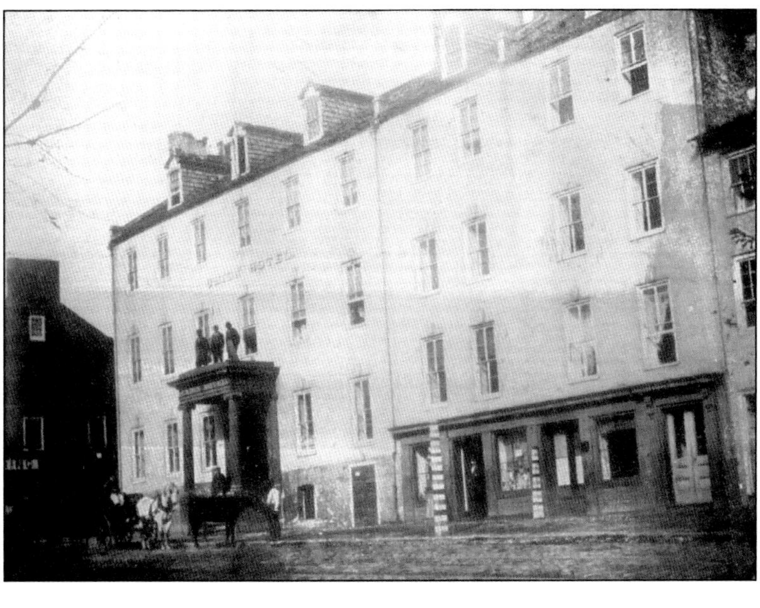

This pre-renovation photograph of the Union Hotel is thought to be from after the Battle of Fredericksburg, dating this to December 1862, when the building was being used as a hospital. The Union Hospital was where Louisa May Alcott, author of *Little Women*, worked during her short time as a nurse in the Civil War. (National Photo Company.)

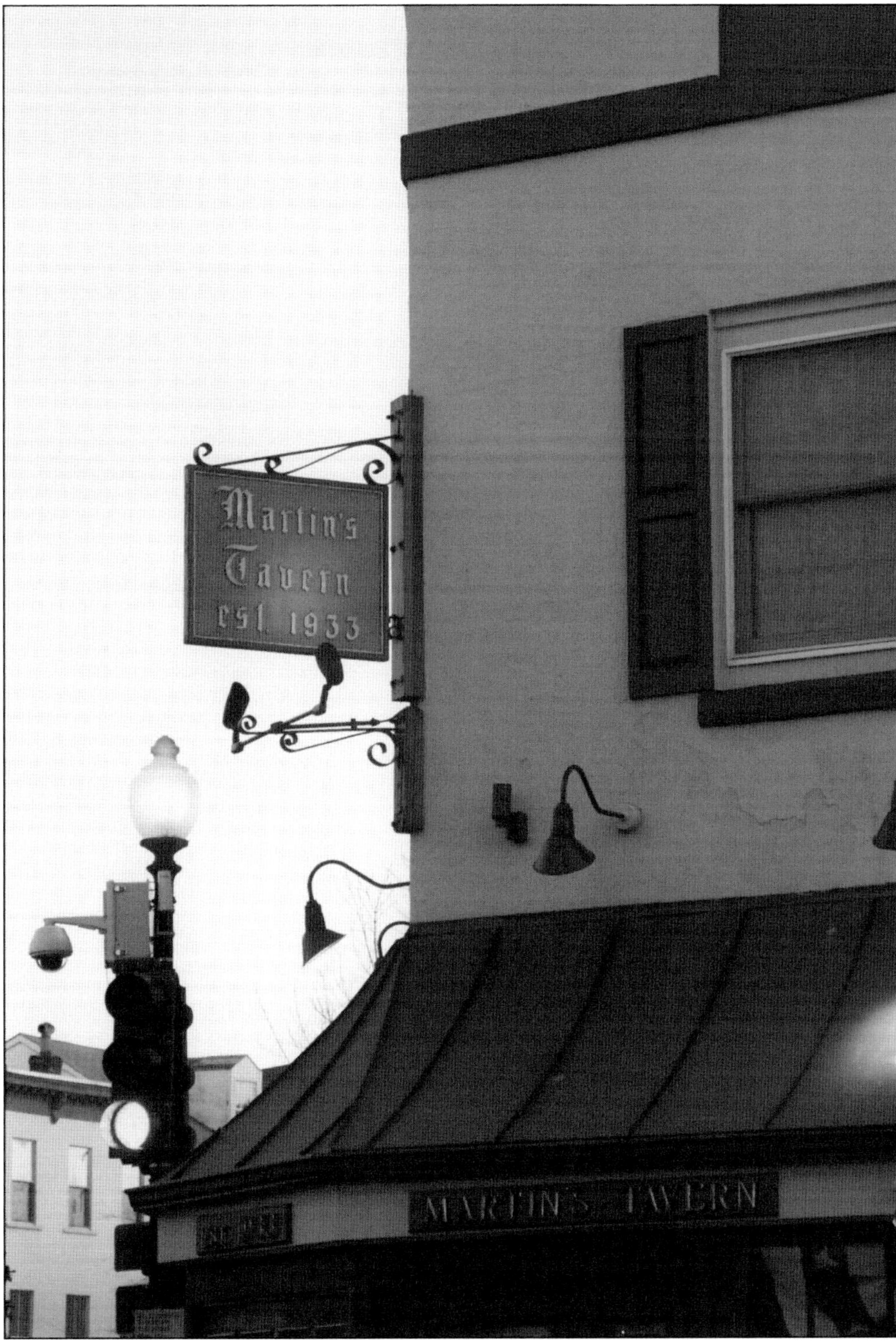

Martin's Tavern is the longest-running family-owned restaurant in DC. It was opened in 1933 by an Irish immigrant, Billy Martin, and is run by his descendants. A well-known local hangout since the beginning, "Meet me at Martin's" was heard throughout the streets of Georgetown during World War II, where military officials and spies unknowingly dined in adjoining booths. It is rumored to be where JFK proposed to Jackie but not proven. At the very least, they likely celebrated their engagement there. (Author's collection.)

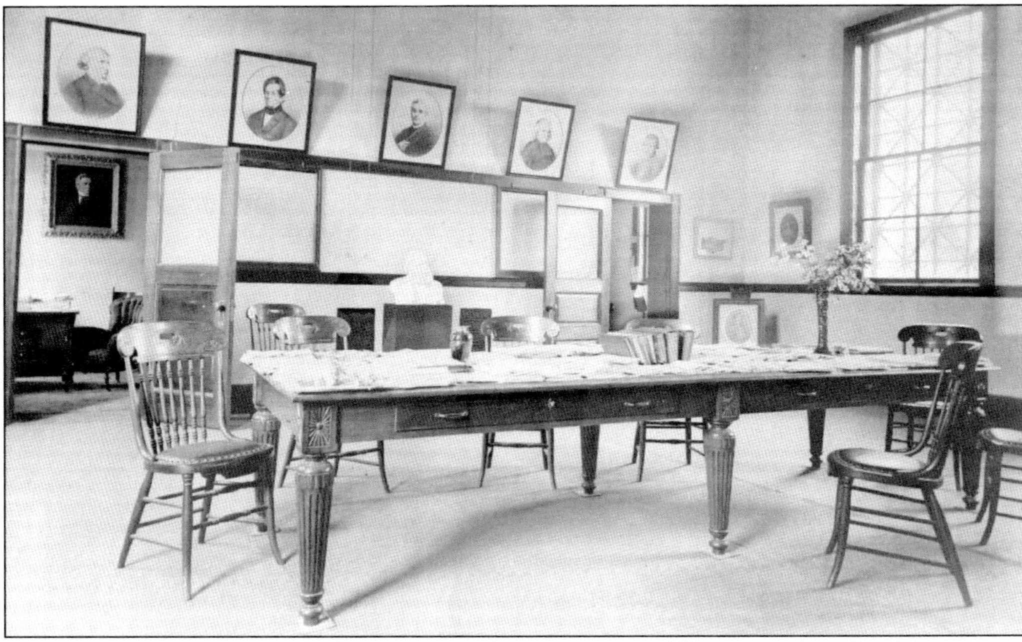

Using funds from his telephone patent, Alexander Graham Bell founded the Volta Laboratory in the 1880s to continue his research. He also used part of his profits to form the Volta Bureau for the "increase and diffusion of knowledge relating to the deaf." The Volta Laboratory improved on the phonograph and rearranged the letters to dub theirs the "graphophone." The American Graphophone Company would later evolve into Columbia Records. (HABS.)

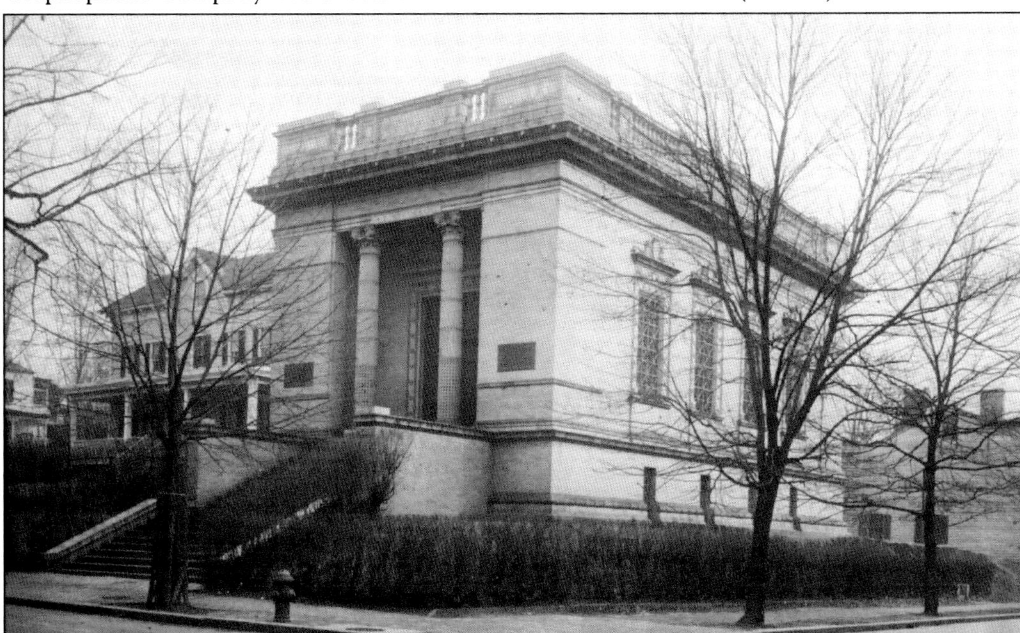

The Volta Bureau began in the carriage house behind Bell's father's Georgetown home but eventually expanded across the street. One of the young girls Bell was working with, Helen Keller, led the ceremony to break ground on the Neoclassical building in 1893. (HABS.)

Located on the busy M Street NW, the Nordlinger Building was named after the owners of the lot in the 1870s. The building was likely erected then and has served as a storefront since the early 1900s. Starting in 1906, it was Baer Clothing Store, followed by a dry goods store in the 1920s. It was then operated as a People's Drug Store for more than 40 years. A prime example of mixed use, this building was a shop on the street level and a residence on the upper levels. (HABS.)

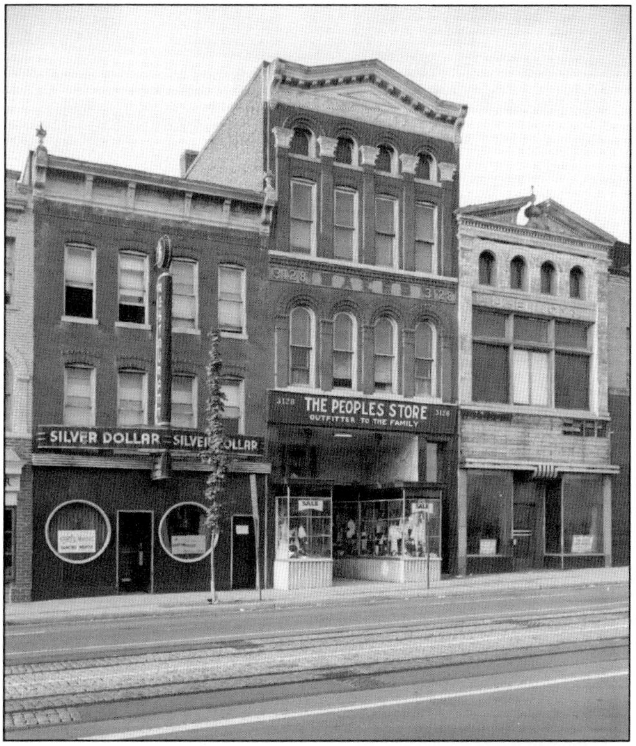

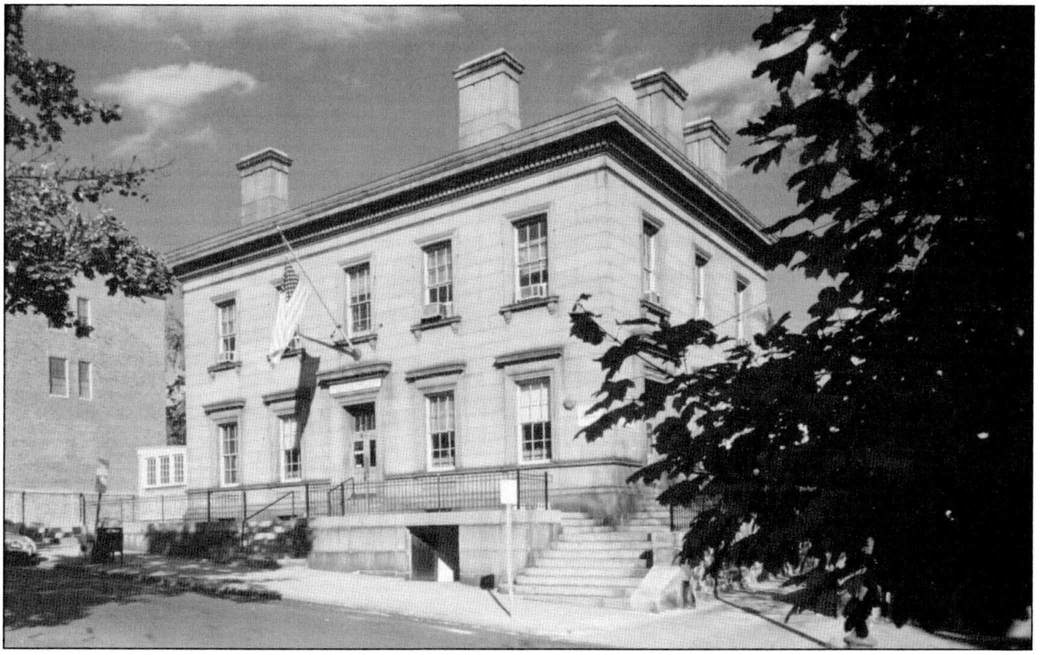

Built in 1868, this was designed to be the official customhouse of the port of Georgetown. It also served as the city hall and mayor's officer for the few years before Georgetown was absorbed into Washington, DC. This revocation of autonomy also meant the Georgetown was no longer the official port. The customhouse, however, remained there until 1967. The Georgetown branch of the post office eventually took over the building. (HABS.)

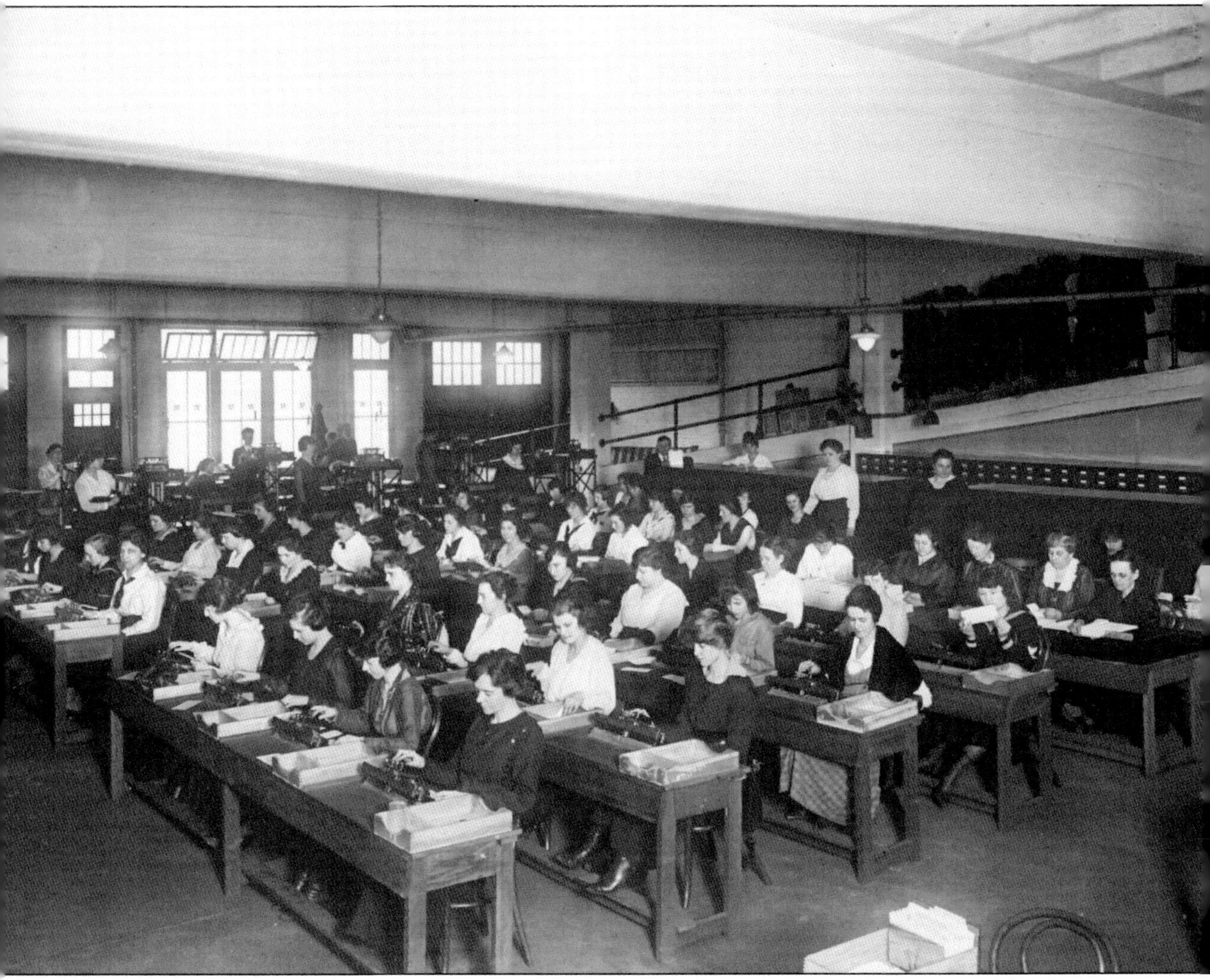

Herman Hollerith, who later rented Mackall Square for his private residence, moved his fledgling punch card factory from downtown Washington to Georgetown in 1892. His company was hired by the census bureau to help calculate the 1890 census. In 1896, it was incorporated as the Tabulating Machine Company. A few decades later, it merged with other companies and became International Business Machines (IBM). (Harris Ewing Photography.)

The Pioneer Flour Mill was established in 1832, but this mill was built in 1845 after a fire destroyed the first. When rebuilding, Gen. George Bomford converted his operations to cotton instead of flour. This only lasted until after the Civil War, when the supply of cotton could no longer meet the needs of the mill, and it was reverted back to a flour mill. (HABS.)

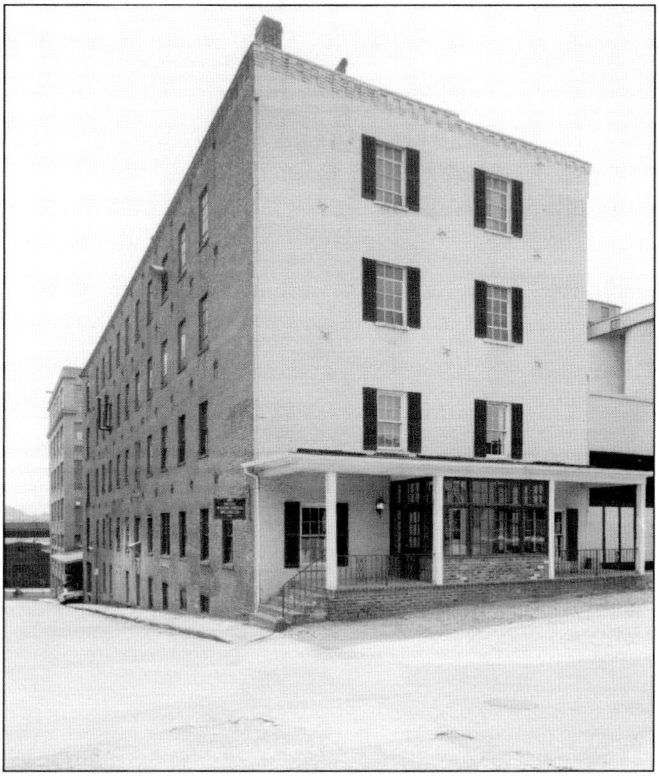

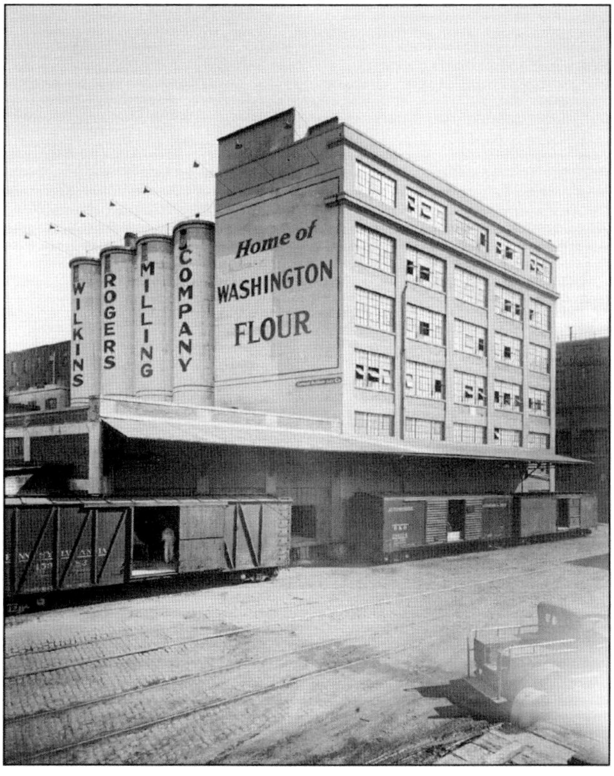

In 1916, Howard Wilkins and Samuel Rogers purchased Bomford's Pioneer mill on the waterfront to produce soft wheat meal and flour. They branded their product as Washington Flour. This photograph, taken between 1918 and 1928, shows their Georgetown mill. In the 1960s, the Wilkin-Rogers Milling Company moved to Maryland. (National Photo Company.)

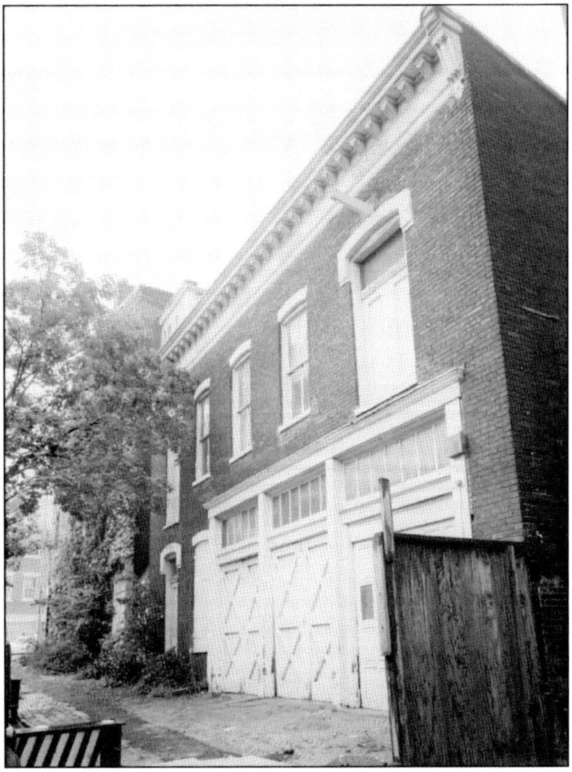

The Birch Funeral Home was already established by 1866–1871, the period during which this building was constructed. The stables are at left, and the front is seen below. It remained in business in this location until the 1960s as a family-run endeavor. Joseph F. Birch, the founder, was both the undertaker and a cabinetmaker, which are very similar to coffins. He began as a cabinetmaker but would make a coffin if requested. A sign of superstitious times, he would not keep a supply of coffins on hand, as that was considered bad luck. This changed when he became a full-time undertaker in 1842. As one of the only undertakers in the area, people would come from rural areas with a stick the length of the deceased and a notch to mark the width, and that is how Birch would measure the coffin size. Birch lived across the street at the Nathan Longborough House from 1858 until his death in 1891. The funeral home then passed on to his sons. (Both, HABS.)

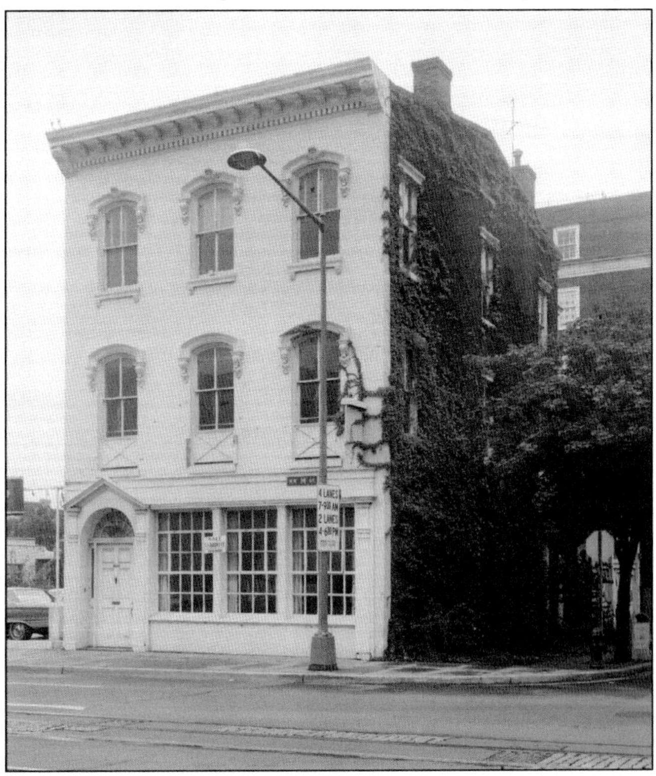

Five

Our Town

Churches, Schools, and Social Clubs

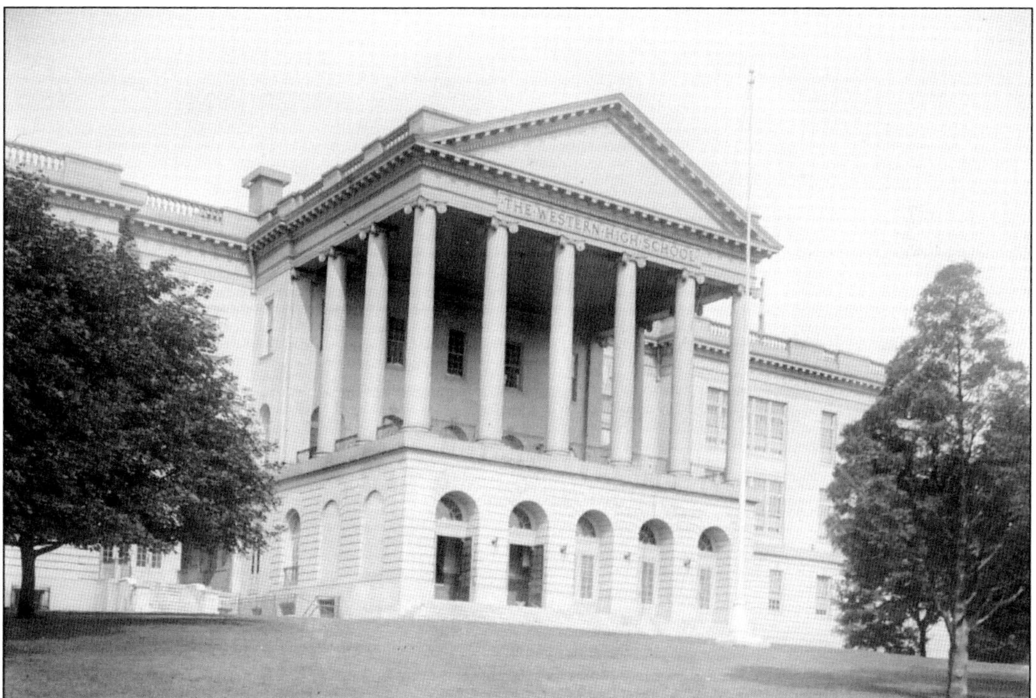

This early-1900s image shows the front entrance to Western High School. Constructed in 1897, it was the high school for much of northwest DC until 1977. Though today many would consider the building to be outside the Georgetown neighborhood, historical records still list it as such. (National Photo Company.)

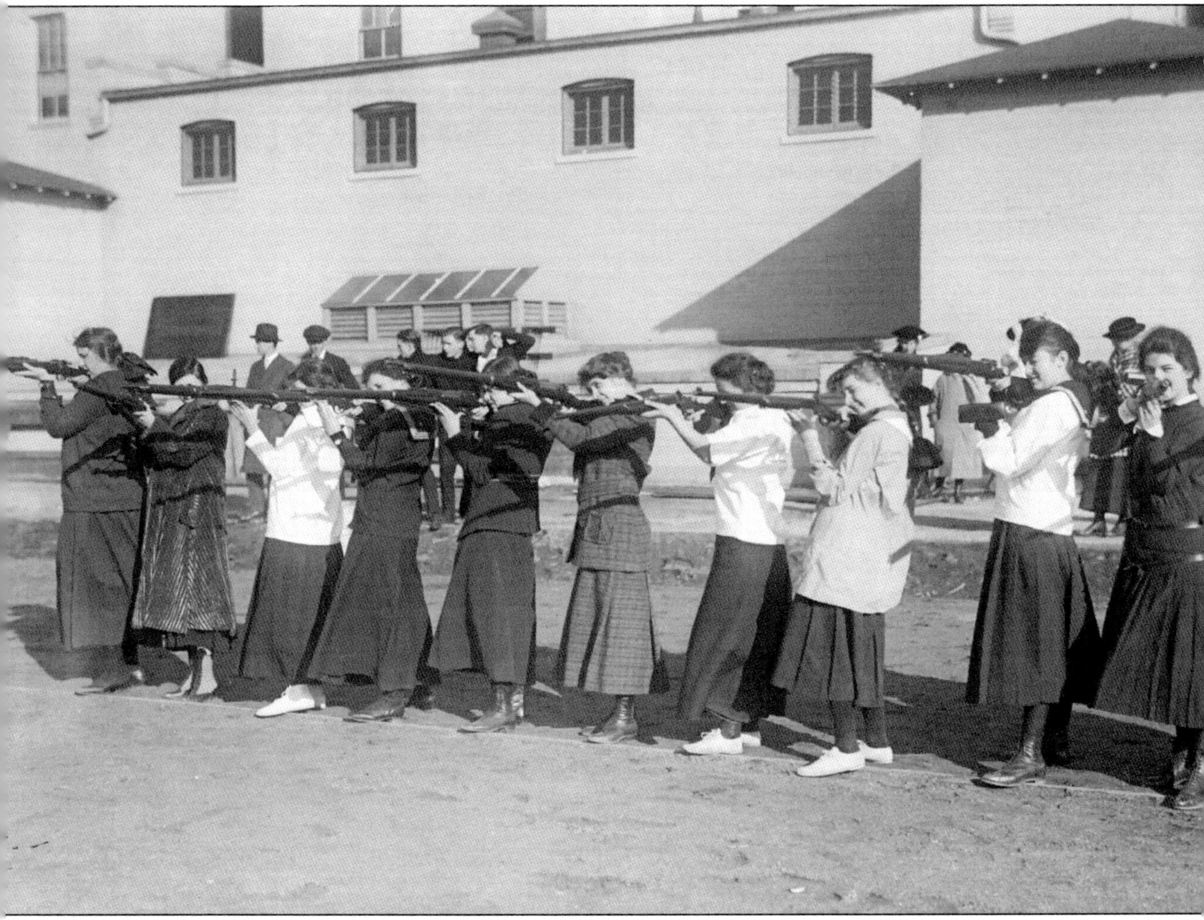

Female students at Western High School organized to form a girls' rifle team to compete alongside the boys in 1916. More than 150 girls were interested in the new club, and they hoped to make the regular team and compete against other area schools. The purpose-built high school even had a drill hall. (Frances Benjamin Johnston, Library of Congress.)

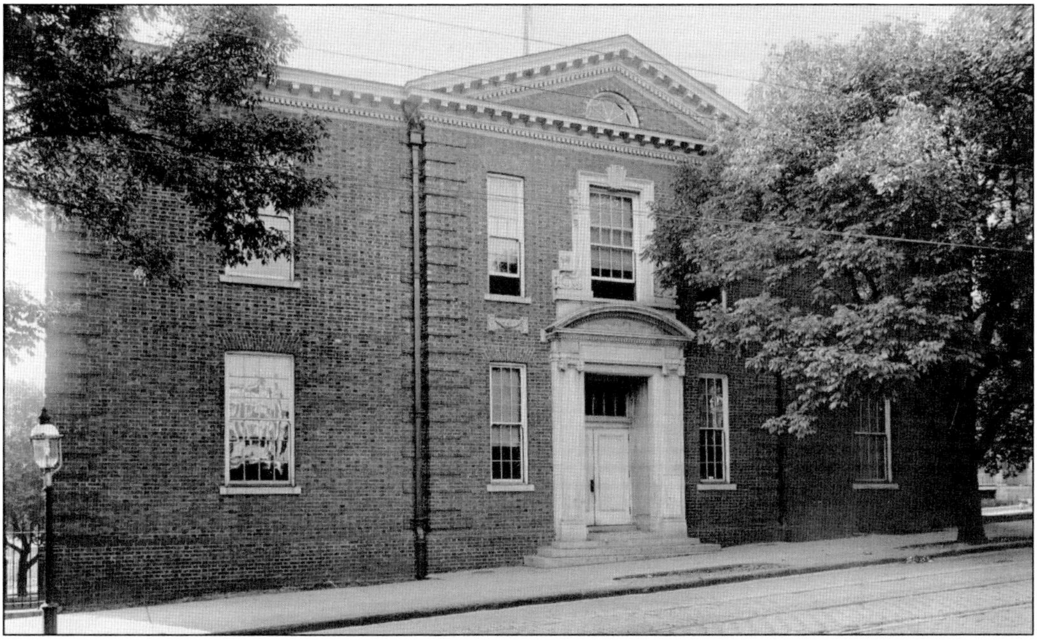

The West Georgetown School, on Wisconsin Avenue NW, was the second school opened at this location. In 1912, it began its new life as a school of culinary arts, teaching local working-class women cooking and food preservation skills. Under Pres. Franklin D. Roosevelt's New Deal, the school was renamed the Central Lunch Kitchen and served hot meals to poor children. During World War II, the school remained focused on kitchen techniques and also taught canning to local residents. By 1950, it was no longer teaching classes. The photograph above shows an undated view, but, sometime before the 1966 photograph below, the building was painted gray, although it remained architecturally unaltered. (Both, HABS.)

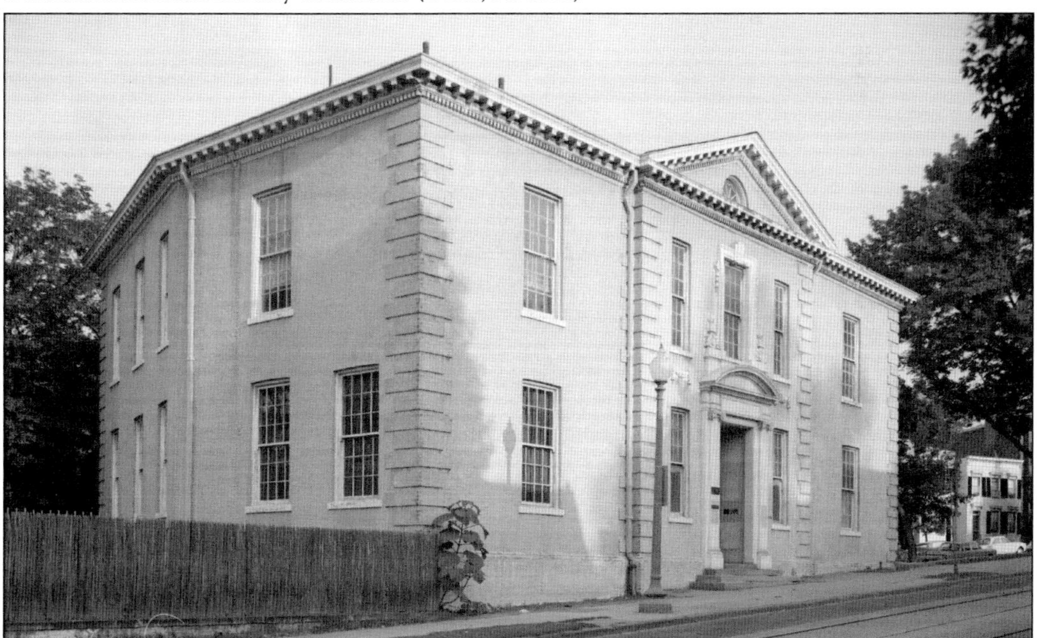

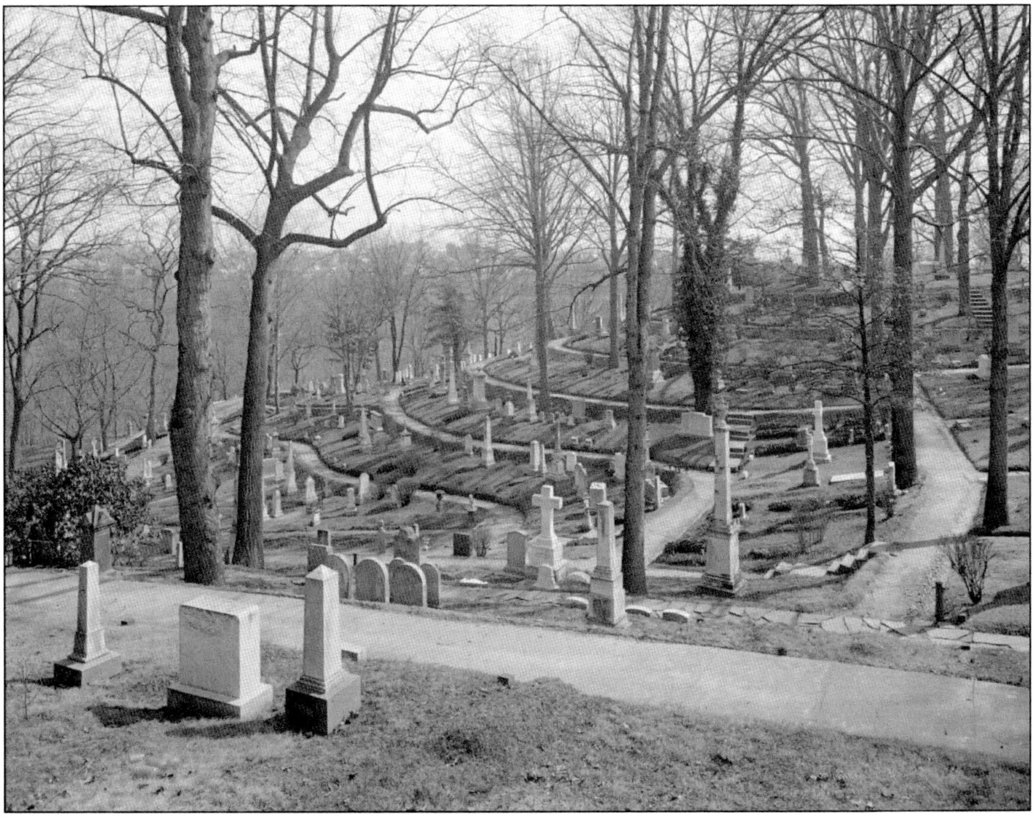

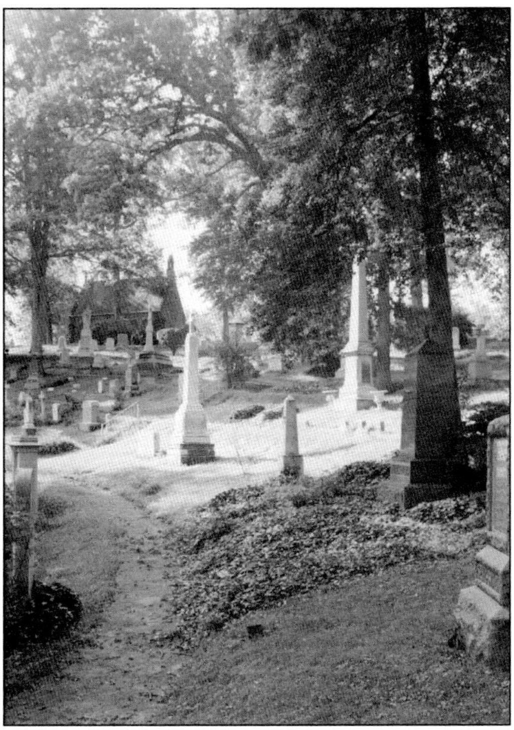

Oak Hill Cemetery was founded by William W. Corcoran in 1848 with the popular rural cemetery movement, which encouraged a botanical landscape surrounding graves. The cemetery is 22 acres, and the grounds were designed by Georgetown resident and civil engineer George de la Roche. Oak Hill is the resting place of Secretary of War Edwin Stanton, Katherine and Peter Graham of the *Washington Post*, William Corcoran himself, and John Howard Payne, who actually died in Tunisia but whom Corcoran had moved to Oak Hill. James Joyce is also buried here, with the plagiarized quote "Laugh, and the world laughs with you. Weep and you weep alone" carved into his headstone. It was actually written by Ella Wheeler Wilcox and published as her poem, but he has now asserted eternal claim to it. (Above, HABS; left, National Photo Company.)

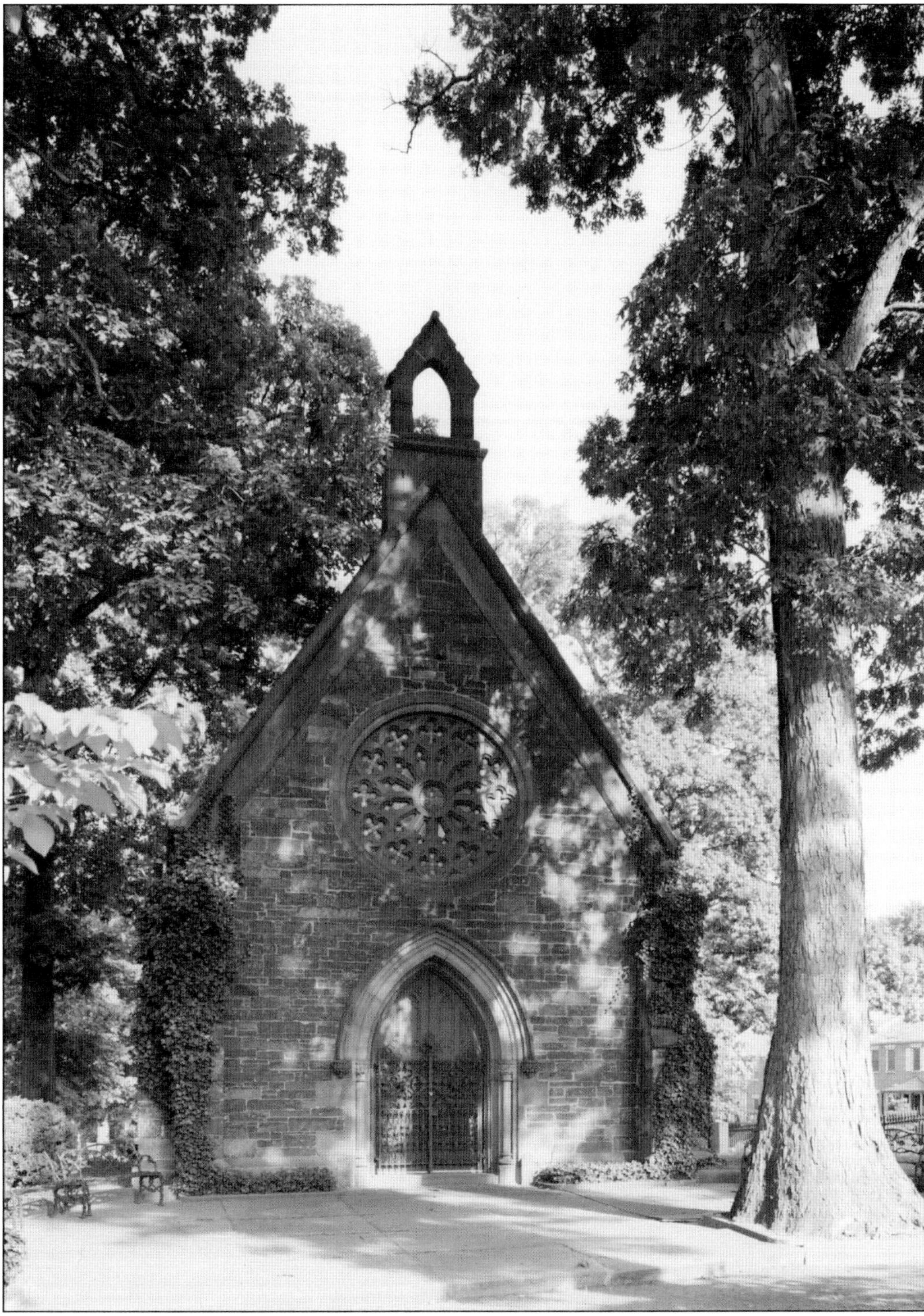

The crowning feature of Oak Hill Cemetery is the James Renwick–designed Oak Hill Chapel. Completed in 1850, it is rare example of Gothic Revival architecture in the nation's capital. The small, one-story chapel was constructed of local materials. (HABS.)

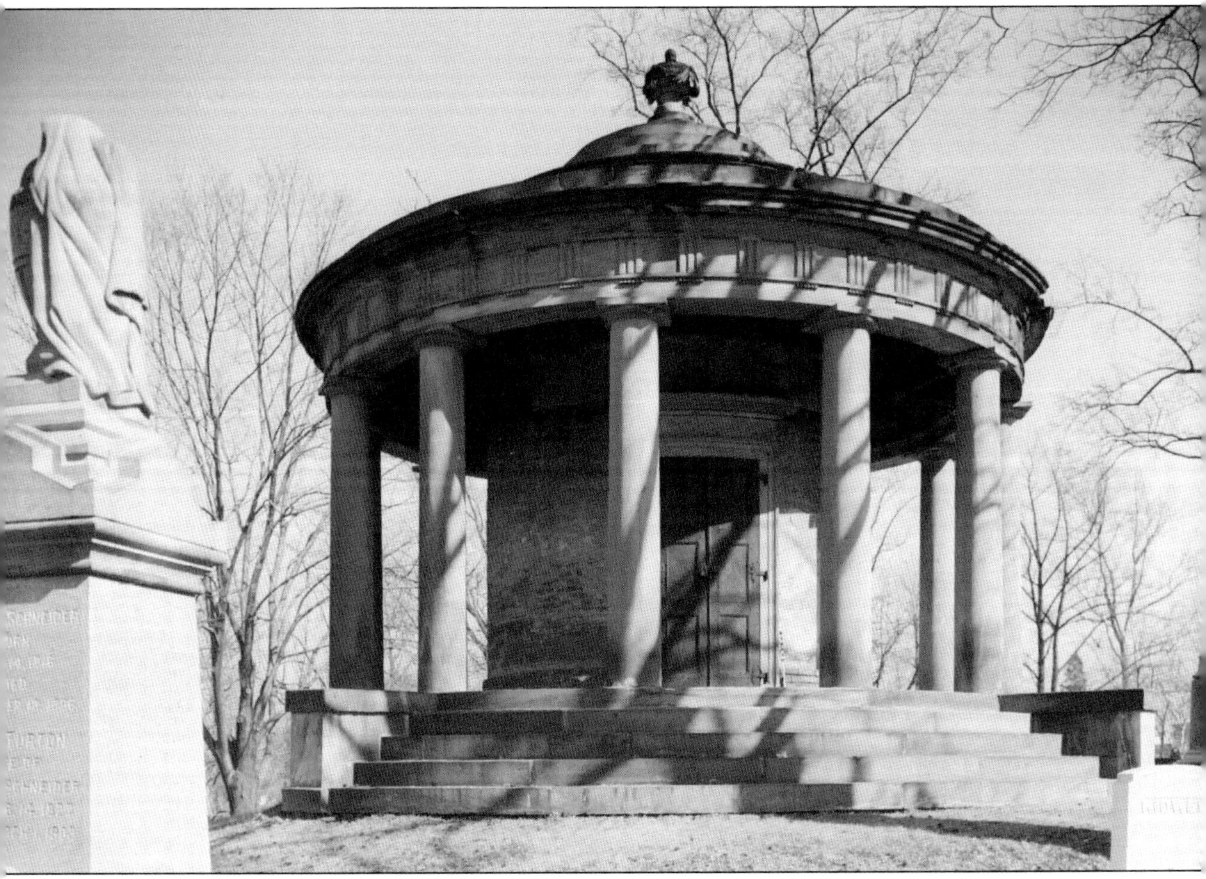

Originally in downtown DC, the Van Ness Mausoleum was built in 1833 for the wife of John Van Ness, a US representative from New York and prominent figure in local Washington politics and the local militia. The mausoleum was moved to Oak Hill Cemetery in 1872, with the remains of the congressman and six other family members. Designed by George Hadfield, it is modeled on the Temple of Vesta. (HABS.)

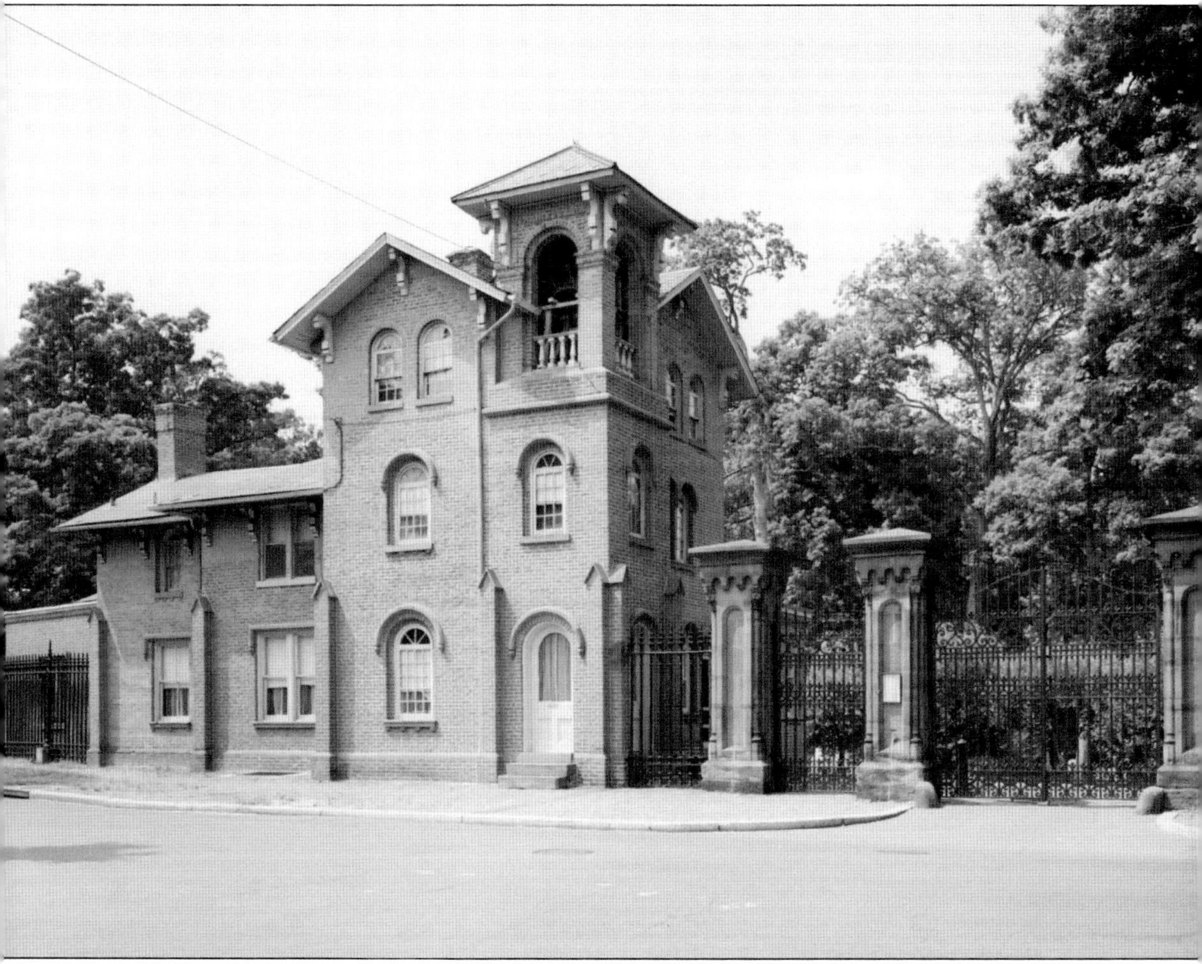

The gatehouse also serves as the home of the superintendent of Oak Hill Cemetery. Though originally built between 1850 and 1853, extensive alterations were made in 1867. The building still stands today, and this 1968 photograph shows it stayed true to the mid-19th-century renovations. (HABS.)

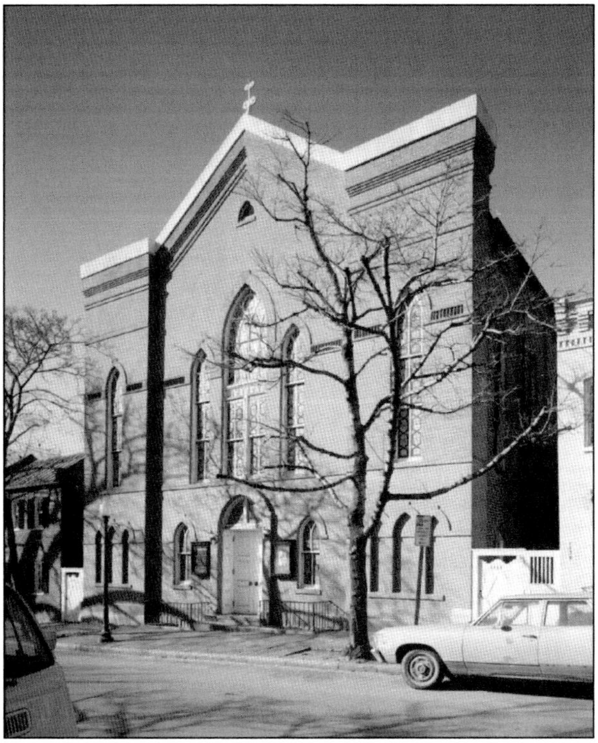

Mount Zion Methodist Church is the oldest African American congregation in Georgetown. In 1814, black members of the multiethnic Montgomery Street Methodist Church left to form their own congregation. A small meetinghouse was built, known as "The Ark," but worship was still conducted by the original minister until the Mount Zion congregation got their own pastor in 1864. (HABS.)

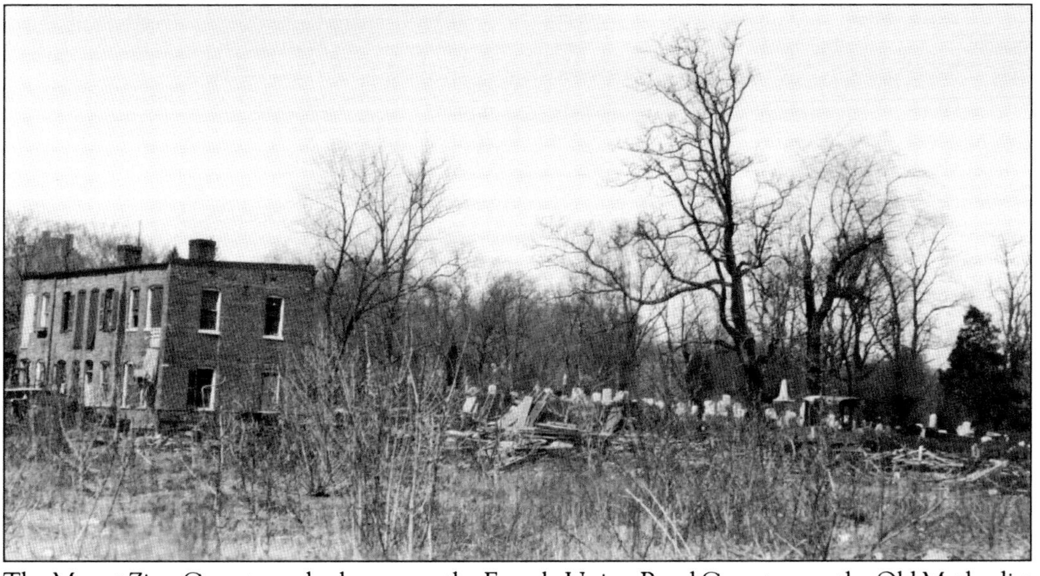

The Mount Zion Cemetery, also known as the Female Union Band Cemetery or the Old Methodist Burying Grounds, was originally a cemetery predominantly for whites, as deeded in 1808. After the creation of the all-white Oak Hill Cemetery, many were reinterred there. In 1842, a parcel of the land was purchased to benefit the Female Union Band, a benevolent organization of freed black women of good moral character who aided each other in times of need and provided a burial plot in the cemetery for members. The combination of multiple graves by various groups makes documenting the number and significance of internments difficult. The estimates range from 1,000 to 2,000 burials, predominately black Americans. (Historical Society of Washington, DC.)

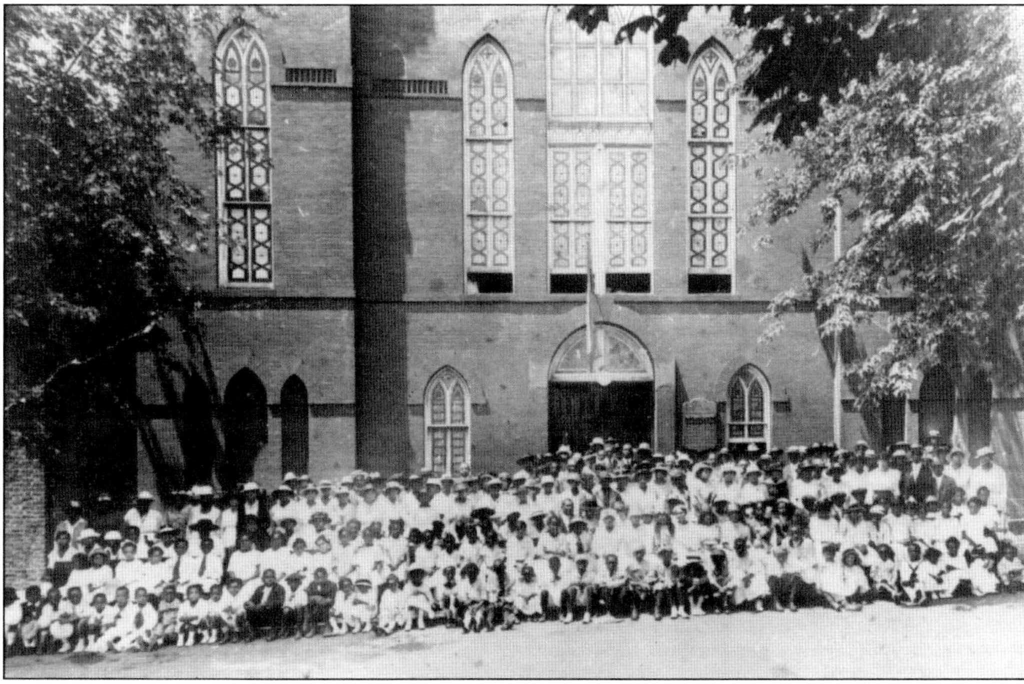

The Women's Day group gathers here in front of Mount Zion Methodist Church around 1917. (Historical Society of Washington, DC.)

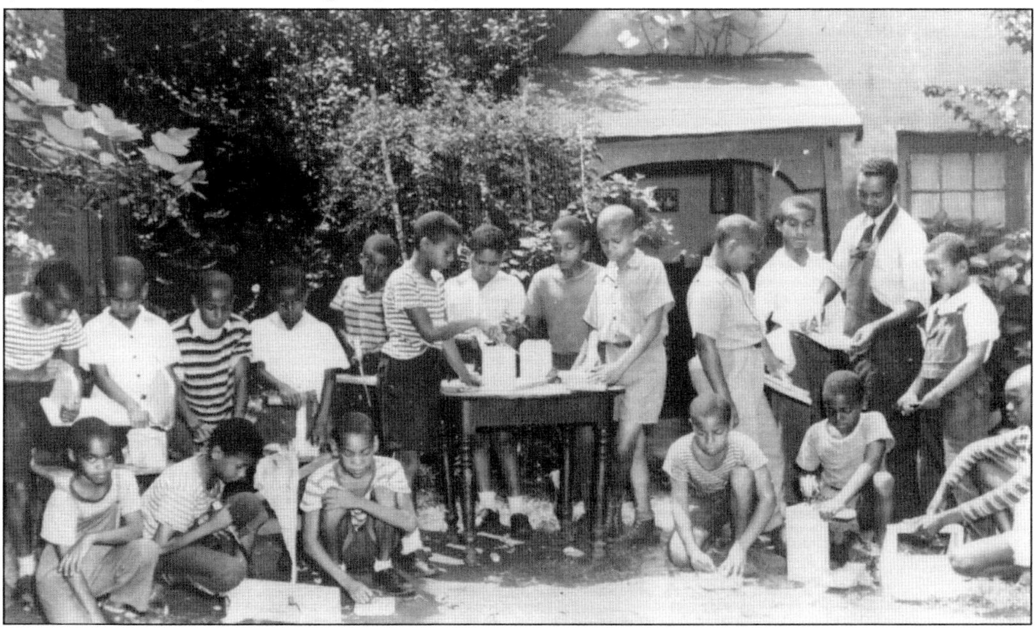

This late-1940s photograph shows the Daily Vacation Bible School at Mount Zion Methodist Church. The Mount Zion United Community House was erected in 1811 and is a rare English-style cottage situated behind the house. Since the 1850s, it has focused on providing resources and education to the congregation that the city does not. Through the years, with the changing demographics of Georgetown, many members of the congregation no longer live in the area. (Historical Society of Washington, DC.)

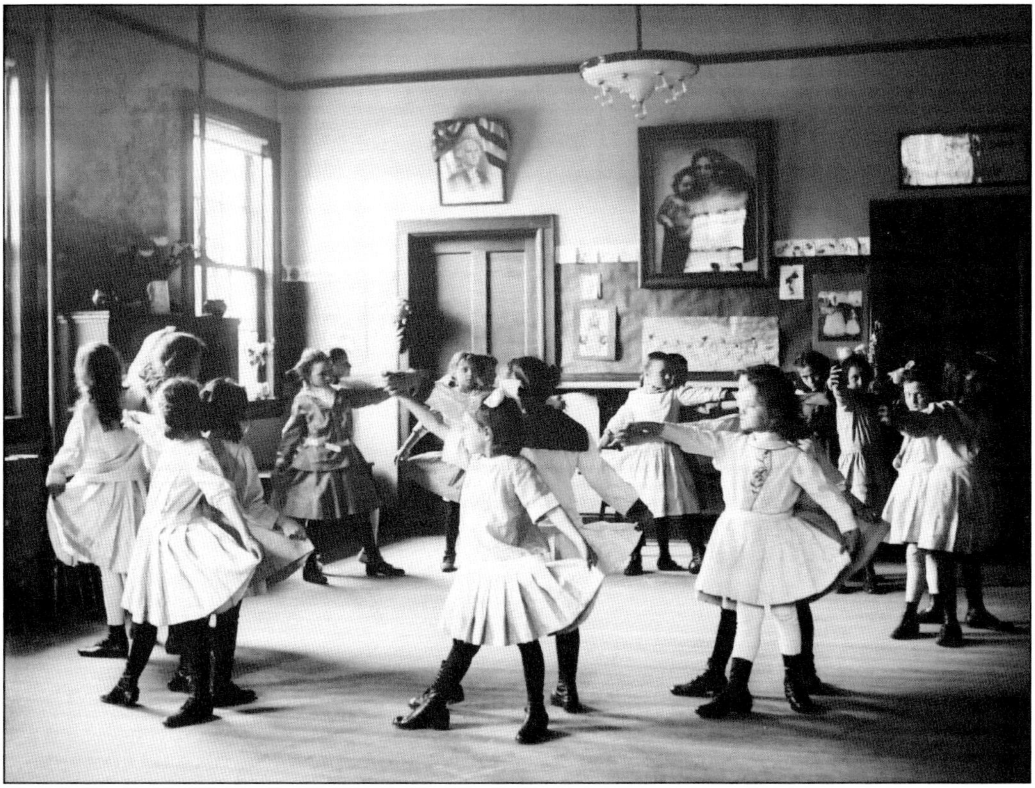

Young students at William Lee's School are seen performing in these photographs from the 1910s. (Both, National Photo Company.)

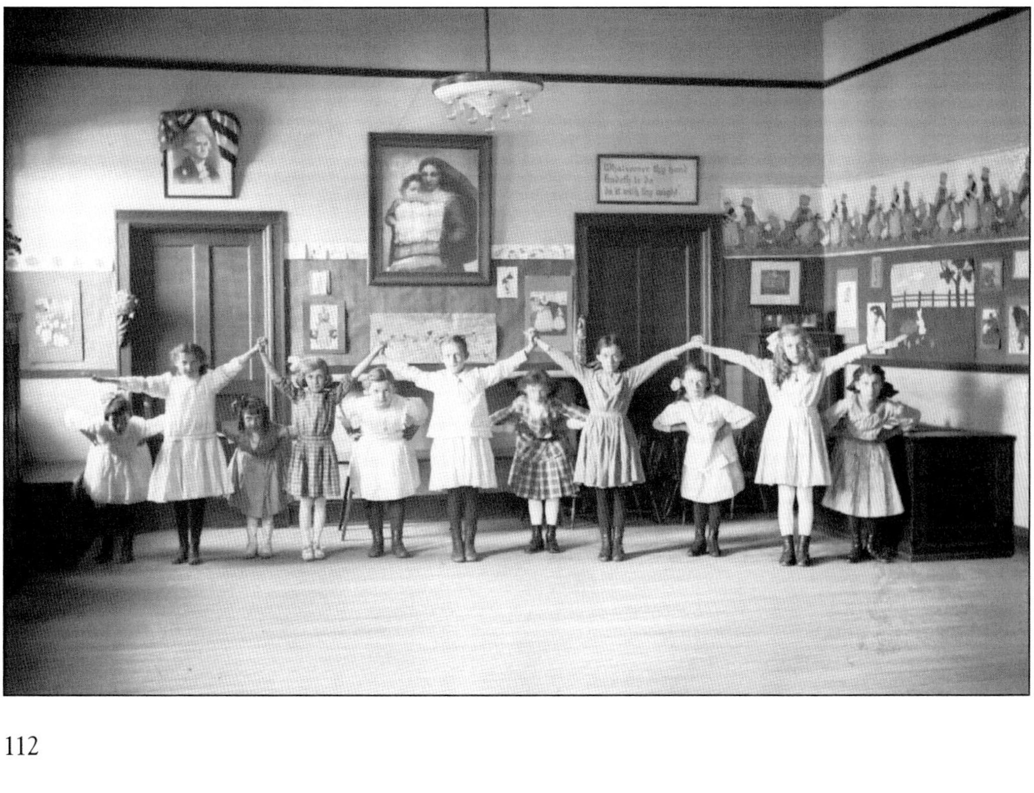

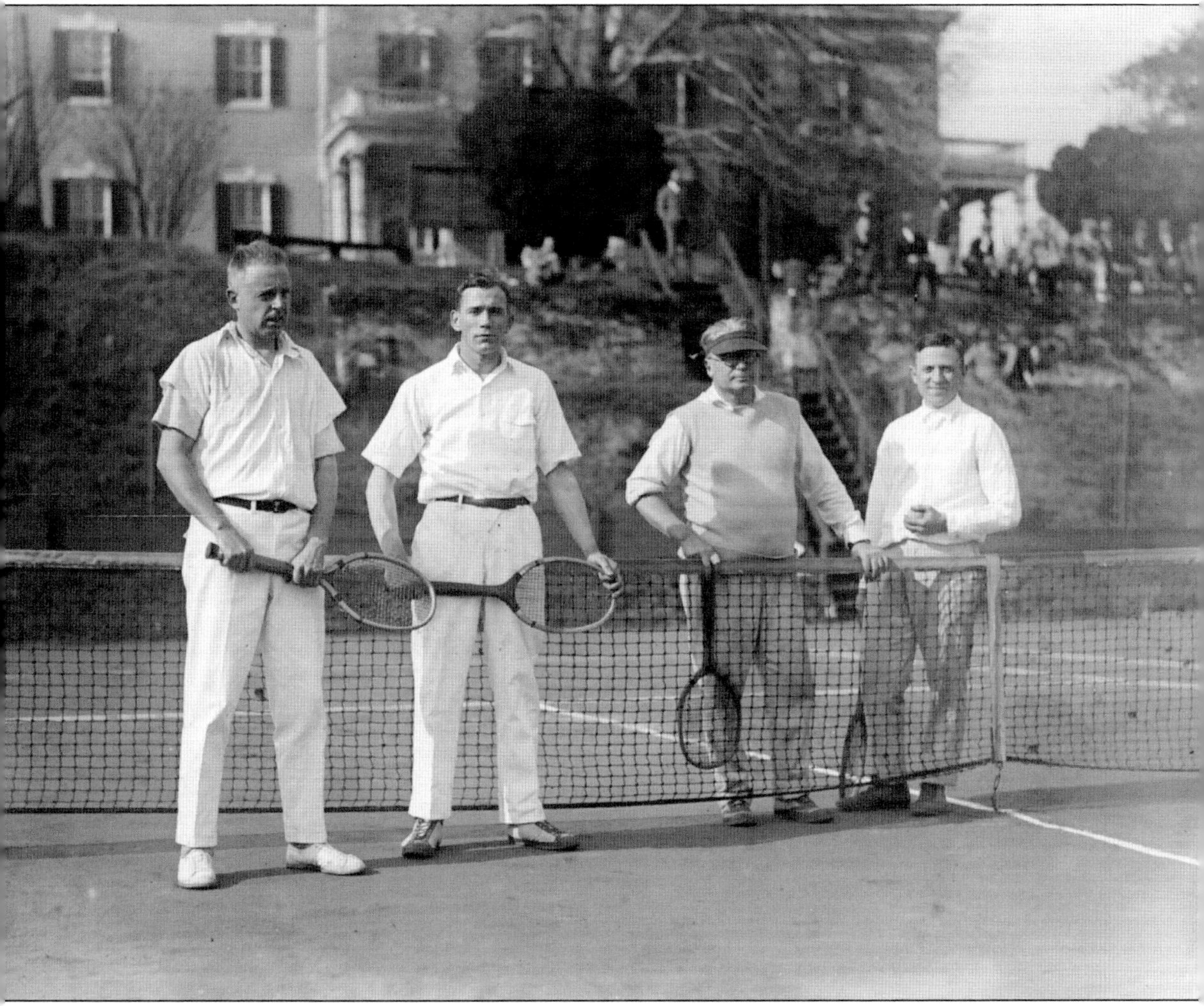

The Dumbarton Club was a social tennis club in 1910s Georgetown. With seven courts, the club's members played friendly matches against other area clubs in doubles and singles. Much akin to a country club, it also had a nine-hole golf course. The club itself was located in the historic Mount Hope home, once owned by Evalyn Walsh McLean. (National Photo Company.)

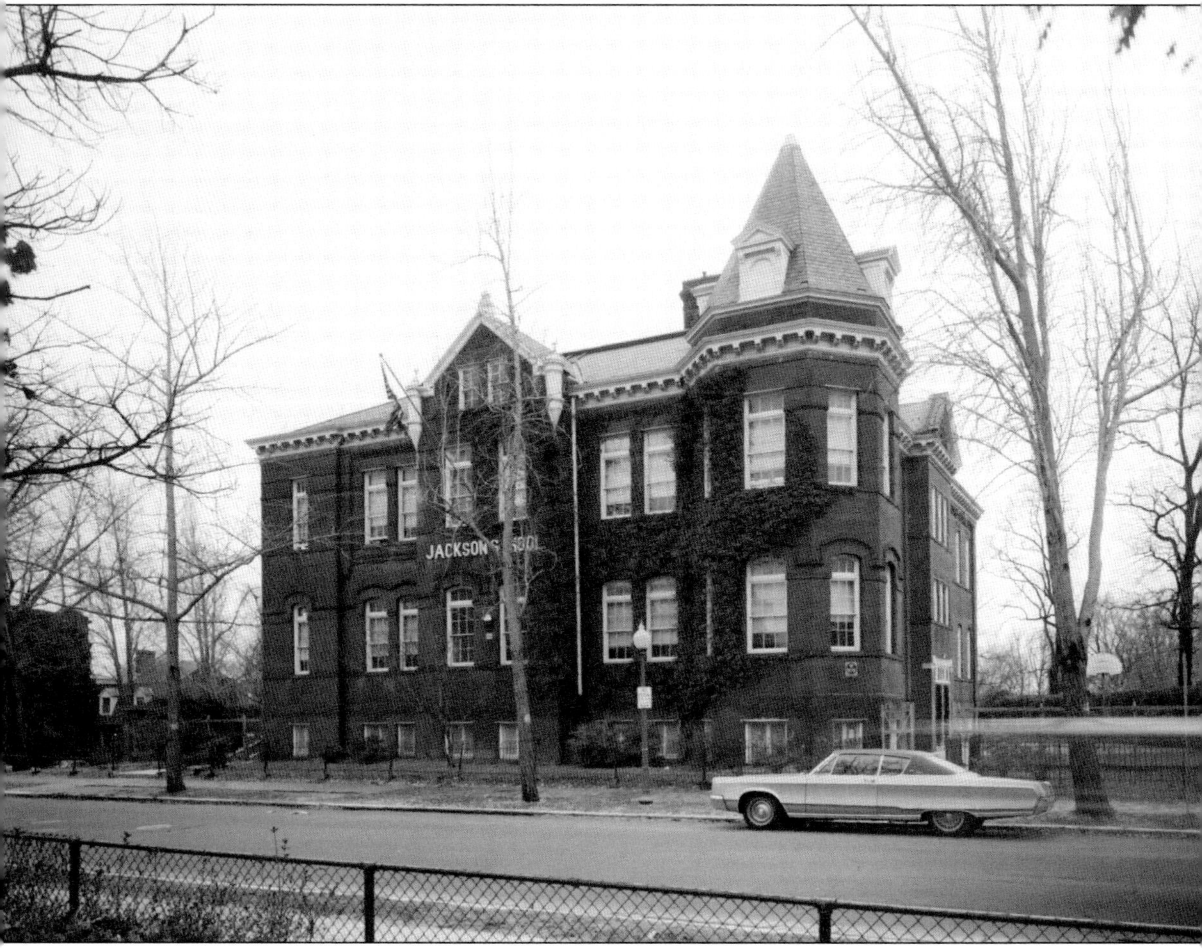

The Jackson School was built in 1890 in north Georgetown as an elementary school for white children only prior to desegregation. Through the years, it suffered from low enrollment, and it has since been closed. In 1942, the board announced only 12 days prior to the school year that it would not be opening. Georgetown parents protested, convincing the school board to reopen the school. It remained open until 1971, when it had an enrollment of 96. (HABS.)

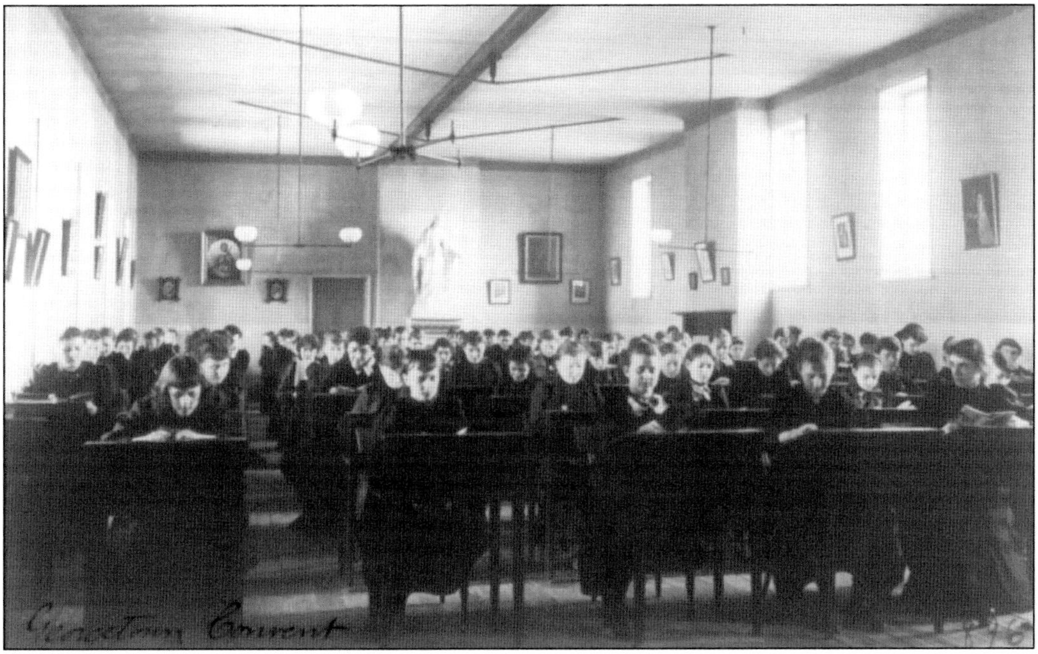

The Georgetown Visitation Preparatory School is the oldest continuously running all-girls schools in DC. Archbishop Leonard Neale, president of Georgetown College at the time, founded it in 1799. Since then, it has educated numerous well-known daughters of presidents and high-ranking officials in the federal government and military. (Francis Benjamin Johnston, Library of Congress.)

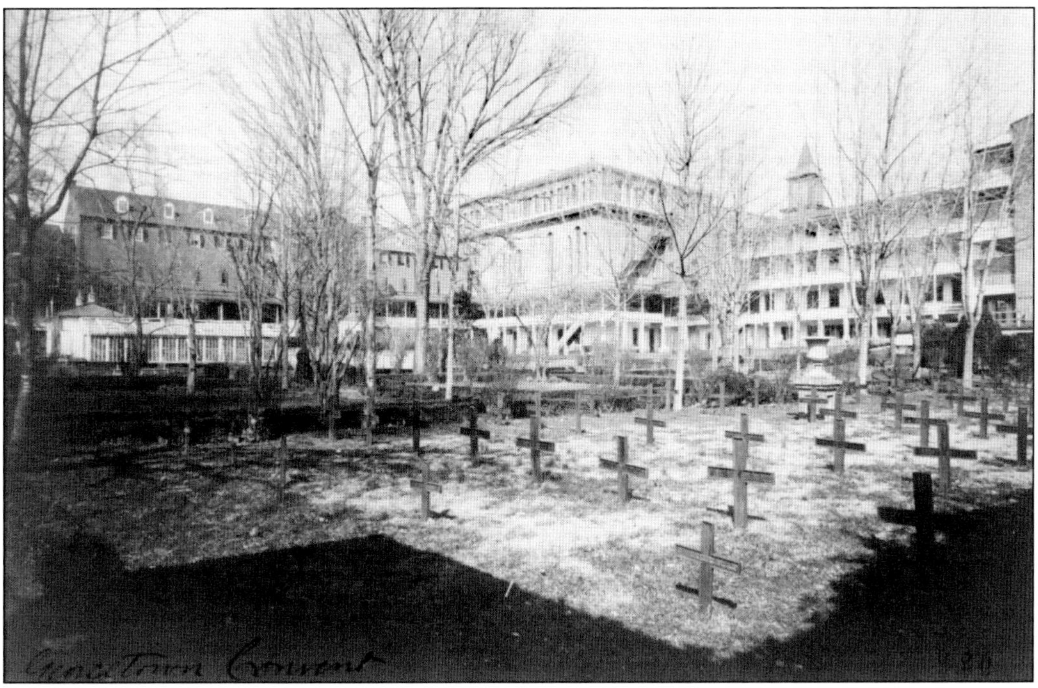

This view shows the cemetery of the Georgetown Visitation Preparatory School in the foreground, with the school behind it, at the turn of the 20th century. (Francis Benjamin Johnston, Library of Congress.)

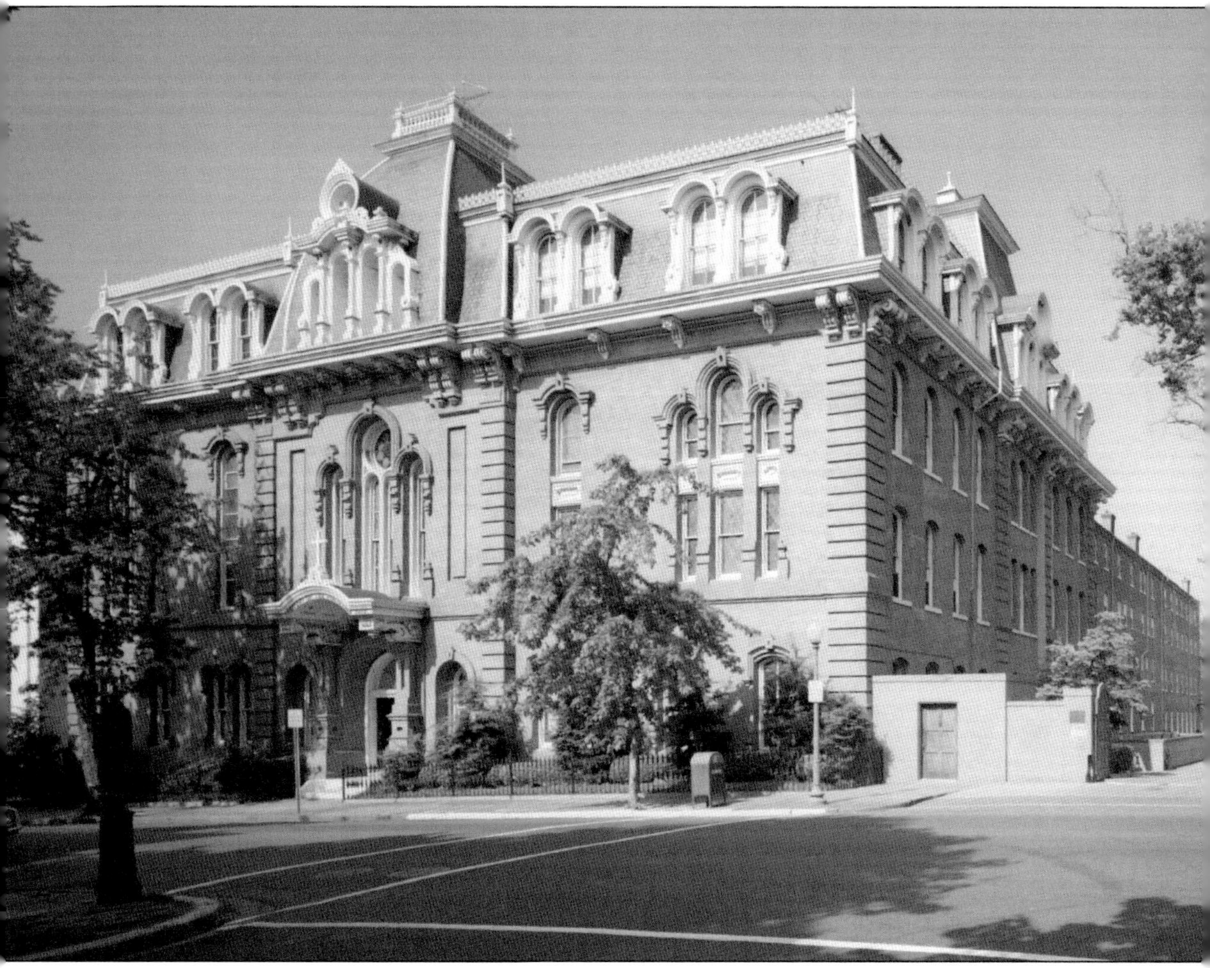

The Georgetown Visitation Monastery was founded as a Salesian community at the same time as the prep school, under Neale and three "Pious Ladies." In 1816, Pope Pius VII granted them the right to be a monastery under the Order of Visitation, making it the first in the United States. (HABS.)

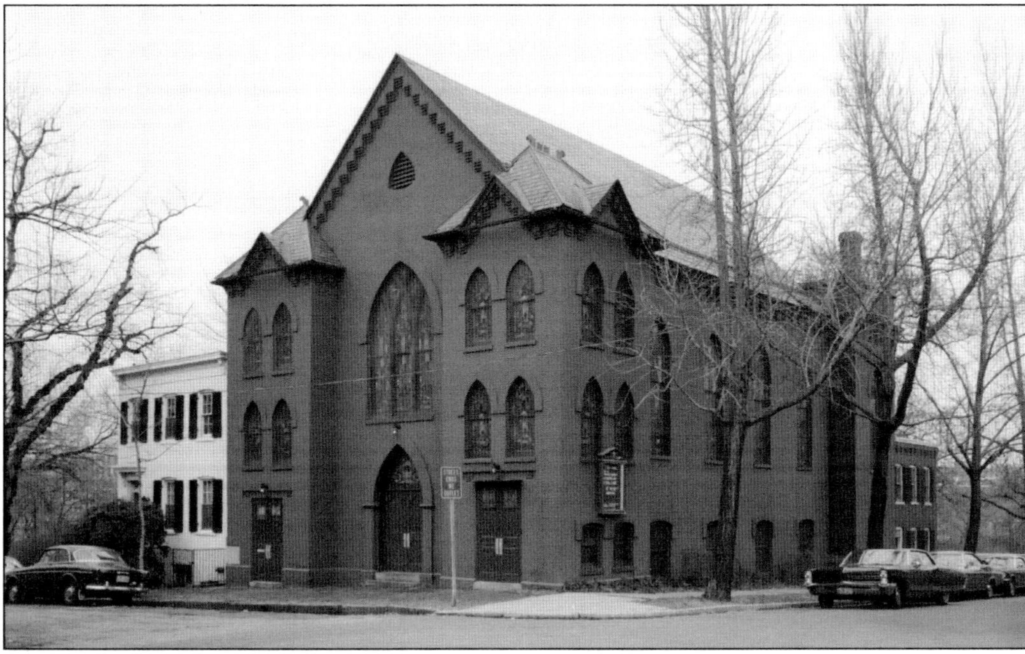

When Rev. Sandy Alexander, a former slave turned ordained Baptist preacher, came to Georgetown to start a Baptist church, he found only two Baptists. He was easily able to convert many members of the community, and they embarked on building a church. When payment was made on the loan, the receipt was made out to "First African Baptist Church," but this was refused until it could be reworded "First Baptist Church," as it would be the first in Georgetown, regardless of race. (HABS.)

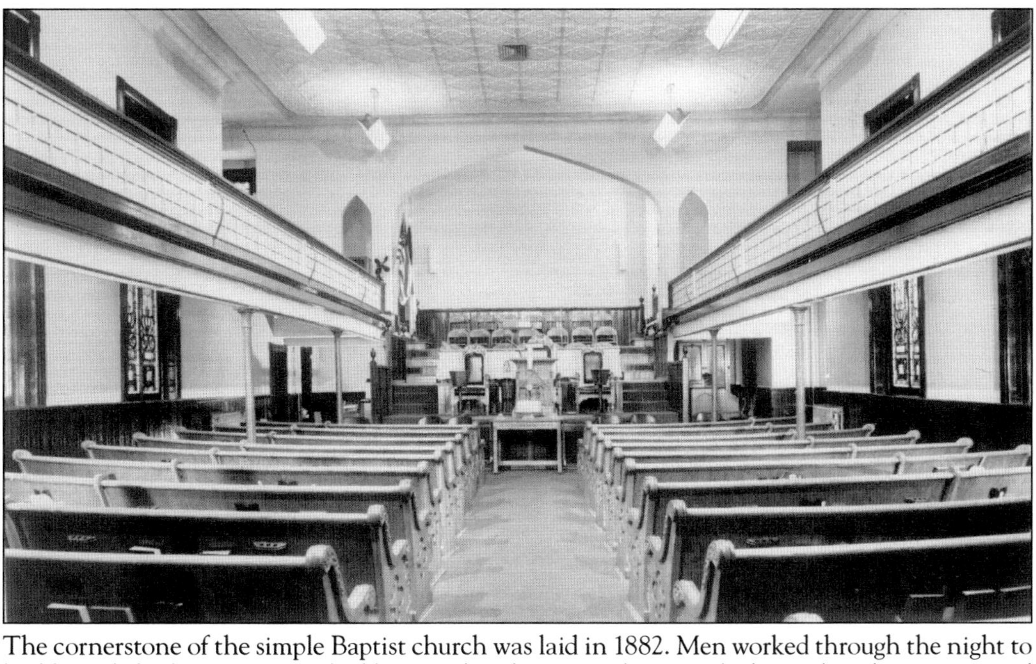

The cornerstone of the simple Baptist church was laid in 1882. Men worked through the night to build it, while the women cooked hot meals. This 1969 photograph shows that the interior and the altar have continued to be without ornate decor. (HABS.)

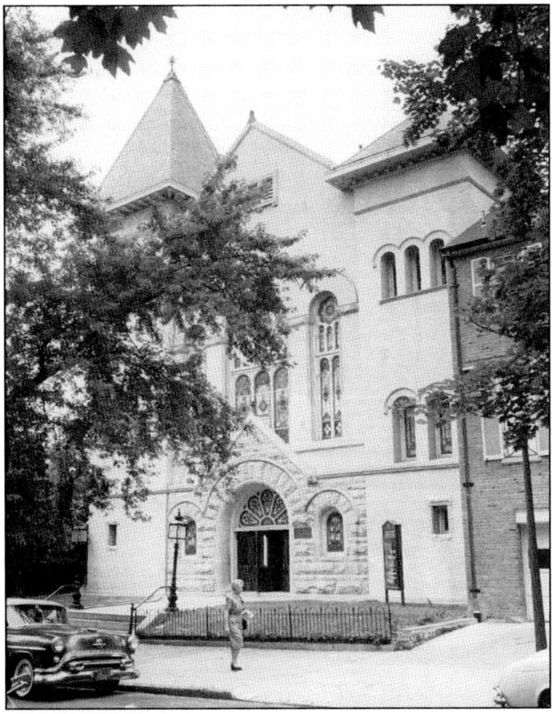

Dumbarton United Methodist Church began in 1772 as the Georgetown Society, before the Methodist Church was even established. It was then named Montgomery Street Methodist Church, before moving to Dumbarton Avenue in 1850. This photograph from between 1965 and 1975 shows the church at its current Dumbarton Avenue location. (Historical Society of Washington, DC.)

The 17-stop Wilson L. Reiley organ in the Dumbarton Avenue Methodist Church was constructed in 1898 by a Georgetown builder. It is seen here around the turn of the 20th century. (Historical Society of Washington, DC.)

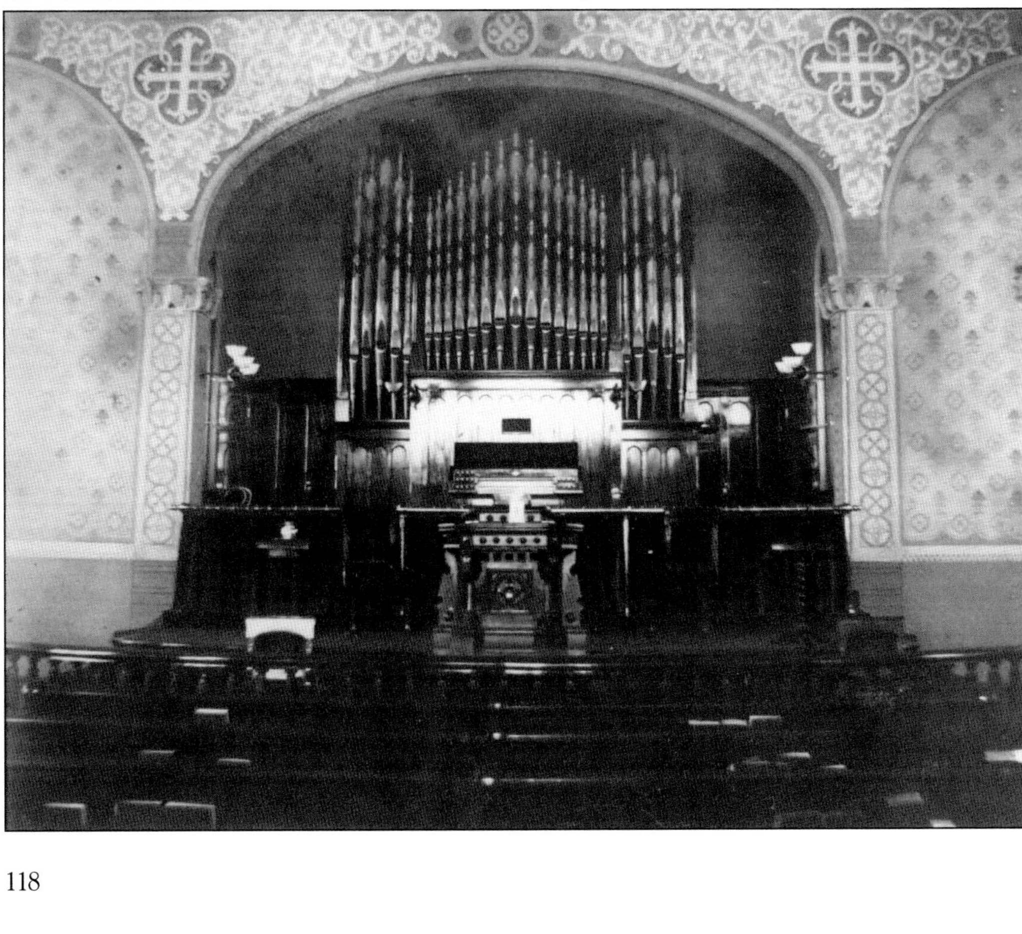

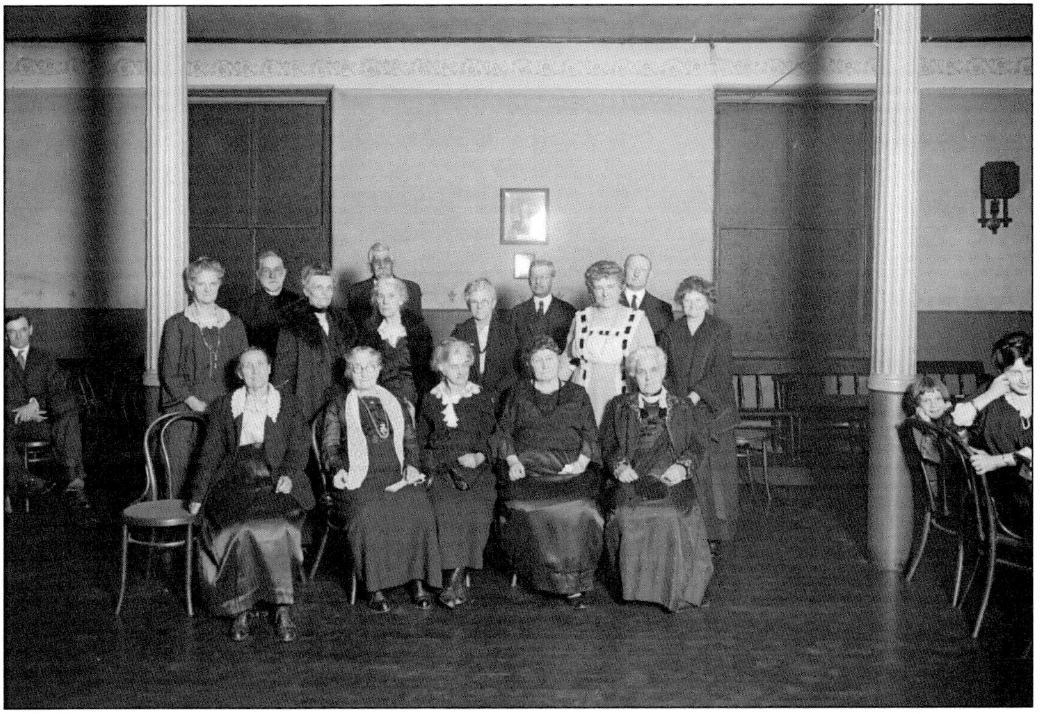

Women and men gather in the 1910s as members of the Dumbarton Avenue Methodist Church. (National Photo Company.)

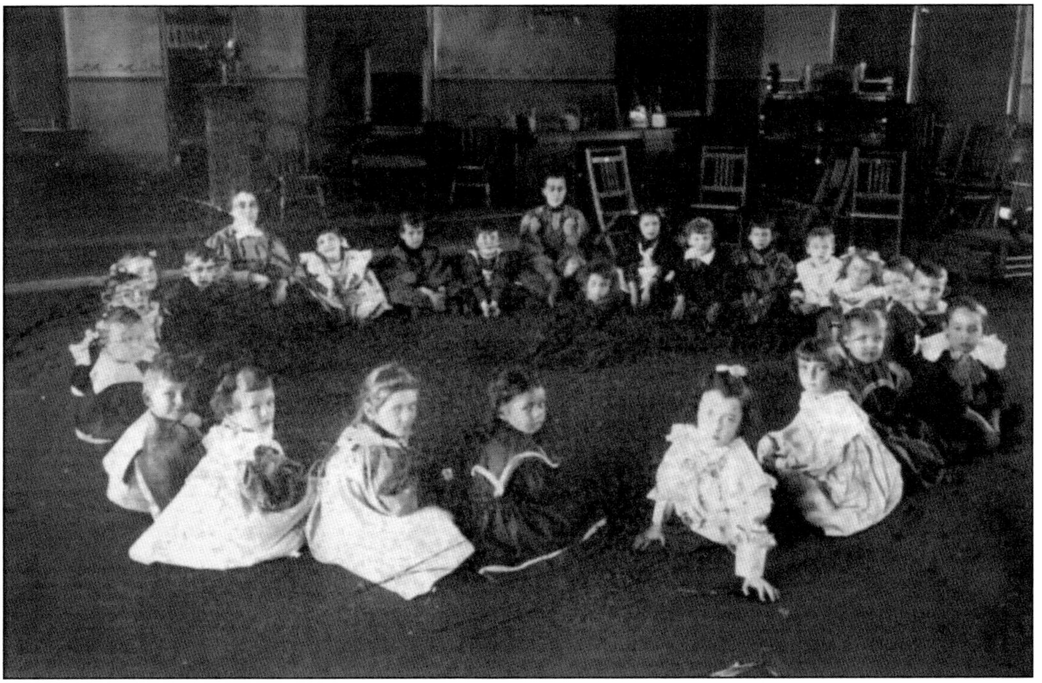

Two Sunday school teachers are seen here with their students at Dumbarton United Methodist Church in 1898. In the 19th century, the Sunday school took an annual excursion to Fort Washington via steamboat. (Historical Society of Washington, DC.)

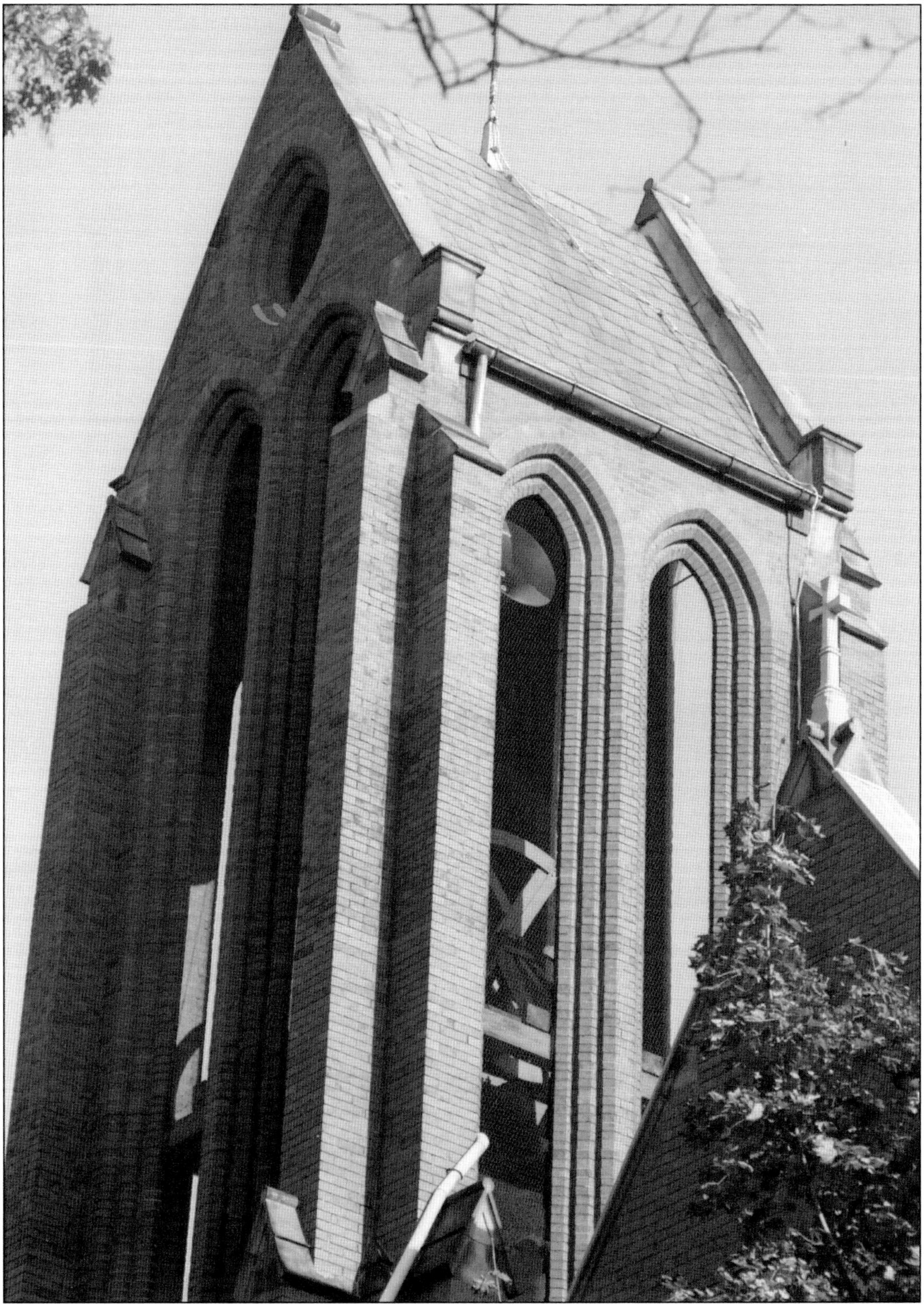

Christ Episcopal Church was founded in 1817 after a small group separated from St. John's Episcopal Church in Georgetown, one of them a lawyer named Francis Scott Key. Not much is known about the original church design, though it was the largest Episcopal church in the area. (HABS.)

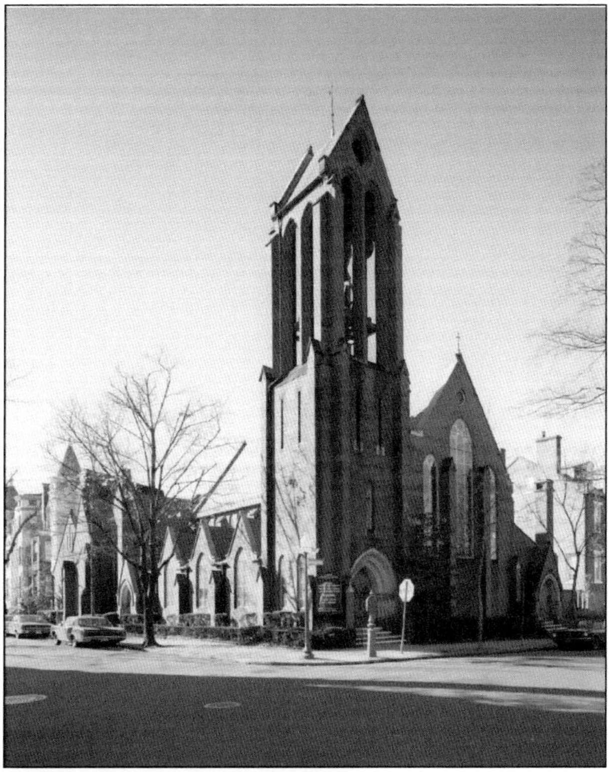

The present Christ Church structure was completed in 1887 as a cathedral in miniature, replacing two previous buildings. The Gothic architecture was not seen in the original buildings but was a result of the rector's desire to emphasize Catholic traditions. (HABS.)

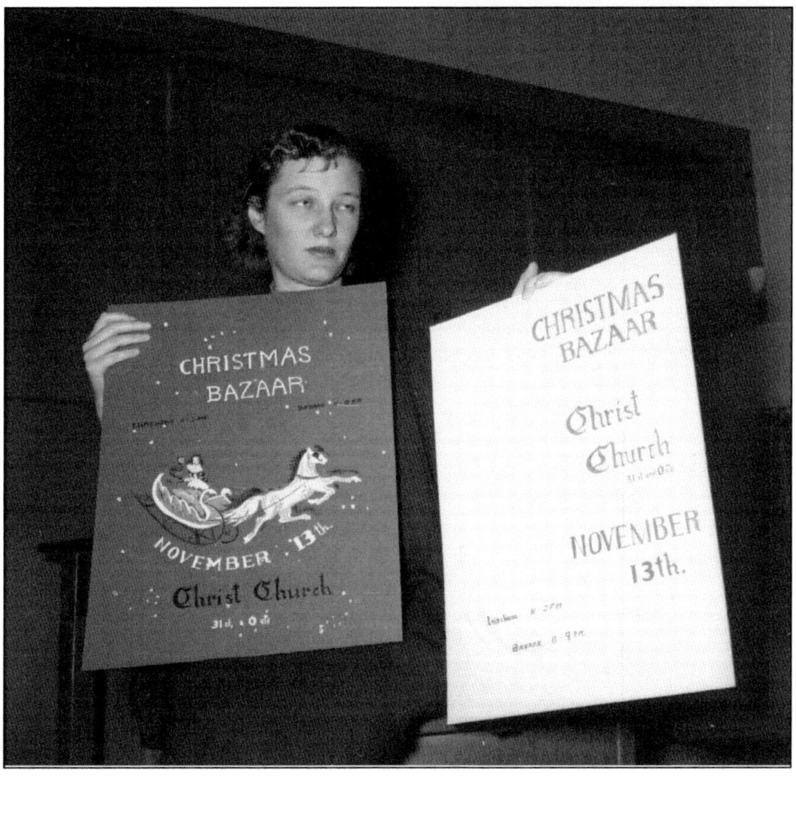

In the 1800s, Christ Church was a neighborhood church comprised of mostly local residents. That has changed through the 1900s, and the congregation has grown from all over the metro area. Candace Shireman holds signs for the Christmas Bazaar at Christ Church in 1956. (Historical Society of Washington, DC.)

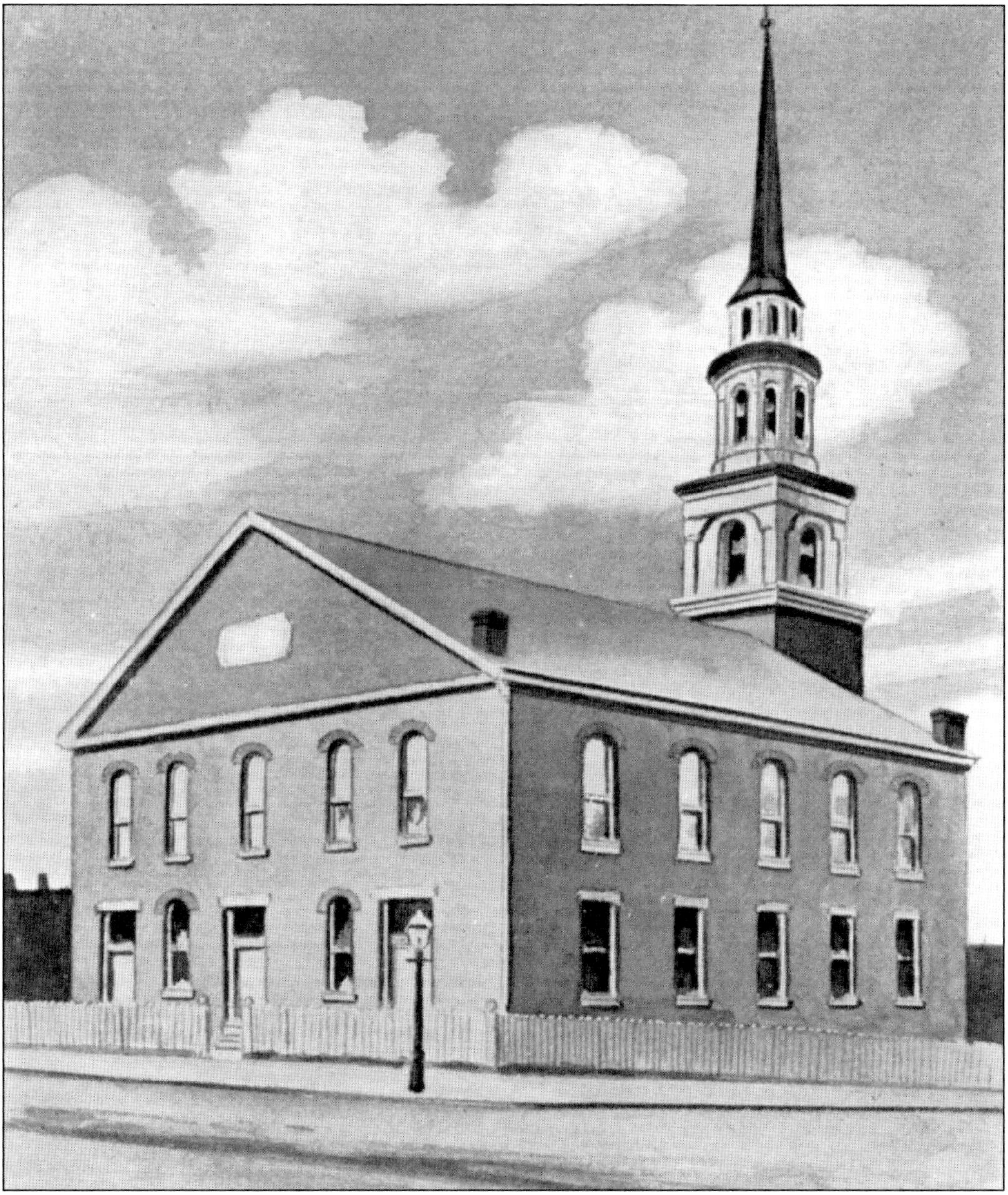

Bridge Street Presbyterian Church is the oldest church of any denomination in the district with continual worship. The congregation was founded in 1760 by Rev. Stephen Bloomer Balch, who lived in the house across the street from what would later be John F. Kennedy's home, at 3307 N Street NW. The church has had many buildings since its original home, constructed in 1782 as the first Protestant church in Georgetown. The second church was built on Bridge Street, before it was renamed M Street NW, and its cornerstone was laid by Pres. James Monroe. In 1871, the building was moved to its current location on P Street NW. While this drawing was made in 1890, it is thought to show the original church location, at what are now Thirtieth and M Streets NW. (Historical Society of Washington, DC.)

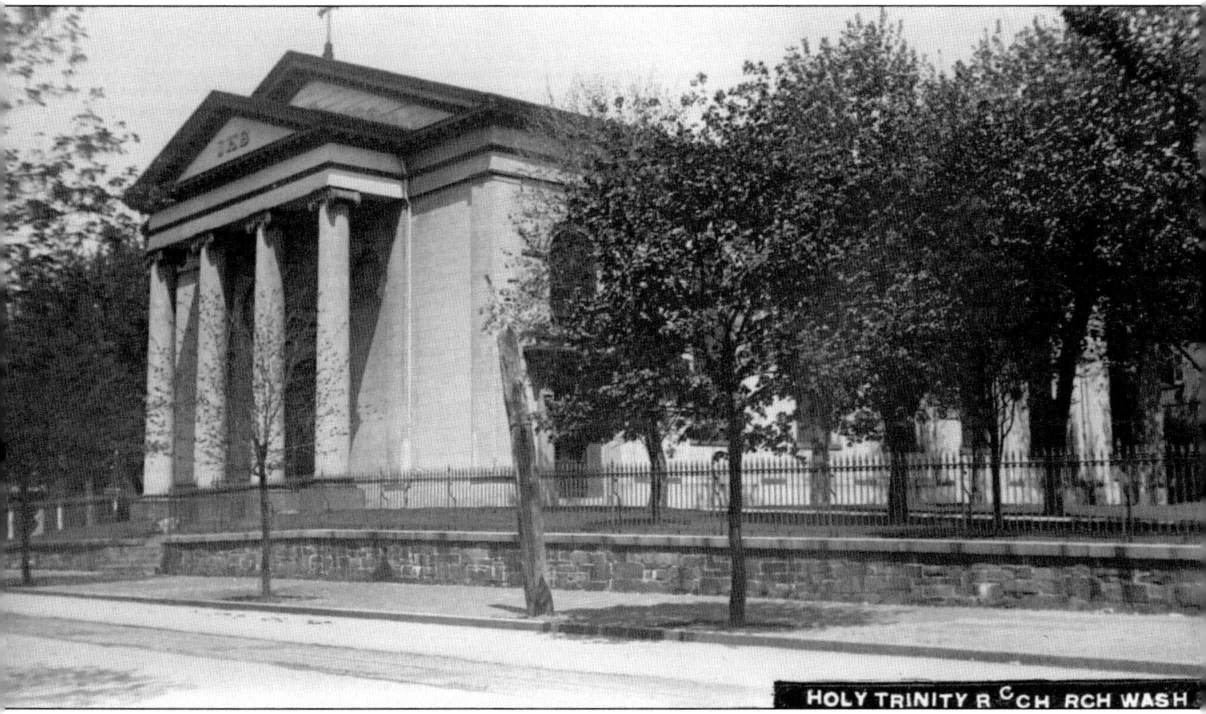

This new building for Holy Trinity Catholic Church was built in 1849. Shortly after completion, it was taken over by the Union government to be used as a hospital during the Civil War. Though the church was returned in 1863, it took 11 years for the government to compensate the church $350. This church was often frequented by Georgetown residents John F. and Jackie Kennedy. (National Photo Company.)

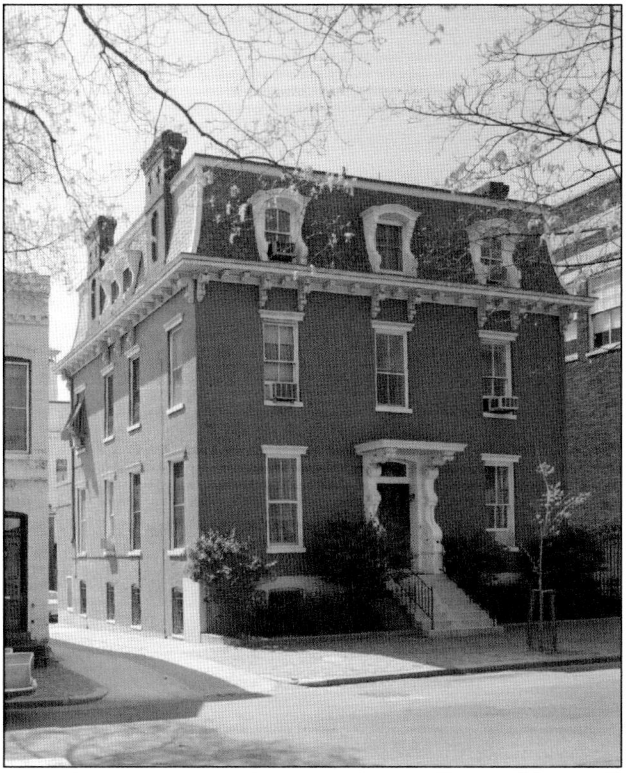

The rectory of Holy Trinity Catholic Church in Georgetown, built in 1869, is shown here in its new location in 1968. In 1917, with the expansion of Holy Trinity's school grounds, the rectory was moved farther down the street. Prior to the building of the rectory, the church pastor and staff lived in dorms at Georgetown College. (HABS.)

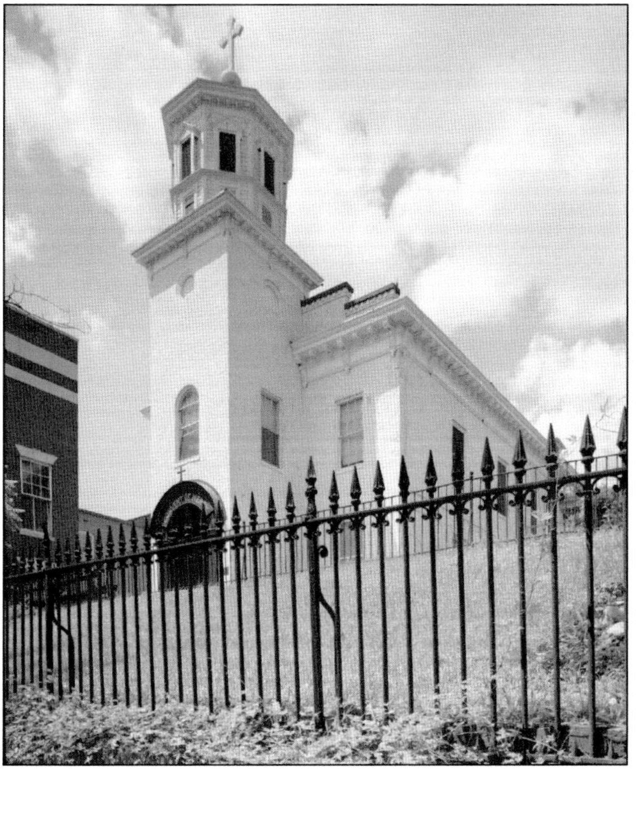

Holy Trinity Catholic Church is the oldest Catholic congregation in Georgetown and also the owners of the oldest ecclesiastical building still in use. This original parish church of Holy Trinity Catholic Church has been rededicated as the Chapel of St. Ignatius. It was built in 1794 but proved too small for the growing church. It has been used as the parish school and convent through the centuries, but it is now a place of worship again. (HABS.)

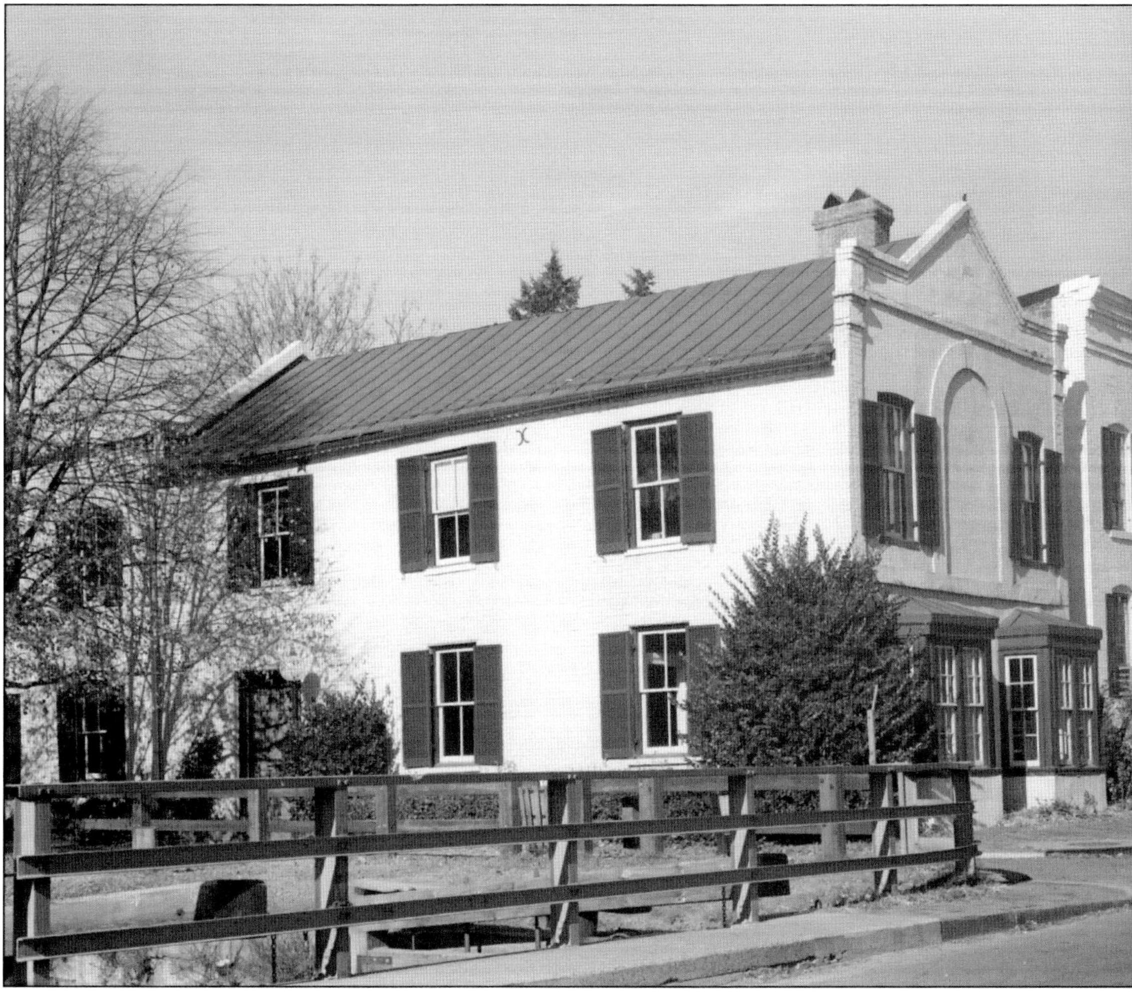

Potomac Lodge No. 5 is the oldest Masonic lodge in the current District of Columbia, though it can trace its history back to when Georgetown was still part of Maryland. The brothers of this lodge helped lay the cornerstone of the "President's House" and the Capitol, in Masonic tradition, of course. In fact, the gavel used by Worshipful Brother George Washington in laying the foundation for the US Capitol Building was given to Potomac Lodge No. 5, then known as Maryland Lodge No. 9. The building was completed in 1811 but only operated as a lodge until the 1840s. Since then, it has been home to a grocer, apartments, and offices. (HABS.)

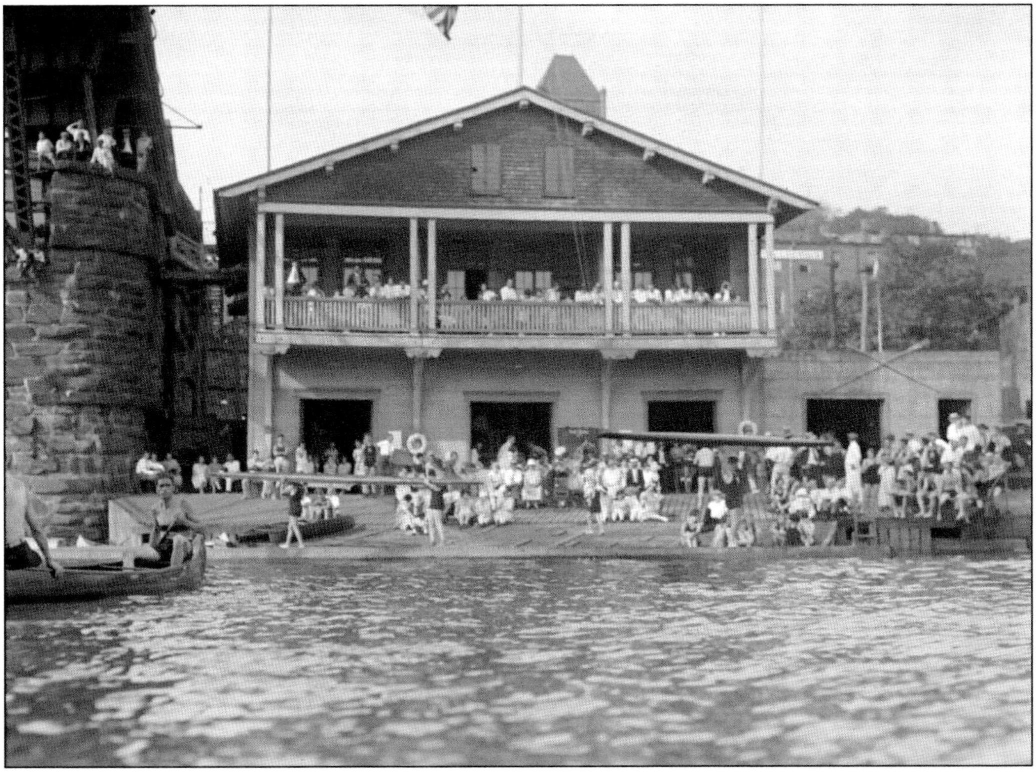

Established when a group of local residents discussed forming a rowing club while having drinks at a local tavern, the Potomac Boat Club won its first race on November 3, 1869. This 1925 photograph shows the boathouse, located in the western part of the Georgetown waterfront. At least the third reincarnation of their headquarters, this boathouse was erected in 1908. (National Photo Company.)

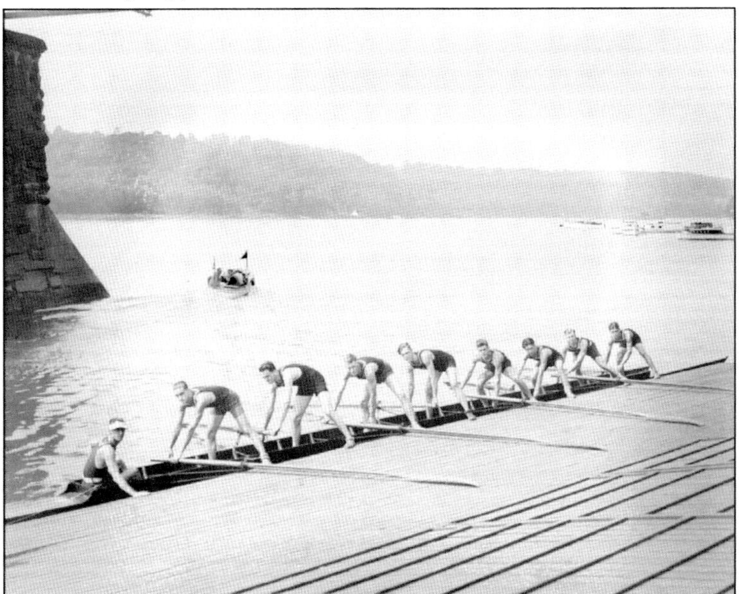

Here, on September 20, 1919, the Potomac Boat Club men's eight team gets ready to push off the dock at the Georgetown waterfront. (National Photo Company.)

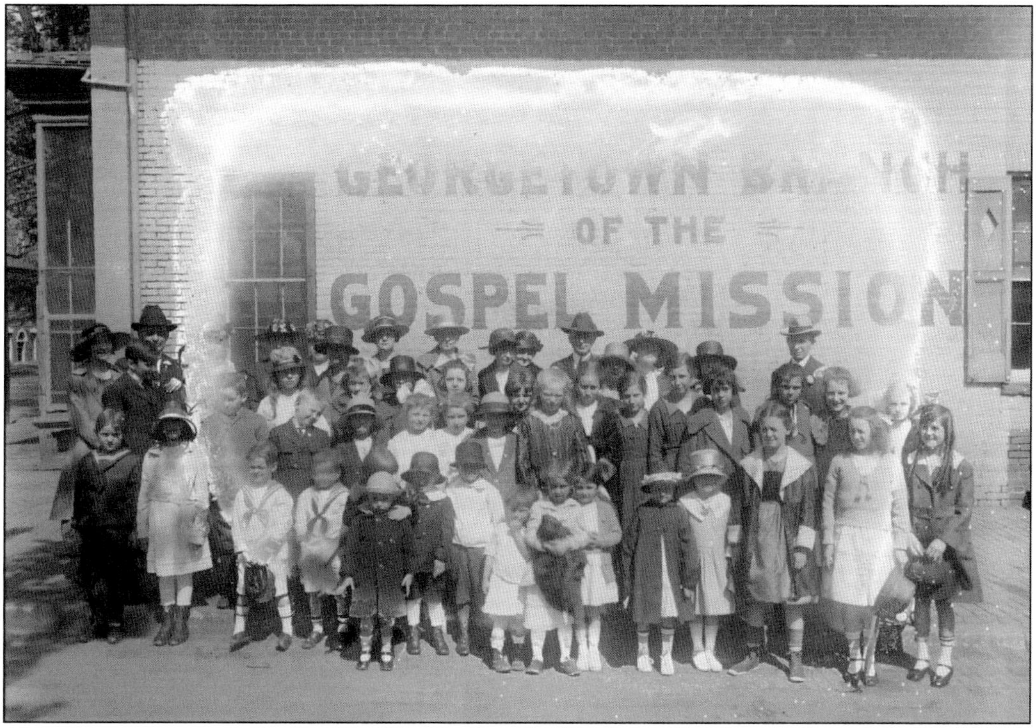

The Gospel Mission, founded in 1906, was a charitable organization originally headquartered in downtown DC. The aim was to provide care for infants, children, and poor mothers in the DC area. As the mission continued to grow, it expanded to all reaches of town. In addition to providing education and nutrition, one of the activities of the Gospel Mission was to take children out on daily trips to provide fresh air and exercise. These photographs from around 1920 show Washington children being taken on these outings by the Georgetown branch of the Gospel Mission. (Both, National Photo Company.)

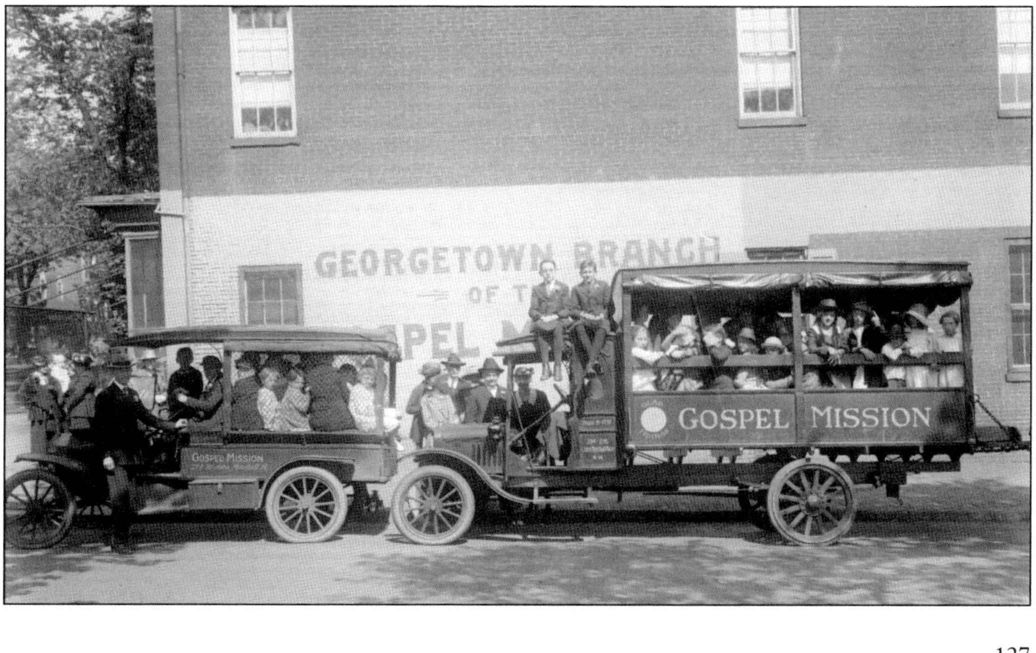